SHAKESPEARE'S WARWICKSHIRE CONTEMPORARIES

SHAKESPEARE'S WARWICKSHIRE CONTEMPORARIES

Charlotte Carmichael Stopes

General Books

A General Books LLC Publication.

Published by General Books LLC.

CONTENTS

1

SECTION 1

SHAKESPEARE'S WARWICKSHIRE CONTEMPORARIES

CHAPTER I

Richard Field (ricardo Del Campo), Printer Of Shakespeare's First Book: 1561-1625.

It is pleasant to remember that the printer who brought out Shakespeare's first book was a fellow townsman, Richard Field, the son of Henry Field, tanner, of Stratford-upon-Avon, a friend of John Shakespeare, the poet's father. The very printer's devil that ran about the office in 1593 was a Stratford boy, his brother, Jasper Field, apprenticed the year before. In going through the Stationers' Registers I was struck by the number of Warwickshire apprentices in the last quarter of the sixteenth century.

The poet may well have had other friends in the trade besides the Fields. Mr. Blades, a printer himself, suggested that Shakespeare spent the early years of his life in London in a printing office, as a printer's apprentice. While finding many cogent reasons againt this theory as a whole, I hold a resembling theory, based on the same preliminary arguments.

When Shakespeare went to London as a stranger, what would be more natural to him than to go straight

to Richard Field, avail himself of his metropolitan knowledge, and very probably share his lodgings ? He would want to know all about his friend's occupation, as he wanted to know about most things, and he learned a good deal about it. The method of Shakespeare's use of printing terms is very different from that of his use of other professional phrases; for instance, legal terms generally illustrate some point in law, or the nature of some legal mind; medical terms have similar applications, but printing language comes forth as a natural and familiar language of the poet, without foundation either in his own art or his development of any special character. For instance, Paulina, a court lady, says to the Lords, regarding Hermione's childl

Although the print be tittle, the whole matter
And copy of the father.
The very mould and frame of hand, nail, finger.

Winter 3 Tale, ii. 3. So Northumberland says in 2 *Henry IV.,* i. 1l

Yea this man's brow, like to a title leaf,
Foretells the nature of a tragic volume.

Mr. Blades collected many such quotations to illustrate his opinion, but readers may find many more of them for themselves.

A still stranger coincidence makes Richard Field's biography of importance to the study of Shakespeare. Much ingenuity hae been wasted to prove the impossibility of Shakespeare acquiring such wide and varied knowledge as his plays exhibit with his limited opportunities in Stratford-upon-Avon," a bookless neighbourhood," as Halliwell-Phillipps scornfully calls it. Even if it had been, which it was not, we have only to follow Shakespeare up to Richard Field's home and office inBlackfriars to find him planted in a good reference library, in the very midst of opportunities such as his works show he could take advantage of. If anyone carefully studies the titles and contents of the books issuing from this printing press, he would not have far to go for the sources of most of Shakespeare's special knowledge, perhaps for all that he shows in his early work beyond Holinshed's Chronicles.

One man alone, the Rev. John Marshall, of Bisbopton, in 1607, left 187 books. See *Atbeiueum,* 23 February, 1907, "Stratford's Bookless Neighbourhood."

To understand this, we must go back a long way and consider facts that, at first sight, appear to be somewhat irrelevant. Mr. Blades does not seem to have consulted the Stationers' Registers, and hence he was mistaken about Field's apprenticeship, asserting that he did not serve with Vautrollier. Field's indenture was a very special and peculiar one. Doubtless the worthy tanner of Stratford-upon-Avon was willing to pay handsomely to give his son Richard the best possible chance as a printer. Perhaps his leather was good for bookbinding, and he had interest with the Company. On the 10th day of August, 1579, an entry is recorded : "George Bishop. Richard Feylde, sonne of Henry Feilde, of Stratford-uppon-Aven, in the Countye of Warwick, tanner, hath putt himself apprentis to George Bishop, citizen and staconer of London, for v11. yeres from Michaelmas next, 2gth Sept., 1579, *is. 6d."* And another entry immediately follows:l "Thomas Vautrollier. It is agreed that this apprentis shall serve yc first v1.

years of his apprentiship with ye said Vautrollier to learn ye arte of printing, and y6 vnth with ye said G. Bishop. 3 Novr." So Field was under two masters from the first, rather an unusual thing for an apprentice. The six years he spent with Vautrollier were those that determined his after career, and, as I think, had a strong influence upon Shakespeare's. It, therefore, becomes of importance to go even further back, and learn who Vautrollier was, and what he did.

According to the Stationers' books, Vautrollier was "a stranger" ; and Ames states that he was "a Frenchman from Paris or Rouen, who came into England about the beginning of Elizabeth's reign." He was made a brother of the Stationers' Company in the same year that Shakespeare was born, on 2nd October, 1564, for the ordinary payment of two shillings and sixpence. This suggests that he had served as a London apprentice ; but there was not full time in Elizabeth's reign to have done so. He might have commenced with one of those friendly foreign printers who through Mary's reign printed Protestant books abroad for the English market. But that matters not to us. He did become, probably through special skill, a distinguished London printer. He seems to have been a man of probity, skill, and cultivation, a scholar of taste and judgement; cca curious printer," Ames calls him, and not without Court influence. For besides the ordinary licence to print, which he secured in 1573, he had a patent for ten' years, from 19th June, 1574, for some books of divinity, for works in foreign languages, for Ovid, Tully, the "Dialectics" of Peter Ramus, and Plutarch's "Lives." No one was to print or import any of these under a penalty of forty shillings, and he was allowed "to keep six foreign workmen, Frenchmen or Dutchmen or such lyke, for the said space and terme of tenne years without any lette or disturbance of any person." The privy seal was attached to this monopoly, granted "to our wel-beloved subjecte Thomas Vautrollier, typographus Londinensis in claustro vulgo Blackfriars commorans." The patent was renewed more than once.

A note concerning Vautrollier's privileges is recorded in the Stationers' Registers, 8th July, 1578; yet in that same year he was fined by the Company for printing Luther's sermons without a licence. In 1582 there was a great outcry made by unprivileged printersagainst such monopolies as hampered free trade, and an investigation was made. Christopher Barker's report shows that "Marsh was allowed the Latin school-books used in the Grammar Schools; Vautrollier the other Latin books, such as Tully, Ovid, and diverse other great works in Latin." "He hath other small things wherewith he keepeth his presses at work and also worketh for booksellers of the company who keep no presses." " Marsh and Vautrollier have certain special schoolebooks wherein yet when they be spoken with, it is thought they will be reasonable." (Arber's Stat. Reg., II., 776.) The commissioners on 18th July, 1583, advise "Marsh and Vautrollier, having the sole printing of school-bookes, may be treated withall to chose some and leave the rest."

Further complaints caused another investigation into monopolies in 1586, when a Royal Commission was appointed that vested, through a Star Chamber decree, the powers of determining these things in the master, wardens, and assistants of the Stationers' Company. Yet they did not disturb Vautrollier in his copies, nor prevent him keeping his two presses.

In 1581 Vautrollier seems to have been abroad, and a dispute arose between his wife and Marsh (Stat. Reg. II., 434, yth July, 1581). "Yt is agreed that Thomas Vautrollier his wife shall finish this present ympression which shee is in hand withall in her husband's absence, of Tullie's Epistles with Lambini's annotations, and deliver to those that have partes therein with the said Thomas. Yf his title be found unsufficient to the said booke, then the said Thomas and his partners to yield such recompense to Mr.Thomas Marshe for this ympression as the table shall think good, for the said Thomas Marshe now pretendith title thereto." On Vautrollier's return he proved that Marsh was wrong and confirmed his own title.

Apprentice Richard Field no doubt enjoyed somewhat more liberty in his master's absence, but seems to have proved faithful to his interests and devoted to his mistress, and her daughter Jacquinetta, who afterwards became his wife. In 1584 Vautrollier had again to leave his presses in the charge of his wife, his foreign workmen, and his apprentices; for in that year, having brought out the works of Giordano Bruno he had to fly the country. This time, however, he only fled to Scotland, and printed notable books there, for a stranger to touch, even. the King's book, " Essays of a prentis in the art of poesie," and "The King's intention regarding the last Acts of Parliament," with his own device and motto," Anchora Spei." He also brought out some of the hymns and psalms for the Scotch Service.

Thomas Baker wrote to Joseph Ames,|"Vautrollier was the printer of Jordanus Brunus in the year 1584, for which he fled, and the next year, being in Edinburgh in Scotland, he first taught that nation the way of good printing, and there staid, until such time as by the intercession of friends he had got his pardon, as appears by a book dedicated 1587 'to the Right Worshipful Mr. Thomas Randolph, Esq.,' where he returns him thanks 'for his great favour, and for assisting him in his distress.'"

During the time he was in Edinburgh his London printing presses were not idle, for some books appeared there of the same date, bearing his name and device. Again Richard Field would be able to prove his ability in the Blackfriars printing office.

It is probable that Vautrollier returned before September, 1585, when Richard Field would have to leave his service and complete his time with George Bishop, probably for bookselling and publishing experience. He would, however, in September, 1586, return to the Blackfriars printing office, to leave it no more. Vautrollier appears to have died in 1587-8. The last entry of a book to him occurs on the 20th February, 1587-8. His widow, "I.V." (Jacquinetta Vautrollier) printed one book dated 1588. But on 4th March, 1587-8, the Court of Assistants recorded an order " That Mrs. Vautrollier, late wife of Thomas Vautrollier, deceased, shall not hereafter print anye manner of book or books whatsoever, as well by reason that her husband was noe printer at the time of his decease, as alsoe for that by the decrees sette downe in the Starre Chamber she is debarred from the same." This sounds extraordinary. Other printers' widows were allowed to exercise the business or to carry it over to a second or even a third husband, as Mrs. Kingston and others did. All the more curious, because in the order of Succession of Master Printers, Thomas Vautrollier is duly given, and it is said that Richard Field married his widow and succeeded to the business. Elsewhere it is stated that he married the daughter. This seems more likely for two reasons: first, because Richard Field's widow " Jakin " succeeded him, when he died in 1625, and carried on the business ; and second, because of the remarkable statement that "Thomas Vautrollier was no printer when he died." It makes one think that Vautrollier must already have handed over his business with his daughter to Richard Field. It is likely that Mrs. Vautrollier also was a Frenchwoman, and there might have been difficulties with her methods. By 1588, then, Richard Field had attained the position of heading a printing business in London, much coveted and difficult to be attained, because only twenty-twomaster printers were allowed in the city; and when a rare vacancy occurred, the Court of Assistants, with the sanction of the Archbishop, claimed the right to elect a successor. Only by inheritance, or by marrying a widow or a daughter, could an eligible young printer evade the risks or an election. Richard Field managed it through matrimony.

Giordano Bruno, born 1548, a monk who had renounced his gown. He had written "On the Signs of the Times," had travelled all over Europe, lectured in Paris on the Thirty Divine Attributes ; and taught the Art of Memory, under the title of "De Umbris Idearum." His conception of the universe as resembling an animal was certainly known to Shakespeare. Bruno anticipates Kepler's view, Descartes' identity of thought and being, Spino2a's of an immanent God, and even the modern theory of Evolution. He was burnt at the stake in I 592.

If Shakespeare, then, went up to London in 1585, after the christening of his twins, he would find Richard Field reigning in the polyglot workshop, where Frenchmen, Dutchmen, and Englishmen worked together at their classical and scientific sheets. Or in 1586 Field might be at Bishop's in a new circle, selling and dealing in books and keeping up an intimate visiting acquaintance with the Vautrolliers, where he probably went of the evenings courting Jacquinetta.

If Shakespeare went up after the sad settlement with the Lamberts in 1587 he might be present at Richard's wedding and Vautrollier's funeral, and see his old friend' installed at the head of the establishment. Then he would have free run among the odd volumes. All Vautrollier's "copies" would be retained, and on his shelves would be many of those that he had " printed for other men," to which we have no clue. Vautrollier's theological, medical, poetical, classical publications were a library of themselves. No critics seem to be aware how much of the learning found in Shakespeare's world might have been acquired from the publications of Vautrollier and Field. He is not familiar with many classical authors, and he quotes few, such as Ovid, Cicero, and the "old Mantuan" John Baptist *(Love's Labours Lost,* iv. 2). These books were in the monopoly of this firm. Shakespeare's "small Latin and less Greek" might have been brushed up in Blackfriars over the Latin "Phrases " of Manutius, Cicero's "Orations" and "Epistles," Ovid's "Metamorphoses," Ovid's "Epistles," and

Ovid's "Art of Love"; his French might become practicable among so many speaking the language around ; his few Italian phrases could be borrowed from "The Campo de Fior, or else the Flourie Field of Foure languages for the furtherance of the learners of the Latin, French, English, but chiefly of the Italian tongue, 1585." Italian proverbs were handy there, and Italian grammars. Everyone knows how freely Shakespeare borrowed from Sir Thomas North's translation of Plutarch's "Lives," Du Bartas' "Divine Weeks," &c. The love of music was evidently a passion in Shakespeare's soul, and Vautrollier's shop held many volumes on this art, chiefly De la Motte's "Introduction to Music," 1574, and "Cantiones Sacrae," &c., by Thomas Tallis and William Bird, of Her Majesty's Chapel Royal, 1575.

Medical books, too, the best of the time, were there, one of them suggesting Shakespeare's study of madness, "A Treatise of Melancholie, containing the causes thereof and reasons of the strange effects it worketh in our minds and bodies, 1586." In some of the Sonnets there are such evident traces of the influence of Giordano Bruno that I long wondered how Shakespeare could' have come in contact with him. That philosopher had, it is true, lectured in Oxford in 1583, but one could hardly fit Shakespeare into a university lecture room. He had visited in 1582 Sir Fulke Greville and Sir Philip Sidney in London; yet we cannot imagine Shakespeare in their company then. But in Vautrollier's shop the sayings of Bruno would acquire tragic interest at his death for a philosophic faith, and not only from the copy kept in the secret cupboard, but from the conversation of the workmen, Shakespeare may have picked up some of these.

The "Dialectics of Aristotle," edited by John Case, of Oxford, came out in 1584. Another book doubtlessread by Shakespeare was a treatise on moral, political, and economical philosophy, by Petrucio Ubaldino, a Florentine, for many years pensioned by Queen Elizabeth (see Dec. Ace. Treas. Chamber, 541-2). Histories there were of many countries, notably Ludovico Guic- ciardini's " Description of the Low Countries " in Master Geffray Fenton's translation. Thus far these were Vautrollier's publications, but Richard Field himself began to print in 1588. A little French volume in the French reformed interest was his first issue.

Published by Vautrollicr, 1579 ; by Field, 1595, 1603, 1607 and 1612.

Thomas Orwin had, on 11th November, 1588, entered as his copy "The Art of English Poesie in three books, the first of Poetes and poesie, the second of proportyon, and the third of ornament," but as he did not pay the fee, it was, with his assent, assigned on yth April, 1589, to Richard Field. This critical analysis of literary elements was dedicated by the author to the Queen, and by Field to Lord Burleigh. It expresses strong objection to rhymed plays, and teaches that vice should' be reproved, even in comedy. Can we not believe Shakespeare learned something from reading this treatise ? In that year also Field brought out an elegant edition of Ovid's " Metamorphoses."

In May, 1589, Richard Field was fined ten shillings for printing a book contrary to order; and on " November 3rd, 1589, for keeping a prentice unpresented according to order, *is. 6d"* Mr. Blades might have rejoiced to see this entry, as possibly representing Shakespeare, but the irregular apprentice seems to have become a regular one, Tor on that date "Launcelot Leafe, son of Richard Leafe of Crawme, in the County of York, fuller, was bound apprentice to Richard Field."

In 1590 there was entered "An account of Sir Francis

I know that there is some doubt about the authorship of this important work, but it is generally believed to be by George Puttenham.

Drake's voyage." In the same year also Field entered as his copy Philip Burrough's " Method of Physicke," a book against the Spaniards, and the " French Littleton "; and in 1591 Sir John Harington's translation of" Orlando Furioso."

In 1592, there came up from Stratford-upon-Avon a new apprentice to Blackfriars : "Jasper Feyld, the sonne of Henry Field, of Stratford-upon-Avon, in the county of Warwick, tanner, hath putt himself apprentice to Richard Field, citizen and staconer of London, for seven years from the date hereof, yth February, 1592-3." (This is the year after Henry Field's death; Mr. Thomas Trussell and Mr. John Shakespeare had appraised his goods on 2 1st August, 1591.) Other apprentices of his were Christopher Waters, of Cambridge, 25th December, 1594; John Hanson, of Nottingham, 2gth September, 1598; John Ryxon, of Oxford, 23rd March, 1601 ; George Myllor, of Northampton, 2gth September, 1604.

Mr. H. Plot's "New Inventions" were entered to Richard Field, 5th March, 1593, and one or two other books shortly after. During the years that Shakespeare, homeless and uncertain of a future, apprenticed to no trade, educated to no profession, inheritor of no property, was being driven with the wind and tossed till he should find a shore, it seems to me that he spent much time and study in Master Field's treasure-house. "The right happy and copious industry of Master Shakespeare," attributed to him by Webster, was true of him even then. While studying the actor's parts that he played, or the old dramas that he patched and tinkered whereby he earned his bread, or the books in Field's shop, wherein he forgot his sorrows, there had dawned upon him the conviction that he, too, was a poet. Was it Ovid or Puttenham during the plague year that acted as the immediate cause? We knownot. But we know that he dedicated his first poem to the young Earl of Southampton; and that his friend, Richard Field, on 18th April, 1593, "entered for his copie under thandes of the Archbishop of Canterbury and Master Warden Stirrup a book intituled Venus and Adonis, *vid."* Probably the dedication facilitated the licence. Then to the press. How lovingly and carefully would Shakespeare read the first proof of "the first heir of his invention"! None of his works are so free from printer's errors as this. It is a credit to Field as a printer, f

I have elsewhere shown how the Earl of Southampton, by active kindness and warm-hearted sympathy, stimulated Shakespeare to a new effort and to "graver labours." In that busy year Shakespeare completed his second poem; but for some reason or other this was entered on gth May, 1594, to Master Harrison, senior, "for his copie under thande of Master Cawood, Warden, a book entitled the ' Ravishment of Lucrece," *vd"* Again, on 25th June, 1594, "Master Harrison, senior, had assigned to him from Richard Field a booke called Venus and Adonis, the which was before entered to Richard Field, 16th April, 1593." But Field printed later editions of the poem for other men. Was this transference merely a business exchange for classical works, or was it a symbol of the loosening of friendly bonds? Was the respectable Richard Field becoming ashamed of his play-acting Stratford friend ? It is possible, because in the list of the inhabitants of Blackfriars that signed a petition in 1596 against the players being allowed to use their theatre in Blackfriars the name of Richard Field occurs. The petition was not successful.

Though Shakespeare seems to have studied some ofField's later publications, we find no proof of further connection between these Stratford men.

Timperley says, in his "Anecdotes of Printing," p. 418, "We find, from a manuscript payment of 12/. for a survey of France and the Venus and Adonis, that by 12th June, 1593, it was in circulation."

f See the Introduction to my edition of the "Sonnets" (De La More Press).

Richard Field was recognised as a master printer in 1596; and was sworn and admitted to the livery on 1st July, 1598, in which year he was chosen with Master Dawson "to goo to my Lord Maiour's feast" (Stat. Reg. II. 35), and on 26th December, 1598, he assisted in drawing up the ordinances of the Stationers' Company.

Master Bishop, under whom Field served his last year, was appointed Master of the Company, February, 1604, and on 25th March Field was elected Renter, for exemption from which office he cheerfully paid ten pounds.

On yth May, 1604, Thomas Vautrollier, junior, was sworn and admitted a freeman of the Company, by Master Legate, but we hear no more of him in this or in any other printing business. It is strange how the son should apparently in this instance have been supplanted by the son-in-law.

Master Richard Field was appointed Warden 1605, and was Master of the Company from 1619 till 1622.f A transcript of the Stationers' Registers was made while he was Master. Some of the phrases illustrate the meaning of words used by Shakespeare. He died in 1625, and his widow, Jakin or Jacquinetta, continued the business, apparently in conjunction with her son.

The name is o rare that I may note that a Sampson Vautrollier, son of James, was baptised in St. Clement's Danes, 15th June, 1631.

J- On 9th May, 1615, a complaint was made of there being too many presses in London, and the Court ordained that " none shall have more presses than are here sett downe:

I. Master Dawson, 2 presses.

II. Master Field, 2 presses," &c.

J " jrd April, 1626, assigned over unto him by Mistres Field, wife of Richard Field, deceased, the following copies to George Miller."

Note A. Warwickshire Apprentices In London Printing Offices.

"Roger Lock, sonne of John Lock, of Stratford-upon-Avon, in the Countie of Warwick, glover, hath puthimself apprentice to Richard Pickeringe, citizen and stationer of London, for tenne yeares, beginninge at Bartholomew-tide laste (24th August, 1577). 2nd September, 1577. *2s. 6d."*

"Raffe Jackson, sonne of Thomas Jackson, of the citie of Coventry, draper, hathe putte himselfe apprentice to Garret Dewce, stationer, for terme of tenne yeares from Mychaelmasse next, 2gth September, 1580. *2s. 6d."*

"John Rampston, son of John Rampston, of Atherston, in the County of Warwick, yeoman, hathe putte himselfe apprentice to James Goneld, staconer, for nine years from Midsomer laste (24th June, 1580). *2s. 6d.* 28th August, 1580."

"8th September, 1580. Michael Mussage, son of Thomas Mussage, late of Barfoot, in ye Countie of Warwick, yeoman, deceased, hathe putte himselfe apprentice to John Bishop for v1 1i. years from Midsomer last (24th June). *2s. 6d."*

"ist March, 1585. Allan Orrian, son of Thomas Orrian, of Stratford-on-Avon, in ye County of Warwick, tailour, doth put himselfe apprentice to Thomas Fowkes, staconer, for the terme of seven yeres from our Lady-daie in Lent next (25th March, 1585). *2s. 6J."*

"Richard Tomes, son of John Tomes, of Stretton-upon- Fauce, in the Countie of Warwick, mason, putteth himself an apprentice to Thomas Styrrope, staconer, for seven yeres from this day, 8th November, 1589. *2s. 6d."*

"22nd August, 1586. Robert Blackham, son of Thomas Blackham, of Sutton, in the Countie of Warwick, tanner, dothe putte himselfe apprentice to Robert Robinson, citizen and staconer of London, for seven yeres from the date hereof. *2s. 6d."* This is erased, and by it written "Gone from his master, and never to be made free."

"i7th Oct., 1586. Morrys Pettifer, sonne of Michael Pettifer, of Anstey, in the County of Warwick, husbandman,putteth himself apprentice to Thomas Brighte, staconer, for 8 yeres, from Michaelmas laste paste, 2Qth Sept., 1586. *2s. 6d."* W12th Jan., 1590. Edmund Mutton, sonne of Thomas Mutton, of Rockbey, in the Countie of Warwick, butcher, hath put himself apprentice to John Penny, citizen and staconer of London, for seven years from the birth of our Lord last, which shall be the day of the date 25 Dec., 1589. *2s. 6d."*

"6th March, 1592. Jasper Feyld, sonne of Henry Field, of Stratford-on-Avon, in the County of Warwick, tanner, hath putt himself apprentice to Richard Field, citizen and staconer of London, for seven years from the date hereof, 7th Feb.,

1592."

"5th March, 1592. Anthony Higgons, son of William Higgons, of Wolverhampton, in the County of Warwick, yeoman, hath putt himself apprentice to Thomas Purfoote, the elder, citizen and staconer of London, for the terme of seven yeres from the date of these presents (6th March, 1592). *2s. 6d."*

"5th March, 1593. Gulimus Winspere, son of John Win- spere, of Exham, in the County of Warwick, taylor, hath put himself apprentice to William Ponsonby, citizen and staconer of London, for terme of nine years from our Lady-day next (25th March, 1593). *2s. 6d."*

Richard Badger, a Stratford-upon-Avon printer, was in 1602 apprenticed to Peter Short.

Note B.

Vautrollier's Publications.

Some idea of the class of books published by Vautrollier may be gleaned from the following notes from the "Stationers' Registers."

1569-70.lThomas Vautrollier's licences.

"A Book of Copyes of Various handwriting, English,

French, and Italian, for the Secretary hand." 1570-1.l"A Booke of Music." 1573.l18th April, for Llodowick Lloyd's translation of

Plutarch's " Lives." For eight years (transferred to

Vautrollier).

Vautrollier's Publicationsl*continued-*

1574.lVautrollier had a patent for ten years for printing several books of Divinity, the worksof Calvin, Luther, Beza, and other theological writers, the New Testament, and digest of St. Augustine; various classical works, such as the works of Ovid, the works of Cicero, with Lambinus' notes; the "Elegant Latin Phrases" of Manutius; the "Dialectics" of Peter Ramus; the"Giardina Cosmographica de B. Sylva"; Plutarch's

"Lives," englished by Sir Thomas North from the French of Amyot. No one else was to print or import any of these, under a penalty of forty shillings. He was also allowed to keep six foreign workmen, Frenchmen or Dutchmen, or such like for the space of ten years without let or hindrance from any one.

1574-5.|"A Brief Introduction to Music," by Paul De La Motte.

1575.|"Cantiones Sacrae," or Sacred Music of Master Bird and Master Tallis of her Majesties Chapell. These two composers had themselves a " patent for all music books whatsoever, and the printing of all ruled paper, for the pricking of any songes to the lute, virginals, or other instruments," but they seemed to have worked their patent through Vautrollier's presses.

1577.| ist Dec. "A Sovereign Salue for a Sin full Soule," by
Nathaniel Baxter, Minister.
"A Right Comfortable treatise containing xiiij points
of consolation for them that labour and are laden."
Unto Master Norton and Thomas Vautrollier "Ye
History of Guicciardini of Master Geffray Fenton's
translation" (from the Latin edition of 1567).
Thomas Vautrollier and Master Wright, "a Booke
in English called Plutarch's 'Lives.'" Eusebius' "Historie" in English.
1578.|Scipio Lentulo's "Italian Grammar," printed by Henry
Grantham.

Charles Merbury's "That Monarchie is the best for the Common Weal," whereunto is annexed, "A book of Italian Proverbs."

Vautrollier's Publications|*continued.* 1578.|"Phrases Linguae Latinae," compiled from Manutius. 18th Sept. Claudii a Sancto Vinculo "de pronun-

ciatione linguz Gallicae, libri duo." 1580.|"A Treatise on French Verbs." 1581.|"A most easie perfect and absolute way to learn the
French Tongue."

1582.|Scipio Gentilis, " Paraphrases of the Psalms of David." "Le Jardin de Vertu et bonnes moeurs," par Jaques
Bellot Cadomois.

"An Astrological Catechism," by Leowitz, translated

by Turner.
"The Life of Admiral Coligny." 1583.|"The French Littleton."
" Campo de Fior or else the Flourie Field of four
languages for the furtherance of the learners in the
Latine, French, English, but chiefly of the Italian
tongues."
1584.|"The Dialectics of Aristotle," edited by John Case of
Oxford.

The works of Giordano Bruno (interdicted).
"The new Godly Garden of Prayers," whereunto is joyned "Bradford against the fear of Death," Edinburgh. (Maunsell's Catalogue.)
"The Essayes of a Prentice in the Divine Art of

Poesie." By the King. Edinburgh. "A Declaration of the Kinges Maiesties intentioun and meaning towards the last Acts of Parliament," cum privilegio Regali. (See Pinkerton.) 1585.|Morgan's "Phoenix Britannicus," Edinburgh. Printed same year in English for Thomas Nelson. See Harl. MS. VII. 4-9.

1586.|Timothy Bright's "Treatise on melancholy, containing the causes thereof, and reasons of the strange effects it worketh on our minds and bodies." "La Main Chretien aux tombes." 1587.|"The Treasons of the Scottish Queen." Sir William Herberte's" Sydney."

Note C.
Richard Field's Publications.

1588.|"Le Politique ReformS."

11th Nov. Allowed to Thomas Orwyn "The Arte of English Poesie in three Books, the firste of Poetes and poesye, the second of proportyon, and the third of Ornament." (Fine not paid and licence granted to Field).

1589.|"The Art of English poesie," beinge before entered for Thomas Orwin's copie is by his consent putt over to Richard Field. (This is Puttenham's book).

"A Book intituled Discours bref mais tressolide monstrant clairement qu'il est loisible, honne'te, utile, et necessaire au Roy de s'allier au Roy de Navarre." (Master HartwelFs hand being to this copy.)

"Le Vray Agnus Dei, pour desarmer le peuple Francois, ecrit pour le Roy treschretien Henri III. Roy de France."

"The Declarations of the French Kingeand the King of Navarre upon the truce concluded between yr Majesties together with the King of Navarres declaration at his passage over the River of Loire."

"David's Faith and Repentance."

" Daniell expounded by Scriptures in Hebrue, Greeke, and English."

These three little bookes following: "Vray Discours sur la Deflaicte de Duc D'Aumalle et Sieur de Battagny, avec leurs troupes, par le Duc de Longue-ville et autres seigneurs." "Lettre d'un Gentilhomme de Beausse a son sien aux Bourgeois de Paris." "Lettre du Roy de Navarre, a Messieurs d'Orleans du 22 May, 1589, a Banqueney."

A Booke intituled "The Furious, translated by James the Sixte King of Scotland, with the Le Panto of the same King." (Both translations from the French of Saluste du Bartas).

"A briefe Dyscourse of the Spanyshe State with a Dyalogue entytuled Philo basilis."

Richard Field's Publicationslcontinued.

1590.l2nd March. "The Methode of Phisicke, Philip Barroughe aucthore." . 16th May. A Booke intituled "Soveraigne Salve for a Sicke Soul, teachinge the right use of a patient bearing the crosse." "A brief discourse dialoge-wyse showing how false and dangerous their reportes are which affirme the Spanyards intended invasion is for re-establishment of the Romische religion." " Her Majesties allyance with ye Netherlanders." "Sir Francis Drake's enterprise three yeares past into the West Indies."

25th June. "The Frenche Lyttleton, set forthe by

Holiband and printed by Vautrollier."

"The treatise of Christian Righteousness, which was

Thomas Vautrollier's copie."

1591.lA booke intituled " John Haringtons Orlando Furioso." 6th Dec. "Parte Prima Delle brevi Dimonstrationi et precetti utilissime de Diversi propositi moral! politic! et Iconomisi, Da Petruccio Ubaldino Cittadine Fiorentino." 1592.lA booke intituled "The French Alphabet, together with the treasure of the French tonge." (This to be void.)

"Saluste du Bartas, the Divine Weeks and Works." 1593.l18th April. "A booke intituled "Venus and Adonis." 1 1th Dec. A booke intituled "The Pearle of Practise, or practisers pearle of Phisick and Chirurgerie." 31st Dec. "A Description of all the principallest Minerals and their properties." 1594.l5th Feb. "A brief discourse of Man's Transgression and of his Redemption by Christ, with a particular survey of Romysh religion and Rome itself." 5th March. "A Brief Apologie of certen new invencions compiled by Master H. Plot."

Walter Bigg's "Summary and true account of Sir

Francis Drake's West Indian Voyage."

David Hume of Godscroft, "Daphnis Amaryllis."

Richard Field's Publicationsl*contd.*

1594.lThomas Cogan's "Hauen of Health for the use of Students."

1st May. "The History of our Lord Jesus Christ in English Meeter." R. H. Holland.

and May. "The first part of Christian passions con- teyning a hundred Sonettes of meditacion humiliation and prayer."

7th May. Assigned over from Master Bonham Norton. "The History of Gwicciardini conteyning the warres of Italy and also the arguments, with a Table &c. Reduced into English by Geffray Fenton."

gth May. "The Theatre of fine devises conteyning an hundred Morrall Emblems translated out of French by Thomas Combe."

" Lyacropedius de Conscribendis epistolis," assigned over unto him from Harrison.

25th June. "Venus and Adonis" assigned over to Harrison.

Thomas Campion's "Observations on the art of English poesie." "A booke intituled Thome Campione Poema."

1595.| I4th Jan. Assigned unto him the printing of Tullie's "Orations" in 16mo in 3 volumes for the Company, and he to allow upon every impression *6d.* in the pound for the use of the poor.

2nd Dec. Harrison and Field. A book intituled "Phrases Manutii."

1596.|3Oth Oct. "A Ne we discourse of a Stale subject called the Metamorphosis of Ajax, with the Anatomy and Apologie of the same, wrytten by Mysacmos to his friend & Cozen Philostilpnos" (Sir John Harington).

nth Nov. "A book called Ecclesiastes in English Verse."

1597.|5th March. "The Elements of Arithmetic," C. Verstitius being the authore and Thomas Hood, Doctor in Phisick translater thereof into English.

Richard Field's Publications|*contd.*

1597.|2gth March. "Aphorisms of Christian Religion a very compendious abridgement of Master John Calvines Institucions by Master J. Piscator, and now Englished according to authors 3rd edition."

1598.|13th May. Entered to Richard Field & Felix Kingston copies formerly belonging to Tobie Cooke, viz., 8 divinity tracts and his "Booke of Wytches."

1599.|22nd May. Richard Field and Robert Dexter. "The Sacred Shield of all Christian Souldyers."

1600.|5th March. Luther's "Commentary on Galatians." Dr. Abbot's "Lectures on Jonas." 28th June. "Oratio Hominis Belgici De Virtute ac laudibus Britannorum."

1602.|"England's View in the unmasking of two paradoxes [by de Malestroict], with a replication to the answere of Master John Bodin by Gerard de Malynes."

1603.|New edition of Plutarch's "Lives."

1607.|Another new edition.

1608.|Matthew Stoneham's Two Sermons.

1610.|4th October. A Booke in French called "Dialogues Rustiques."

1611.|271!] Sept. A Book intituled "In Assertorem Chymicae sed verse Medicinae desertorem Franciscum Antho- niuui. Matthaei Gwynne."

14th Oct. A Booke called "Analysis Logica 30ta psalmorum a primo scilicet ad inum Authore Gulielmo Templo Dublinensis apud Hybernos Col- legii Praeposito."

1612.|20th Jan. A Booke called "Vis Naturae et Virtus Vitas, &c., Aucthore Gulielmo Sparke."

1613.| 17th Jan. "De Numeris Geometricis. Of the Nature and' properties of geometricall numbers written by Lazarus Sconerus, englished by Master Bedwell."

1614.|1st March. "Trigonium Architectonium or the Carpenter's Square, that is a table serving for the measuring of a board, Glasse, Stone, and such like playne and sollides by William Bedwell."

Richard Field's Publications|*contd.*

1615.|16th Jan. A booke called "Mohammedis Imposture

translated out of Arabic by William Bedwell." 22nd June. The following 8 copies. A book of Copies in English, French, and Italian; Luther on Galatians; A History of " Fortunatus"; A Commentary of Luther on the 15 Psalms of Degrees; Eusebius' "Ecclesiastical History" in English; Declining of French Verbs and the "French A.B.C." 1616.|15th March. "Principles of Arithmetic written in Latin by Barnard Salignac, now englished by William Bedwell. "Tobacco tortured or the filthy fume of Tobacco refined."

This does not pretend to be a complete list, it is only what has been gleaned from the Stationers' Register. Many other books were printed by Field, some for other men and some even for himself, such as Juvenal's "Satires" and Histories of England and Scotland, but there are sufficient to show where Shakespeare had the opportunity of acquiring a considerable amount of learning. I give no publications after Shakespeare's death, but it may be noted that Field entered for publication the French edition of Camden's"Elizabeth,"4th November, 1623.

2

SECTION 2

CHAPTER II

Sir Thomas Lucy The Elder,
The Real And The Traditional: 1532-1600.

Sir Thomas Lucy was the chief person in the immediate neighbourhood of Stratford-upon-Avon during the latter half of the sixteenth century, and there is no doubt that he must have often come into contact with Shakespeare. But we have no clue to the circumstances thereof. Mr. Halliwell-Phillipps says "No record of the least value bearing directly on the Shakespeare traditions has ever been found in Charlecote" ("Outlines," vol. ii., 383), and the minutes of the Court of Records and the Chamberlain's Accounts are likewise silent. The untrustworthy nature of the traditions that have come down to us concerning these two men can best be shown by a careful historical criticism of authentic facts and a psychological analysis of apocryphal anecdotes, founded upon mistaken association of ideas.

Sir Thomas Lucy came of a long line of distinguished ancestors, who had dwelt at Charlecote over four hundred years, and had given commanders, councillors, sheriffs, knights of the shire, and justices of the peace repeatedly to the service of their country. Dugdale supposes Thurstan de Charlecote to have been a younger son of Thurstan de Montford, whose son and heir Henry granted to Walter the son of Thurstan of Charlecotethe lordship of the village, which grant King Richard I. confirmed by letters patent at Dover, 6th December, 1191, and John again confirmed with all the privileges therein noted in the fifth year of his reign. " From this Walter de Charlecote (who was a knight) by Cecily his wife, descended William, who assumed the surname of Lucy." This makes Dugdale think that his mother Cecily must have been a " Lucy." There were many Lucys on the fellowship of The Guild of Knowle. In 1494 was introduced Domina Alicia Lucy Vidua de Charlecote; and prayers were requested for the soul of Sir William Lucy. Thereafter appeared Master Edmund Lucy Armiger and Johane his wife, and Thomas, Edward, William, Anna, and Marie Lucy. Prayers were requested for the souls of Alicia and Edmund in 1523.

The owner of Charlecote at the opening of the sixteenth century was Sir Thomas, who married Elizabeth, the widow of George Catesby, and daughter of Sir Richard Empson, of Easton Neston, Northamptonshire. He was Sheriff of Warwick and Leicestershire, and was buried at Greyfriars, London, leaving three sons, William, his heir,f Thomas and Edmund, well provided for, and three daughters, Anne, Radegund, and Barbara. Of this William many notices may be gleaned from the Domestic Series of State Papers. Among those yet uncalendered is a list of soldiers furnished by the noblemen and gentlemen of Warwick for the Vantguard, 1544:l"John Gryvell 31 fotemen, Thomas Arden 16, William Lucy 20," &c. But the only records important to our after history are his will, and the Inquisition Post-mortem, because therein we find many domestic particulars as well as details of his inheritance, his debts, jewels, and estates, his children and his plans for their up-bringing.f

Some entries in the Testa de Neville suggest another name for the lady. "Matilda de Lucy holds in the Hundred of Barlichway the villa of Hulenhalle of John de Screiveila, one carucate of land and *j* virgates of land," p. 88. A tenant "holds Mineli and Lantian (Cornwall and Devon) of the honour of Matilda de Lucy, and Robert, the son of Walter." "Robert, the son of Walter and Matilda de Lucy holds Mineli and Lantian," &c. This might be a second son's portion from his mother. But the eldest son is also noted. "William de Lucy holds half of Charlecote from Peter de Monte Forte and half of the Earl of Warwick." " In Charlecote 4 parts of a fee which William de Lucy holds of the Prior of Coventry." " The aid granted to the King on marrying his sister to the Emperor of Romel William de Lucy, 1 Mark."

j The Dictionary of National Biography states that he married Anne, daughter of Richard Fermor, of Easton Neston.

Thomas, his eldest son, was born on the 24th April, 1532. He did not go to the university, but seems to have been educated by private tutors at home. The Dictionary of National Biography states that he was educated by John Foxe, the martyrologist, and that he imbibed from him his Puritan tendencies. But we must not forget that Foxe only left Oxford in July, 1545, and that he was in London eighteen months later.- During this period both he and Thomas Lucy got through their courtship and marriage, so there was not apparently much leisure for a wide education at that time. On the 1st of August, 1546, Sir William drew

Another may be here noted, only because it may prove of local interest, and has not been printed, concerning William Lucy, John Greville, and John Combes, who, on the 15th day of March, 30 Henry VIII.- examined Robert Mawde, clerk,

parson of Whatcope, because he would not read the "King's injunctions" from '
'['',

his pulpit on Sunday, but entertained sturdy vagabonds in his house at Knoll, playing cards with them. A lively account is given of the irregular manners of this parson.

I Tli' I Registers of Charlecote have preserved gome facts concerning the family:

"Susane Lucye, ye daughter of Mr. William Lucye Esquier was baptized ye 15 of January 1543 [-4].

Martha Lucy daughter of Mr. William Lucy Esquier was baptized ye 15 of Augut 1545.

Joyes Lucye ye daughter of Mr. William Lucye Esquier was baptized ye last of September 1546.

Tymothie Lucye ye sone of Mr. William Lucye Esquier was baptized ye 16 of November, 1547.

Edwarde Lucye sone of Mr. William Lucye Esquier was baptized ye 30 of June, 1549."

Among the marriages : "Thomas Merson and Margret Lucye were married the z1st of October, 1543."

The Burial Register notes:

"Susane Lucy buried i.;tii April 1546.

Anne Lucye buried 16th of July 1549. Mrs. Anne Lucye 12th July 1550.

Mr. William Lucye Esquier, buried ye 24th of June 1551."

up the marriage settlement between his eldest son and Joyce Acton, the only child and heir of Thomas Acton, of Sutton Park, Worcestershire. Thomas could only, therefore, have been fourteen at the time of his marriage, and his bride is stated on her parents' tombstone to have been twelve, though she is reckoned as being a year older on her own tombstone in Charlecote church.

In January, 1546-7, a few months after the marriage, Thomas Acton died, and Joyce Lucy inherited his great estates, deer park and all, subject to her mother's dowry. In February, 1546-7, Foxe left Charlecote for London, having married a dependant of the Lucys, and therefore no doubt he found his stay at Charlecote so pleasant. Sir William Lucy died in 1551, and Thomas succeeded at Charlecote in the nineteenth year of his age. There were various debts of his father to be cleared, portions for the other sons, Edward, Richard, William, Timothy, and for the daughters Elizabeth, Mary, Jane, Martha, and Joyce, so he must have been' forced to live economically at the first. On 22nd April, 7 Edward VI., just when he came of age, he was granted Sherburne and Kingsford, which he afterwards sold to Mr. Dabridgecourt. His Puritanism was not impassioned enough to let him suffer for conscience' sake in Mary's reign. His biographers state that he had a gift of Hampton Lucy from her; but a note in Egerton MS., 606, f. 27, implies that it was paid for.

By 1558 he had probably paid up his sisters' portions, and settled his brothers' incomes, for he was able to

Near Sutton Park, the inheritance of Joyce Acton, in the church of Tenbury, Worcestershire, *is* the tomb of the Actons, with this inscription :l" Here lieth Thomas Acton, of Sutton, Esquire, who at the age of seventy years departed this life January 2, 1546, and Mary his wife, daughter to Sir Thomas Laycon, of Willy, Knight, being of the age of 58 years, deceased April 28, 1564, having issue in their lifetyme two sons, Launcelot and Gabriel, who dyed before them in their infancy, and Joyce their only daughter and heir, being then of the age of 12 years, was espoused to Sir Thomas Lucy, of Charlcot, knight, which Dame Joyce, in dutiful remembrance of these her loving parents, hath erected this monument, 1581.l T.A.M.A."

rebuild Charlecote in a sumptuous manner. To honour the Queen, he designed it in the pattern of a royal E. He was elected sheriff of the county in that year. He was interested in Archery.

Sir Thomas Lucy wrote to Lord Robert Dudley:l

Right honorable and my singular good lorde pleaseth it youar honor to be advertised that according youar lordships request and my one promise I have sent you my servaunt Burnell whom I fear will not be liable to doo yor lordshipp such sarvice as I could wish nor as his hart woold sarve, for that by occasion of longe sickness his strength is greatly decayed, and thereby his shuting much hindered. Your lordshipp must take hede in making off yor matches that Burnell be not overmarked for that at this instante he is hable to shute no farr ground (which iff youar lordshipp forsee I doo not mistrust but he will be able to shute with the best). Thus as one off the best off youar lordship's friends in power or habilitie to doo youar lordshipp any sarvice or pleasure (although as willing as the greatist in hart and good will as youar lordshipp shall well understand when occasion shall sarve) I commend you unto almightie God who send you long life in the feare off God with increace of honor according to your lordship's one desier from Charlecot the viiith off Aprill at your lordship's commandemant during life.

Thomas Lucy.

(Addressed) To the Right Honorable and his singuler good Lord my L. Robert Dudleye, Mr. of the Quenes horse, &c.

There is no date to the letter. Dudley was appointed Master of the Horse 1558, and he became Earl of Leicester 1563. It must have been between these dates.

Mrs. Acton died in 1564 (a few days after Shakespeare was born) and her dowry came back to her daughter's estate. Sir Thomas was knighted in 1565 (tradition says in his own house), and became later a justice of the peace and Commissioner of Musters forWarwickshire. From the register of the University I find that his brother, Timothy Lucy, became B.A. of Oxford 26th April, 1567, and M.A. shortly afterwards. Sir Thomas was elected knight of the shire for the Parliament of 1571, in which he seems to have been an active and respected member. He was appointed to be on the Committee to discover which of the members had taken money for their voices ; of the committee to consider abuses of religion as suggested by Mr. Foxe's book; and of the conference touching the Bill against priests disguising themselves as serving-men, which had been drawn up after the Pope's ill-advised Bull against Elizabeth.

The photogravure in the British Museum is headedl"Facsimile of a Letter from Sir Thomas Lucy of Charlecote, the Justice Shallow of Shakespeare, to Lord Robert

Dudley, Master of the Horse, from the original among the papers of the Marquis of Bath at Longleat, co. Wilts, by whom this is presented."

The Charlecote Registers say that "Mr. Thomas Lucye Esquier was married to Dorothee Arnoll sone *(sic]* to Sir Nicholas Arnoll Knight, 27 Jan. 1574[-5]-" That is, of course, Sir Thomas's only son and heir.

Another entry isl"Mr. Edward Aston, ye sonne and heir of Sir Walter Aston Knight, and Mrs. Anne' Lucy, daughter of Sir Thomas Lucye, Knight, were married y 27 of April 1580."

Sir Thomas was again elected sheriff of the county in 21 Elizabeth, but was not returned as knight of the shire for the next Parliament, which lasted eleven years. A Bill had been brought forward during its sitting concerning the preservation of game, which had been rejected on its first reading.

The chief act of the session of 1581 was that which, in order to keep her Majesty's subjects in due obedience, had decreed new penalties on the exercise of the Romish religion, and had added new terrors to the preaching thereof. A commission had been instituted with truly inquisitorial powers. Sir Thomas, as justice of the peace, was associated with it, and he was not slow to exercise his privileges, so as to prove his loyalty through his family motto "By Truth and Diligence." There isnothing to show that he was not upright in action and conscientious in intention, while he obeyed the Government, then represented by Leicester. We must allow somewhat for the customs and circumstances of the time, and for the blinding effect of religious and party passions. Nevertheless, he seems to have acted harshly, even by the standard of his own generation, in relation to recusants.

The first victim of the new commission was the noble and high-minded Catholic gentleman, Edward Arden, of Park Hall, a far-away kinsman of Shakespeare's mother. Dugdale, Camden, and others openly attribute his cruel death to the malice of Leicester, but Sir Thomas Lucy was the instrument through which Leicester worked. He received into his house Thomas Wilkes, clerk of the Privy Council, sent down to investigate "the plot" ; he personally searched Arden's house, and sent his own servants up with him as prisoner to London. I later tell the interesting story more fully. It is quite possible that Sir Thomas Lucy's energy on this occasion embittered Shakespeare's mind, and added other anxieties to his monetary and domestic troubles.

In January, 1583-4, Sir Thomas Lucy and Sir Fulke Greville were made arbitrators between Hamnet Sadler and Ananias Nason, and the Corporation granted a bottle of wine "when they were made friends" (see Chamberlain's accounts). Many other entries are made of gifts of wine and sugar to Sir Thomas by the Corporation, when he was in town performing the duties of a justice. Mr. Halliwell-Phillipps found in the accounts of the Coventry Treasurer for this year the unexpected entry, " Paid to Sir Thomas Lucie's players Xt. "; so he was not severe enough to restrain theatrical performers.

On 2yth November, 1584, Sir Thomas was againreturned as knight of the shire to Parliament; was energetic in promoting the Bill against the Jesuits and seminary priests ; impeached Dr. Parry, the solitary member who had courage to speak against its tyrannical spirit; and when he was proved a traitor, petitioned the Queen for his execution. A Bill for " The Preservation of Grain and Game," a curiously-worded production, was upon its second reading committed to Sir Thomas Lucy and others, but it seems to "have been discontinued with divers others of no great moment" (see Sir Symonds d'Ewes' Journal, p. 344). Therefore, it never became law. A private Bill was passed that session for the "assurance of certain lands which are not defined, to Sir Thomas Lucy and others." The Parliament was prorogued 29th March, 1585, and after being again prorogued six times was finally dissolved 14th September, 1586.

Baptised in Charlecote Church, loth February, 1552.

In the Domestic Series of State Papers, 12th April, 1586, is preserved a letter dated from Warwick from. Sir Fulke Greville and Sir Thomas Lucy, in which it is stated that Francis Smith, Esq., was not a recusant, but a good subject, and went to church. The same papers contain the draft of a letter of thanks to Sir Thomas Lucy, 5th September, 1585, for "sending up the two Abingtons, recusants, from Hucknoll." He was elected sheriff of Worcestershire, through the estates brought to him by his wife; and he also sat on the Commission for Tiplers in Stratford-upon-Avon this year. These facts show that he had not hung about London waiting for the predetermined dissolution of Parliament. His party thought him more useful in the country. The certificates of the justices of the peace within the Hundred of Kineton about their proceedings in executing the orders of the Council for the supply of the market with grain were signed by Sir Thomas Lucy and Richard Verney, 28th February, 1587.

It is evident that his "truth and diligence" had been appreciated in high quarters; though I have been unable to find his name among the associations of the nobility and gentry in defence of the Queen's person that Leicester suggested after the Somerville-Arden affair. He appears as Commissioner of Musters during 1588 in the Stratford-upon-Avon Records. On 16th December, 1590, among the State Papers (Dom. Ser. Eliz., 234) is preserved a letter to the Lord President of Wales, for the election of the Earl of Worcester, Lord Chandos, Sir Thomas Lucy, Sir Richard Berkeley, Sir Wm. Herbert of Swansea, and Serjeant Owen, into the Council for the Marches of Wales. And on 22nd April, 1591, Lucy wrote a letter from Charlecote to Mr. Rokeby, Master of Requests, to the effect that he and Richard Verney, justices of the peace for Warwickshire, recommended the case of Thomas Cater, the bearer, who was their neighbour, and had a good title for life to certain lands near, but was wrongfully kept out of them by his adversaries through his poverty. It was probably about this time that a John Shakespeare's name was first included in the list of recusants sent up to the Privy Council by Sir Thomas. The second certificate of all such as have been presented to them was set down at Warwick, and signed by Sir Thomas Lucy 25th September, 1592. It has always been sup- osed that this John was the poet's father. I do not hink so, for two reasons: first, because *Mrs. Shake- peare's* name is not associated with her husband's, as is :he case with the Wheelers and other known recusants; second, because 1592 is just the time of the turn of the tide, in which prosperity came back to the house of Shakespeare, instead of departing from it. But the *other John Shakespeare* of Stratford-upon-Avon, Master of the Shoemakers' Company there, was then a *widower.* He evidently was in trouble at the time, and he disappeared from Stratford immediately after this recusant list was sent in.

In 1593 Sir Thomas Lucy's only son Thomas was knighted; so for a time there were two knights of the same name at Charlecote.

On i0th February, 1595-6, Lady Joyce Lucy died, and was buried in Charlecote Church, where Sir Thomas set up a grand monument for her and for himself. The epitaph he wrote is very singular, and seems intended to answer widespread gossip. The only trace of its nature is preserved in a letter from Sir Edward Aston of Tixhall, who had married his only daughter Anne. He describes his mother-in-law as a perfect vixen, but sons-in-law are apt to revenge themselves by strong language for curtailed privileges ; so we need not altogether believe him. Sir Thomas died on yth July, 1600, and was laid beside his wife on yth August following. He had a grand funeral, but nobody wrote his epitaph, so we do not know how he appeared to his family or. his friends when he had completed his life's work. I think we may believe he closed an honourable career by a fitting end.

It has generally been believed that Shakespeare had some spite against Sir Thomas Lucy, and that he intentionally and bitterly satirised him in the character of Justice Shallow. A story of deer-stealing, trial, threatened imprisonment, mockery in a lampoon, flight to London and keener revenge on the stage, has taken solid shapt

Lady Joyce Lucy, "who departed out of this wretched world to her heavenly kingdom in the year of our Lord God 1595, and of her age 63 ; all the time of her life a true and faithful servant of her good God, never detected of any crime or vice, in religion most sound, in love to her husband most faithful and true; in friendship most constant; to what in trust was committed to her most secret; in wisdom excelling, in governing of her house and bringing up of youth in the feare of God, that did converse with her, most rare and singular. A great maintainer of hospitality; greatly esteemed of her betters; misliked by none unlcsse of the envious. When all is spoken that can be said, a woman so furnished and garnished with virtue as not to be bettered and hardly to be equalled by any. As she lived most vertuously, so she died most godly. Set down by him that best did know what hath been written to be true.lThomas Lucv."

after the pattern of "The Three Black Crows." By degrees this shadow has crept over and obscured the real facts of both lives. The demand for particulars produced the supply. All apocryphas appear after date, and contain some element of confused truth. The ordinary methods of determining authenticity when applied to these traditions prove their unreliability, and elucidate their genesis. Supposing the story to be true, Shakespeare would have been the more hot and angry the nearer the cause of offence happened. He writes of "Sir William Lucy" calmly and pleasantly in Part I. *of Henry VI.* "Shallow" was a much later conception, about ten years after the date of the traditional *story,* and any such "revenge" would have been taken much earlier in his career. But I am sure that "Shallow" was not intended to represent Sir Thomas Lucy; that there was no foundation for the tradition, and that the whole story was built upon a misreading of Shakespeare's plays, and a misunderstanding of his art. His genius was too well balanced to produce a meaningless caricature from superficial associations. To understand what I mean, it is necessary to forget for the time being all preconceived notions whatsoever, and consider analytically the *rtle* of Justice Shallow as a real man. The reason of this creation seems to have been in order to add a new shade to the intricate character of Falstaff, the sot, the braggart, the coward, always impecunious, who risked highway robbery to fill his pockets, and told any number of lies to keep up his credit. *(Henry IV.,* Part I.) It was the ready wit of Falstaff that made him acceptable to the Prince, and popular with the audience. The rags of his conscience were only aired when he was alone, as in *Henry IV.,* Part I., Act iv., scene 2, when he had been made a captain, and allowed to find his own soldiers. "I have misused the King's press damnably; I have got in exchange of a hundred and fifty soldiers three

hundred and odd pounds . . . and such have I to fill up the rooms of them that bought out their services that you would think that I had a hundred and fifty tattered prodigals lately come from swine-keeping," &c. In *Henry IV.* Part II., he is sent on another campaign to separate him from Prince Henry; and he asks the Lord Chief Justice "to lend him a thousand pounds to furnish him forth." This he is refused. On his recruiting tour in Gloucestershire he meets Justice Shallow, whom Shakespeare uses as a foil to his bright parts (Act iii., scene 2). Each sees in the other a means to advance his private ends. Falstaff is a knight of good parentage and upbringing, once page to the highest nobleman in the land, and despite his rollicking ways still in good society, known to be on familiar terms with the young Prince, and now sent in honourable command to the King's wars. Shallow, of meaner descent, of poorer upbringing, evidently a younger son of a younger son, had comparatively lately, either through legal conveyancing acquired at Clement's Inn, through farming or trade, or through a late and unexpected inheritance from some far-off relative, received the honours of a three-hundred-year-old family name and coat of arms, and had become possessed of property important enough to allow him to be appointed a justice of the peace and Commissioner of Musters, a great rise in the world for him. But he wants to rise higher. He is not very wealthy even yet, though wealthier than he seems. Stern training in adversity had taught him to live sparingly, to consider the markets, and never to miss the chance of turning a penny. He is short of servants, and overburdened with petty economies and domestic supervision. His good fortune had come to him too late in life to suggest matrimony, and he was a lean old bachelor still. Davy, his general servant, had been so invaluable to him through the eight years sincehe had come into his property as companion and economiser in the country solitudes of Gloucestershire that he was willing to pardon even the knavery of Davy's friends to secure Davy's allegiance. He was, it is true, kind to the relatives who flattered him in his day of prosperity, as he flattered FalstafF, laughing at poor jokes, and paying far-fetched compliments. He was seemingly honest about wishing the King served with the best soldiers he could find. He was honest also in wishing to do well with his gifts.

There is no conscious humour in Shallow. The audience laugh at him, not with him, when he boasts of his wild youth and of the mad pranks that he had played at Clement's Inn. FalstafFs soliloquy shows the whole situation. He could see the bottom of Justice Shallow. " Every third word was a lie." " At Clement's Inn ... 'a was the very genius of famine, ever in the rearward of fashion," and "now is this Vice's dagger become a squire . . . Well, I'll be acquainted with him . . . and it shall go hard but I will make him a philosopher's two stones to me." Falstaff symbolises himself as an old pike, snapping at one as foolish and ignorant as a young dace.

Shallow's desire of Court influence makes him hospitable. The form that his ambition takes is suggested in the song of his drunken cousin, Silence:

"Do me right
And dub me Knight,
Samingo."

Knighthood was an honour of value in those days, not too easily attained, and even Shallow had wit enough to know the difficulties of an unknown man like himself attaining it. Pistol brings news of the King's death, and Falstaff, showing his intuition of his host's dream, cries: "Master Shallow, my *lord Shallow,* be what thouwilt, I am fortune's steward: happy are they which have been my friends." On the strength of this promise, we can see that Falstaff had got out of Shallow the thousand pounds he had begged in vain of the Lord Chief Justice. They had travelled together to town, were standing together as the young King passed to his coronation, were humbled and disappointed together, and carried off together to the Fleet. Every point in the picture is contradictory to the life and circumstances of Sir Thomas Lucy, except that of being a justice of the peace, as many another householder in England was. It may be that a love of archery and pride in his garden distinguished Sir Thomas, but these were common English tastes. It may possibly be that he had a little habit of repeating his words as Shallow does, but it is perfectly certain that Lucy's familiar oath was not "By the Mass." He had no memories of Clement's Inn, he had never been wild, and, above all, he had always been wealthy, and, so to speak, had always been " Benedict the married man."

A man of many friends, and high social position, he needed no backstairs influence at Court. Knighthood came to him the year Shakespeare was born; in his own house. Is there anything in the action that could suggest Sir Thomas Lucy to a theatrical audience ?

Though the plot of *The Merry Wives of Windsor* is a thing apart from the *History of Henry IV.,* in which Falstaff flourished, and the *History of Henry V.* in which he died, yet the characterization of the principal part is carried over. It is said that Elizabeth expressed a desire to see Falstaff in love, and that Shakespeare picked up the dropped threads of the story as he left it in *Henry IV'.*, Part II. Shallow had quarrelled with Falstaff, doubtless on that memorable occasion when he discovered he had lost his thousand pounds, without a prospect of taking it out in Court patronage.Probably the imprisonment was short, but it was imprisonment, a disgrace all the more galling to the justice that he might not speak of it in public. Apparently he had acted on Shallow's old invitation, had been refused hospitality in the house, and had taken a humorous revenge by hunting the deer in his park. This was an actionable offence, and it was quite creditable to the dignity of Justice Shallow to complain of it, and thereby pay off old scores. He would bring Sir John into a fine of three times the amount of the damage, and three months' imprisonment. This would satisfy his soul in many ways, and would advertise himself and his possessions. Therefore, he hurries after Falstaff to London, scorns advice and mediationl"Were he twenty Sir John Falstaffs he shall not abuse Robert Shallow, esquire." The thousand pounds and his imprisonment stuck in his throat. His servility to Sir John Falstaff is over ; it is clear he can help him no more. "Knight, you have beaten my men, killed my deer, and broke open my lodge." "But not kissed your keeper's daughter." This, probably, had been entered in the formal complaint he had threatened to make to the Council. It was a custom of the time for lawyers to say: "You must plead to the indictment as it stands, aye or no." Sir John Falstaff knows that, and evades the whole on the one point; then allows the whole indictment, and advises Shallow to forbear, or he would be laughed at. For Falstaff knew, what Shallow evidently did not, that such cases must be tried in some open Court of Record in the same county where the offence was committed. Falstaff knew also the old proviso in the Forest Laws, that any one called to the service of the King might take a deer in any park by the way if so be he blew a trumpet; and he knew too his power of ready wit and unconscionable lying would browbeat a Justice Shallow in any court. Was Shallow's park enclosed ? Who werethe men Falstaff had beaten ? Slender seems to have been one of them. "Slender, I broke your head." Then comes Slender's charge against Bardolph and Pistol for stealing his purse when he was drunk, and Falstaff's airy way ofdeciding it. Falstaff would seem to have carried out the humour of the thing by presenting some of Shallow's venison to his host Page, who thanks Shallow for it, as if it had come from himself. He is evidently mollified somewhat thereby, but grumbles, " It was ill- killed." Even in Windsor, Shallow is still poorly attended. Childless and single, he seems affectionate towards the foolish young kinsman who appears to be his heir presumptive. The idea of a rich marriage for him changes the current of his ideas. Slender, awake to his chances, is willing to do anything in reason to please Shallow, even to the extent of marrying the well-endowed daughter of FalstafFs host. Shallow's wrath cools, his sense of importance is satisfied, and he henceforth becomes entirely subordinate to the principal characters. One has only to use Hamlet's words, " Look here upon this picture and on this."

In all this, there is only one point suggesting Lucy, the talk about the coat of arms. There was an opportunity of a play on words such as always delighted the London groundlings, and Shakespeare might have meant a little pleasantry in this discussion, or even a little bitterness. It is quite possible that Sir Thomas Lucy had been at the back of those who opposed the grant of arms to Shakespeare's father; and he might want to show that all associations of an old coat were not necessarily dignified. Lucy did not bear the dozen white luces, but only three luces argent. Other families bore the same, such as "Way" and the family of "Geddes." The representation of twelve for three made a "patible difference," the phrase the heraldsused of the Shakespeare coat when objectors said it was too like another's. Shakespeare's humour may have lain in illustrating the meaning of a "patible difference" between the resembling crests of Shallow and Lucy, men so different in other points.

Much difficulty has been made of Shallow's remark, "The luce is the fresh fish; the salt fish is an old coat." Shakespeare may have done this to show his ignorance of heraldry in using the term "salt" instead of "haur"; or he may have intended an allusion to the "Company of Stock Fishmongers," whose coat of arms also bore "two luces in saltire argent," and perhaps he meant to suggest that Shallow's money had come from a Stock Fishmonger.

I may add, further, that the acting copy of *The Merry Wives of Wlndsor* is taken from the Folio Edition of 1623. But a Quarto Edition was allowed to Busby in January, 1601-2, printed by Creede 1602, "as it had been divers times acted by my Lord Chamberlain's Company both before her Majesty and elsewhere." A second issue appeared in 1619, but in neither is there the slightest allusion to the coat of arms. Of course this was a pirated edition, taken down in rough notes by one of the audience. But we may be perfectly certain that all the points that tickled the ears of the groundlings would have been seized, as it was "played divers times."

It may be suggested that the passage was added after the publication in 1602. But Sir Thomas Lucy died in 1600. Can we imagine Shakespeare base enough to wait to take his revenge until after a man was dead ? Nothing else in the play would have suggested Sir Thomas Lucy. He never had a deer park to steal from, as we may learn from his father's will, from Leland's "Itinerary," and from his grandson's purchase ofFulbrooke in after years. Even Fulbrooke in his time was disparked, and the Act of 5 Elizabeth only concerns deer taken in a chase enclosed, and made a statutable park by Royal permission. His free warren could not count. Manwood has noted " The hare, the conie, the pheasant, the partridge, and none other, are accompted beasts or foules of warrens."

Sir Thomas Lucy never presented deer to the Corporation of Stratford-upon-Avon as other neighbouring park holders did. The park of Sir Thomas Lucy was of his wife's inheritance, far away in Worcestershire. That Shakespeare might have chased and slain many a deer is quite possible, as that was considered a proper part of the training of every youth of spirit.f And there were so many loopholes of escape. Even in the Forest Laws it is said, "And although men may kill such wild beasts in their wildness, when they are found wandering, being out of a forest, parke, or chase, yet noman hath any property in them until they have *killed* them." If, therefore, there was no penalty possible even had Shakespeare been clever enough to secure one of Sir Thomas's home-stalled deer, how could the story arise of Shakespeare's flight to London, when it should have been Sir Thomas's chase to London ? Doubtless out of the materials of *The Merry Wives of Windsor,* by some realistic romancer. (See my article in the *Fortnightly,* February, 1903, " Sir Thomas Lucy not the original of Justice Shallow.") The ballad on Sir Thomas Lucy needs only to be analysed to be discredited. The production is evidently of later date, and the story is based on the play, except in the particulars regarding Lucy's value as a Parliament member, which we have seen to be untrue. "Poets are born, not made." Even in his youth Shakespeare could never have written these poor lineslldisconnected, far-fetched, unjust, and untrue.

" A fayre park called Fulbrooke. In this parke was a praty Castle made of Stone and bricke. There is a little lodge or Piece of Building in this parke, called Bargeiney, made, as I conjecture, by some Lord or Lady Bargeiney. This Castle of Fulbrooke was an Eyesore to the Earles that lay in Warwick Castle, and was cause of displeasure between each Lord. Sir William Compton, keeper of Fulbrooke Parke and Castle, seeing it go to mine, helped it forward, taking part of it (as some say) for the Building of his house at Compton by Brayles in Warwickshire, and permitted others to take pieces of it down. ... A mile and a halfe lower down the Avon leaveth Charlecote, Mr. Lucie's ancient manor place on the left ripe."|Leland's "Itinerary." No park mentioned.

Fulbrooke was granted to John Dudley, Earl of Warwick, by Edward VI. Mary gave it to Sir Francis Engldidd, but disparked it. He went abroad on Eliiabeth's accession, as he was a Catholic. His estate was seized in 1571. Sir Thomas Lucy's grandson bought it in James's reign.

In Sir Philip Sidney's "May-Lady" deer-stealing is described as "a pretty service." Francis Osborne, born 1589, regrets he had not had the chance of such a training.

The students of Oxford had always been notorious poachers. An Act in the fifteenth century banished "disorderly hunters" from the university. But this seems to have been ignored. Their depredations led to the disparting of Radley Park near Abingdon, four miles from Oxford, in the time of Henry VIII. (see Leland). Dr. Forman relates how two students in 1573 "never studied or gave themselves to their books, but to go to schools of defence, to the dancing schools, to steal deer and conies, and to hunt the hare"; and one of these was John Thornborough, afterwards Dean of York and Bishop of Worcester.|(See Halliwcll- Phillipps' "Outlines.")

Other causes guided Shakespeare to London.

Is it possible that Sir Thomas Lucy demeaned his character for justice in personal revenge for some such offence ? Is he likely to have warped the law to suit his own ends ? I cannot think it. He must have been too well acquainted with the letter of the law, too much experienced in its bearing, to have attempted anything of the kind, which would have defamed the honour of a noble race and the credit of the Bench. There is not a trace of any prosecution either in the Records of Stratford, Warwick, or the Star Chamber.

The one play that above all others gives Shakespeare's dreams and thoughts about a forest and the chase is *As You Like It,* and there, I think, is to be found the nearest approach to a portrait that Shakespeare has given us of Sir Thomas Lucy, as a justice, the reverse of thin,

With eyes severe, and beard of formal cut,
Full of wise saws and modern instances.

3

SECTION 3

(42)

CHAPTER III

Sir Thomas Lucy The Second: 1551-1605.

Some confusion has arisen, even in high quarters, owing to the fact that three succeeding Sir Thomas Lucys were contemporary with Shakespeare. Of the second considerably less is known than of the first and third. Dugdale does not give the date of his birth, nor have I been able to find it in any other printed notice. Malone mentions the Inquisition Post-mortem of Sir Thomas Lucy the Elder, taken at Warwick, 26th September, 1601, and speaks of its contents in the "Prolegomena." But at the Record Office only a fragment of the Inquisition remains, enough to identify the person and the place, but insufficient for literary criticism. The age of the heir has disappeared.

But the Inquisition Post-mortem of Dame Joyce Lucy, who died on the 10th of February, 1595-6, was taken after the death of her husband (43 Eliz., 160 Wigorn., Part I.). This gives full details of her property, and states that at the time of his mother's death, her only son and heir Thomas was forty-four years old and more, which throws back the date of his birth to 1551. As there is no entry of his birth in the Charlecote Register, it probably took place in Worcestershire. His parents must have been still very young, his father being nineteen and his mother seventeen. Perhaps Sir William Lucy saw his infant grandson before he died that year.

This second Thomas was probably educated at home, like his father. There is no notice of his having travelled, though he seems to have been studious and literary. As Dugdale says of one of his ancestors, there is nothing noticeable about him except his marriages. He first married Dorothy, the heiress of Nicholas Arnold, Esq., of Kingsholm, Highnam, and Upleaden Manor, county Gloucester. She is always stated to have been the daughter of Sir Nicholas, but I find from a Chancery case that she was not. She was the only daughter of his eldest son Roland, who died before his father. The date of their marriage is given in the Charlecote Register. "Mr. Thomas Lucye, Esquier, was maried to Dorothee Arnoll sone *(sic)* to Sir Nicholas Arnoll Knight 27 Jan. 1574[5]." The estates were delivered to Thomas Lucy, Esq., in right of his wife (see Rudder's "Gloucestershire," p. 342). In the State Papers, Dom. Ser. Eliz., 117, f. 8, is preserved a "Brief of Mr. Richard Arnold's proofs that there was an entail of the lands of his brother, Sir Nich. Arnold, with Mr. Lucy's answers to the same, about 1580." By Dorothy Arnold Thomas Lucy had a son, named Thomas, who died young. Among the young gentlemen willing to serve in arms in Warwickshire, 1583, appears the name of "young Lucie" (see State Papers, Dom. Ser. Eliz., 165, f. 46). I used to consider this a reference to Thomas Lucy the Second, but since I found the dates of his birth and marriage I think the entry must. refer to some other member of the family. The young couple had also a daughter: " Mrs. Joyes Lucye, daughter of Mr. Thomas Lucye Esquier was baptized ye 8 of July 1578." She was married to William Cooke,a relative of Sir Francis Bacon. An interesting letter, probably written in 1597, to Sir Thomas, in connection with this affair, is preserved in Spedding's " Life of Bacon."

A Chancery case arose from this wedding in 1607. Sir Thomas Lucy the Third and his mother Dame Constance Lucy, executors of the will of Sir Thomas Lucy the Second, and a number of tenants appealed against the husband of Joyce, now Sir William Cooke, that he would not repair dilapidations, or confirm leases and made forcible entries on copyhold tenures. That Sir Nicholas Arnold, seised

To Sir Thomas Lucy.

Sir,|There was no news better welcome to me this long time than that of the good success of my kinsman; wherein if he be happy he cannot be happy alone, it consisting of two parts. And I render you no less kind thanks for your aid and favour towards him than if it had been for myself, assuring you that this bond of alliance shall on my part tie me to give all the tribute to your good fortune upon all occasions that my poor strength can yield. I send you, so required, an abstract of the -lands of inheritance, and one lease of great value which my kinsman bringeth, with a note of the tenures, notices, contents, and state, truly and perfectly drawn; whereby you may perceive the land is good land, and well countenanced by scope of acres, woods and royalties; though the total of rents be set down, as it now goeth, without improvement; in which respect it may differ somewhat from your first note. Out of. this what he will assure in jointure I leave it to his own kindness; for I love not to measure affection. To conclude, I

of Highnam, &c., had left it to his heiress Dorothy, who married Sir Thomas Lucy deceased, and held her lands after her death by the courtesy of England. And shortly after the marriage of his daughter Joyce in 39 Eli?., she and her husband agreed that Sir Thomas Lucy should continue the tenure, and grant leases of twenty-one years. But since his death they refuse to act on their agreement. The answer to this Bill of Complaint was signed by Francis Bacon as well as by Sir William Cooke and his wife. It states that Sir Nicholas Arnold did not die seised of the lands, as he had conveyed them to his wife first and then to Dorothy and her heirs; that his wife died before him, that Sir Nicholas died 22 Eli/., and Dorothy five or six months later, that Dorothy had not entered into possession, and her husband could not hold the lands by the courtesy of England. 1t farther stated that Sir Thomas Lucy had asked the right to make leases, ic., before their marriage, which Cooke refused, thinking it to be very unreasonable ; that Sir Thomas Lucy had acquainted his daughter Joyce of this, and said that Sir William Cooke only sought the marriage for her wealth and lands, and seemed to be discontented, and to dislike the marriage, and tried to persuade Joyce to refuse Sir William. But Sir William, by entreaty of Lady Joyce, gave in, to win the favour of Sir Thomas, and agreed to be as good to him as he could, and allowed him the courtesy of England in the lands for his life. But Sir Thomas had allowed great waste, had cut down timber to the amount of 5'jo/., and the property, which amounted to 15,ooo/. at least during the minority of the said Joyce, had been much depreciated. That the executors of Sir Thomas should pay the waste and damages, and give up all claim to leases.l6 Oct. 1607. Chan. Proc. James I., L. xiii. 55.

doubt not your daughter mought have married to a better living, but never to a better life; having chosen a gentleman bred to all honesty, virtue, and worth, with an estate convenient. And if my brother or myself were either thrivers or fortunate in the Queen's service, I would hope there should be left as great an house of the Cookes in this gentleman as in your good friend, Mr. Attorney-General. But sure I am, if Scriptures fail not, it will have as much of God's blessing, and sufficiency is ever the best feast.

(See " Resuscitatio" Supplement, p. 92, Spedding's "Life," ii., 369.)

Mrs. Dorothy Lucy, we see, did not live very long, and the young widower married secondly, Constance, daughter and heir of Richard Kingsmill, Esquire. They had a large family, six sons and eight daughters. There is little recorded of their married lives, but everything points to domestic happiness. In the absence of other details one little incident may be noted in connection with the great flood of the Avon on the 18th of July, 1588. In the Parish Registers of Welcombe it is mentioned that the Avon drowned the bridge, broke down Grange Mill, washed away much hay and many carts, " and three wains with the furniture of Mr. Thomas Lucy." He would therefore seem at that time to have been moving his residence.

He was knighted in 1592-3, as may be seen in Met- calfe's " Book of Knights." (This entry does not occur in the Cotton MS.) The young couple appear to have stayed occasionally with Mr. Kingsmill at Hurstborne. The Dictionary of National Biography states that their fourth son, William, was born there.

On 28th November, 1595, among "the gentlemen of account living in London," I find in " Tower Warde, Sir Thomas Lucye, of the county of Gloucester, knight " (Lansd. MS. 78, f. 67). He would be entered thus on account of his first wife's possessions in Highnam.The same manuscript curiously enough gives the name of another Warwickshire contemporary of less note. "An examination of certain idle and masterless men and women at the Old Bailey by the Commissioners, July 22, 1595." "Agnes Robinson, a poor lame woman, dwelleth at Stafford-upon-Raven *(sic)* Warwickshire, and was sent thither with a passeport." (Lansd. MS.

78, f-531-)

Sir Thomas the Second was therefore in London

when the new poems of the Earl of Southampton's *pro- tlge* were stirring the literary world. Already they had been noticed in William Herbert's "Epicedium of Lady Helen Branch," in "Willobie his Avisa," in Drayton's " MatiWa," in W. Clarke's " Polimanteia," in "L'Envoy to Narcissus," by Thomas Edwards, and (probably) in Spenser's "Colin Clout's come home again." Sir Thomas Lucy could not but have heard of his Warwickshire neighbour. Probably he returned to Charlecote on his mother's death, 10th February, 1595-6, remained with his father, and succeeded there on yth July, 1600. His first act was to solemnise with great magnificence the funeral ceremonies of his father on yth August in Charlecote Church. Three heralds came down from London, among whom was William Camden, Clarencieux, the author of the "Britannia." But Sir Thomas, by some oversight, placed no epitaph on his father's tomb. The only son and heir, he was handicapped by no brothers' portions, and no mother's dowry. His sister Joyce had already received her portion. So he proceeded at once to make his will on I3th August, 1600, in "perfect health of body and mind." He left his heir his due share of "Landes, tenementes and here- ditamentes" (no park), made arrangements for the maintenance and education of his younger sons, and assigned property for the "preference in marriage" of his daughters. He left "to his entirely beloved wife,the Lady Constance, the house of Charlecote, with all demesnes and as much copse wood out of Hampton Woods as is yearly cut for Charlecote, for fuel. The use of all the household stuff in Charlecote," though she was "to leave it there for the heir." "I give to my wife all my plate, goods, and chattels at Overton in Wiltshire, and all the plate, goods, and chattels I have in all England, except such as I otherwise dispose of." "To my son and heir Thomas, the gilte bason and ewer graven, which was my father's, with the two gilded engraven lyverye potts, and a nest of gilded holies, with a cover, and a gilded saulte, together with a dozen of gilded spoones, to whom I also give all my household stuff at Sutton and my best horse and furniture at his choice, bothe to be chosen by him. And all my Frenche and Italian bookes." "To my second son, Richard, my second best horse and furnyture, to whom I appoynte no porcion of land, for that his grandfather, my most lovyng father-in-lawe, hath promised to assure him in Hurstborne. But towards his placing there I give him one hundred pounds of current English money." There is no mention of his third son, but he may have been "placed" during his father's lifetime. Dugdale merely names him George. "I give my fourthe sonne, William Lucie, part of my lease at Rudforde, which I hold of the Deane and Chapter of Gloucester for three lyves, whereof his life is one ; the lyvinge that Richard Restall holdeth from me in Rudford; the lyvinge which Robert Griffith holdeth from me in Rudforde, and the myll which Geoffrey Suckley holdeth from me in Rudford, paying the Dean and Chapter their old rent." "I give to my fifth son, Robert Lucye, the remainder of Rudford. I give unto my sixth sonne, Francis Lucy, when he shall accomplish the age of one and twenty yeares, the manner of Cherington, in Warwickshire, and the rent of Hugford Myddleton, in the county of Salop,or thirtye pounds by the yeare. And until theis my three laste younger sonnes shall be possessed of their several livinges, to have for their mayntenance and breeding up in learning the profits of the manors of Cherrington and of Hugford Mydleton and Wooten Howe, and twenty pounds a yeare out of the mannor of Kingston in Herefordshire." To all his daughters he left one hundred marks for a jewel. To his "trustie and true servant Thomas Gwillim fortye pounds of current English money and my best trotting gelding." To his servant Thomas Addis thirty pounds. All other servants to have one year's wages. The executors were to be "Lady Constance Lucie and my heir, Thomas Lucy . . . my approvers, my good friend Mr. William Walter, and my moste kinde, and loving brother-in- lawe, Mr. William Wroughton." For their pains they were to have one hundred marks each. "And the overseer of my will, my most loving father-in-lawe, Richard Kingsmill, Esq., my best ambling gelding and a hundred pounds in money." The witnesses were William Walter, Geoffrey Suckley, his marke, Richard Haile, William Cleeve, John Llad.

He was lieutenant of the county in 1601 (43 Eliz.). Dugdale says that he died in 1 James I. (1603). But the Charlecote Register gives the date as two years later:|" Sir Thomas Lucy, Knight, departed this life the Sixteenth day of July, 1605, and was buried the xx day of August, 1605, in the 3rd year of the King's Majesties reign."

The will was proved in London on the 20th of November, 1605, by Lady Constance Lucy. On the sumptuous monument in Charlecote Church there are carved neither dates nor epitaph. Perhaps Lady Lucy thought the fourteen kneeling children and the sorrowing wife in marble sufficient record of the many virtues ofthe deceased. The Inquisition Post-mortem of hisgoods was taken at Warwick before Thomas Leigh and William Hart. It is blotted at the date, but it took place on the 15th of July, a year all but a day after his death.

Though the dates are contradictory, the facts mentioned regarding the second son in the Dictionary of National Biography are: "Richard (1592-1667) matriculated from Magdalen College, Oxford, in 1607, aged 15, and graduated Bachelor ofArts from Exeter College in 1611. He became a student at Lincoln's Inn in 1608. Through his marriage with Elizabeth, daughter of Sir Henry Cock, and widow of Sir Robert Oxenbridge (d. 1616), he became life-owner of Broxbournbury, Hertfordshire. He was knighted at Whitehall 8 January, 1617-18, and was created a baronet on 1 1 March following."

Elizabeth Kingsmill left by will on 9th December, 1605, "To my cousin, Richard Lucy, my whole game of Swannes in the river."

He and his wife had a suit in Chancery (Chancery Proceedings, Jac. I., L. x. 18, 5th July, 1622) against Edward Turner, of the Middle Temple, London, who had been formerly steward in the demesnes of Brox- bourne, Cheshunt, and Austen, in the county of Hertford, and had retained the Court rolls, charters, and muniments. As they cannot give the dates, and do not know how they are kept, they cannot apply to Common Law for redress. He had another suit later (Chancery Proceedings, Jac. I., L. xiii., 10th February, 1622-3).

In the State Papers, 8th May, 1639, there is an amusing *contretemps* recorded between him and Lord Ker at Ware, when the latter was carrying letters to the Queen.

He was elected Member for Old Sarum to the Long Parliament in 1647, and sat in Cromwell's Parliaments of 1654 and 1656 as Member for Hertfordshire. His

Somerset Home, 18, Stafford.

son, Kingsmill, of Facombe, Hampshire, the second baronet, was a Fellow of the Royal Society and Doctor of Civil Law. He married Theophila, second daughter of George, Earl of Berkeley. His son, Sir Berkeley, also a Fellow of the Royal Society, died the 1gth of November, 1759, and the title became extinct.

Burke says that George was slain in France, but in Charlecote Register there is the entry, "Mr. George Lucye was buried the 19 day of August, in the year of our Lord 1646."

The fourth son was William Lucy, whose dates the Dictionary makes 1591-1677 (it must mean 1594 or 1595, seeing his elder brother was born in 1592). He was born at Hurstbourne, entered Trinity College, Oxford, 1610, graduated Bachelor of Arts 13th November, 1613, and the following year studied at Lincoln's Inn. He afterwards studied at Cambridge, 1615, and became Master of Arts in 1619. He lived for several years there upon his estate, and then took the degree of Bachelor of Divinity. By the special recommendation of the King he was made chaplain to George Duke of Buckingham, and took his doctor's degree at once. Some objections were made to this. There is a curious statement among the State Papers for July, 1623, by his brother, that William Lucy, being descended from an ancient and honourable family of barons, came within the limits of the statute enclosed, and was admitted at once to a doctor's degree, which certain ignorant persons appealed against. Dr. William wrote a letter with this statement to Secretary Conway, thanking him for his favours, and requesting a continuance of the same. He was granted the living of Burgh Clere and of High Clere in Hampshire, where he quietly studied for some years.

He was dispossessed during the Civil Wars, when he lost his library, which he had been at great pains tocollect (see Tanner MS., 146, 133; Hobbes' "Leviathan," 1657, Epistle to the Reader; Clarendon State Papers, No. 664; Walker's "Sufferings of the Clergy," p. 298). After the Restoration he was appointed Bishop of St. David's on 18th November, 1660. He had rather a stormy time in his See, as he expressed his views very definitely, and would not submit to any infringement of his rights. He wrote several philosophical and religious works (see Wood's "Athenae Oxonienses," vol. iii., r 127). He was the ancestor of the Castle Cary Lucys.

Of the fifth, Robert, Dugdale says nothing. The only point I have found that may refer to him is from Le Neve's "Book of Knights." He states that Sir Edward Atkins, of Kensington, Gloucestershire, Lord Chief Baron of the Exchequer, married the

daughter of Lucy, of the Strand, brother of Sir

Richard Lucy, Baronet. Probably Robert was the "orphan" his mother mentions. One entry in Charle- cote Register may refer to him :l" Bridget Lucye, the daughter of Robert Lucye, Esquier, and Margaret, his wife, was baptised the 6th of September, 1655."

Francis, the sixth son, matriculated from Trinity College, Oxford, 5th May, 1615, aged 15, became a Barrister-at-Law at Lincoln's Inn in 1623, and was elected Member for Warwick in 1624, 1625, 1626, and 1628. Of his affairs, besides what is mentioned in his father's will, I have only found the notice in the State Papers, July 3rd, 1632.

"Mr. Corderoy desires to sell Conholt Farm. Francis, the son of Lady Lucy, offered him two thousand three hundred pounds for it." The will of Martha Lucy, one of Sir Thomas's daughters, is preserved at Somerset House, dated 1618 (27 Meade).

Lady Constance survived her husband many years. Besides the Chancery case already mentioned (see footnote, p. 43), she had another in regard to property atHigh Gere, Hampshire, in 1608. There was a little wood at Asmersworth in the parish of East Woodhay in the county of Southampton, of which two shares belonged to her father, and the third to her mother, Alice. Sir Robert Oxenbregge (Oxenbridge) had got hold of some papers, claimed the right of the woods, had cut down the trees, and had taken up for trespass the servants she had sent to protect them. She, as heir to her father, prayed relief. (Chan. Proc., Jac. I., L. xii. 51.) Various notices of her occur in the State Papers. "On Nov. 30, 1611, from Blackfriars, Constance, Lady Lucy, writes to thank Earl Salisbury for accepting her orphan son to his service."

Another Chancery case was initiated by Lady Constance against Sir John Hungerford, whose son, Sir Anthony, had married her daughter Elizabeth. Her late husband, Sir Thomas Lucy, had assured his daughter of two thousand pounds after marriage, and Sir John had promised them two hundred pounds a year and- the right to live in his house; but since her husband's death Sir John Hungerford had been stirred up against his son and his wife, and had turned them out of his house, without making any provision for them to dwell elsewhere. When they had found a home in the house of their brother-in-law, Sir John had entered in their absence, broken open a desk belonging to Sir Anthony, taken out the obligation he had signed, and had removed some of their furniture. (Chan. Proc., Jac. I., L. xv., 48, 1617.) I have not found the decision. She had yet another suit about letting some property in Clifton, Warwickshire, 26th June, 1623. (Chan. Proc., Jac. I., L. xviii., n.)

On the 26th of November, 1624, a warrant was drafted permitting Dame Constance Lucy, widow, of St. Giles Without, Cripplegate, to reside in London on account of her age and infirmities. In this was encloseda certificate by Dr. William Paddy and Dr. Thomas Mountford that Lady Constance Lucy, of St. Giles, Cripplegate, was too ill to be removed from her house into the country, 1gth November, 1624.

The Lady Constance was in the habit of having a grandchild to stay with her. It seems suggestive of unhealthy surroundings that two of these died in her care. Dugdale mentions the tomb and epitaphs of both, as also does Fisher. On the south side of the Choir of St. Giles, Cripplegate, is the inscription: "To the memory of Constance Whitney, eldest daughter to Sir Robert Whitney, of Whitney, the proper possession of him and his ancestors in Herefordshire for above five hundred years past. Her mother was the fourth daughter of Sir Thomas Lucy, of Charlecote, in Warwickshire, by Constance Kingsmill, daughter and heir of Richard Kingsmill, Surveyor of the Court of Wards. This Lady Lucy, her grandmother, so bred her since she was eight years old as she excelled in all noble qualities, becoming a virgin of so sweet proportion of beauty and harmony of parts; she had all sweetness of manners answerable, a delightful sharpness of wit, an offenceless modesty of conversation, a singular respect and piety to her parents, and religious even to example. She departed this life most Christianly at seventeen, dying to the grief of all, but to her grandmother an unrecoverable loss, save in her expectation she shall not stay long after, and the comfort of knowing who she is, and where in the resurrection to meet her."

In the same choir lies her cousin, whose tomb is also mentioned in Fisher's "Monuments." "Here lies Margaret Lucy, the second daughter of Sir Thomas Lucy of Charlecot, in the county of Warwick (the third by immediate descent of the name of Thomas) by Alice, the daughter and heir of Thomas Spencer, of Claverdon, in the same countie, Esq., and Custos Brevium of theCourt of Common Pleas at Westminster, who departed this life the 18th of November, 1634, and about the nineteenth year of her age. For discretion and sweetness of conversation not many excelled, and for piety and patience in her sickness and death few equalled her, which is the comfort of her nearest friends, to every of whom she was very dear; but especially to her old grandmother, the Lady Constance Lucy, under whose government she died, who having long expected to have gone before her, doth now trust by faith and hope in the precious blood of Christ shortly to follow after, and be made partaker together with her and others of the unspeakable and eternal joys in His blessed kingdom," &c.

Lady Constance died in 12 Charles I. The Charlecote Register says, "Domina Constantia Lucy, obiit apud High Clere in Comitatu Hamptoniensi, cujus corpus hinc translatum magna cum solemnitate sepultum fuit vicesimo octavo die Martij 1637." The Inquisition Post-mortem of her goods was taken in 13 Charles I., though entered at the Record Office as 15 Charles I. (Part II., 112, Southampton.) The name of Thomas Cooke is mentioned. The age of the heirs is not clear.

In the State Papers, 2jth January, 1637-8, we find on a list, signed by John Button, late Sheriff of Hampshire, of persons in arrear for Ship-money," Hurstborne Tarrant, Lady Constance Lucy, deceased, 3/." Eleven others had refused to pay. She must have attained a good old age before she departed, and left her dowry in Charlecote back to her husband's heir, Sir Thomas Lucy the Third.

4

SECTION 4

CHAPTER IV
Sir Thomas Lucy The Third: 1585-1640.

In the Inquisition Post-mortem of his father, Sir Thomas Lucy the Third is entered as being "19 years and 50 weeks old" at the time of his father's death. If (as Dugdale states) this happened in 1603, ne would have been born in 1584. This date is supported by the epitaph on his tomb, which says that he was fifty-six at his death in 1640. If his father's death took place in 1605, as the Charlecote Register gives it, the date of his birth would be 1586. This latter date is supported by the Students' Register in Oxford, where he matriculated from Magdalen College, the 8th May, 1601, aged fifteen. The heraldic visitation of Warwickshire, taken in 1619, states that Sir Thomas was thirty-three at that date.

He became a student at Lincoln's Inn about 1602, and was knighted early, though at what place and under what circumstances I have hitherto been unable to find. Metcalfe's "Knights" does not inform us. He was fond of travelling, delighted in riding, and studied all the arts and accomplishments of the fashionable young knights of the period. He became much more a public man than his father or grandfather. His great friend was the young Lord Herbert of Cherbury, famous alike for his philosophic thought and his personal vanity.From the "Autobiography" of that young nobleman we learn something of the travels, in 1609, of his friend, Sir Thomas Lucy the Third. At page 107 of the edition by Mr. Sidney Lee, he says :l

Having passed thus all the winter until the latter end of

January (1609)! took my leave of the French King

at which time the Princess of Conti desired me to carry a scarf into England and present it to Queen Anne on her part, which being accepted, myself and Sir Thomas Lucy (whose second I had been twice in France, against two cavaliers of our nation, who yet were hindered to fight with us in the field, where we attended them), we came on our way as far as Dieppe in Normandy, and there took ship about the beginning of February, when so furious a storm arose that with very great danger we were at sea all night.

The master of our ship lost both the use of his compass and his reason ; for not knowing whither he was carried by the tempest, all the help he had was by the lightnings, which, together with thunder very frequently that night, terrified him, yet gave the advantage sometimes to discover whether we were upon our coast, which he thought by the course of his glasses we were near approached. And now towards day we found ourselves, by great providence of God, within view of Dover, to which the master of our ship did make. The men of Dover, rising betimes in the morning to see whether any ship were coming towards them, were in great numbers upon the shore, as believing that the tempest, which had thrown down barns and trees near the town, might give them the benefit of some wreck, if perchance any ship were driven thitherwards. We coming thus in extreme danger straight upon the pier of Dover, which stands out in the sea, our ship was unfortunately split against it; the master said, *Mes amis, nous sommes perdus ;* or, My friends, we are cast away. When myself who heard the ship crack against the pier and then found by the master's words it was time for every one to save themselves, if they could, got out of my cabin (though very sea-sick) and climbing up the mast a little way, drew my sword and flourished it.

They at Dover having this sign given them, adventured in a shallop of six oars to relieve us, which being come with great danger to the side of our ship, I got into it first with my sword in my hand, and called for Sir Thomas Lucy, saying, that if any man offered to get in before him, I should resist him with my sword ; whereupon a faithful servant of his taking Sir Thomas Lucy out of the cabin, who was half dead of sea-sickness, put him into my arms, whom after I. had received, I bid the shallop make away for shore, and the rather that I saw another shallop coming to relieve us ; when a post from France, who carried letters, finding the ship still rent more and more, adventured to leap from the top of our ship into the shallop, where, falling fortunately on some of the stronger timber of the boat, and not on the planks, which he must needs have broken, and so sunk us, had he fallen upon them, escaped together with us two unto the land. I must confess myself, as also the seamen that were in the shallop, thought once to have killed him for this desperate attempt ; but finding no harm followed, we escaped together unto the land, from whence we sent more shallops, and so made means to save both men and horses that were in the ship, which yet itself was wholly split and cast away, insomuch that in pity to the master Sir Thomas Lucy and myself gave thirty pounds towards his loss, which yet was not so great as we thought, since the tide now ebbing he recovered the broken parts of his ship.

After being received at Court and performing his commission, Lord Herbert returned to his wife and studies. He delighted in riding the great horse.

No horse yet was so dear to me as the jennett I brought from France, whose love I had so gotten, that he would suffer none else to ride him, nor indeed any man to come near him, when I was upon him, as being in his nature a most furious horse. ... Sir Thomas Lucy would have given me 2OO/. for this horse, which, though I would not accept, yet I left the horse with him when I went to the Low Countries, who not long after died.

Mr. Sidney Lee, the editor of this autobiography,makes an error in adding a note to the effect that this Sir Thomas was the son of Shakespeare's Sir Thomas. "Richard Lord Dorset" had Lord Herbert's portrait, which he had got as " a copy of a picture which one Larkin (or Lockie) a painter drew for me, the original whereof I intended before my departure to the Low Countries for Sir Thomas Lucy" (p. 127). This portrait, painted on copper, is still preserved at Charlecote.

Sir Thomas Lucy was a great patron of literature. We may notice the epigram ofjohn Davies of Hereford, written in 1610, in "The Scourge of Folly," n.d., printed by E. A. for Richard Redmer :|

To my much honoured and beloved Sir Thomas Lucy, Knight. Epigram 103.

Bright sparke of Wit and Courage ; yet ynow
To set a world of hearts in love, on fire ;
Whose influence provokes my Muses Plow

To cast thy Beames abroad, that be intire,
Thou all-belou'd and highly-prized Jemme
That in the Courts Browes (like a Diamond
Or Hesperus in Heaven) dost lighten them
For men to see their way on glorie's ground;
Of thy most honoured nature, take in gree
This offer of my Muse to honour thee.

He seems to have been more interested than any of his family in game as well as horses. He made a Star Chamber matter of a deer-stealing case in his Worcester estate of Sutton Park. He petitioned, July, 1610,against those who had unlawfully taken the deer from his enclosed park, that the " pernicious example " might be checked, praying that the punishment might be awarded the offenders which had been decreed in 3 James I.; and that the severer punishment might be added of contempt of law. He indicted William Wall, of Rooke, in the county of Wigorn, gentleman, Rowland Harnage,of Kynlett, in the county of Salop, gentleman, and other abettors. William Wall pleaded " not guilty " (June, 1611). (See *Notes and Queries,* Third Series, vol. xii., p. 181.) The extremely bitter form of the petition has suggested to my mind a possibility that some of the parties prosecuted might have written on him "the satirical ballad," and might have fixed it to his park gates: might, indeed, have suggested the comparison to Justice Shallow, afterwards fathered on Shakespeare. Thus many a picture, first modestly entitled "after" Rubens, Teniers, or Titian, in later days takes the credit of a master's name. This Sir Thomas purchased Fulbrooke Park, had it united to Hampton Woods, enclosed, and licensed by King James.

He was also more politically inclined than his immediate predecessors. He sat as knight of the shire in six successive Parliamentslin 1614 along with Sir Richard Verney; in 1620 with Sir Fulke Greville; in 1624 with Sir Clement Throckmorton, and in 1625, 1628, and in April and May, 1640. He seems to have taken a thoughtful and disinterested view of his duties to his country. He was lieutenant of the county in 10 James I. and in 9 Charles I. That he was also justice of the peace is evident from the State Papers.

On the 20th of July, 1613, there was a grant to Sir Thomas Leigh, Baronet, of Stoneleigh, and Sir Thomas Lucy, of Charlecote, Warwickshire, of an annuity of 200/. for the use of Lady Alice, the wife of Sir Robert Dudley (son of the Earl of Leicester), during her life.

On the 26th of November, 1622, a letter was written from Warwick by Sir Thomas Leigh, Sir Richard Verney, and Sir Thomas Lucy to the Council aboutthe dispute regarding a coal mine owned by some Coventry men.

He was the first Lucy to give a buck to the Town Council of Stratford-upon- Avon :l"*1tem,* given to Sir Thomas Lucie his keeper for his fee, and in wyne bestowed on him whenas he brought us a bucke, 121. *6J."* (Chamberlain's Accounts, Stratford-upon-Avon, 1632.)

On the 5th of July, 1625, a demise of property was drawn up by Henry Lord Worley and Monteagle, Richard Catesby, Walter Stafford, and Anthony Pen- ruddock to Sir Thomas Lucy of Charlecote and John Penruddock as sureties.

On the 19th of October, 1635, Bishop Wright of Coventry and Lichfield invited the sheriff, Sir Thomas Puckering, Sir Thomas Lucy, and Mr. William Purefoy to meet him at Coventry about martial affairs.

In April, 1639, an indenture was signed between Sir Thomas Leigh, Sir Thomas Holt, Sir Thomas Lucy, and William Boughton, deputy-lieutenants of the county of Warwick, with Lieutenant Moses Tresinell to conduct two hundred and thirty men newly pressed in the county to Selby, Yorkshire.

On the 24th of February, 1639-40, letters of attorney were written by Sir Thomas Lucy and Richard Catesby of Drury-lane, to William Ewer and Ursula Catesby against Sir William Saunders and others to recover money due. These entries are from State Papers. The last notice is touching to read. On the 25th of March, 1640, Sir Thomas writes :l

I have received commandment from the Council to give my personal attendance for some reasons to be communicated to me at my coming up. The truth is for this ten weeks I have been so indisposed that I have scarcely peeped out of my chamber, and a short journey of four miles on Monday last to Warwick completely distempered me, so that I find, without much danger, I shall not be able to endure so long a journey. I pray you, therefore, if occasion be offered to move the Board that I may be dispensed with until I may undertake the journey with probable safety; but if I must come, it is fit, though I had a hundred lives, I should hazard them all to testify my obedience.

He died on the 10th of December, 1640.

On the 3rd of January, 1640-41, from Ragley, Fulke Reed wrote to Edward Viscount Conway:

Though it be conceived somewhat early to send to Chalcot about what you commanded me, there being a heavy house, and the funeral not yet finished, yet I sent Mr. Prescot, a friend, to know what purpose there is for disposing of such of Sir Thomas Lucy's estates your lordship is desirous to deal with.

The entry in the Register runs thus:|"Dominus Thomas Lucy placide dormivet in Christo, 10 die Decembris, et summo cum honore sepultus fuit 20 die Januarij, 1640. Anno Regis Caroli xvj."

Sir Thomas married about 1610 (see funeral sermon) Alice, only daughter and heir of Thomas Spencer, of Claverdon, and granddaughter of Sir John Spencer, of Althorpe, Northamptonshire, by whom he had a large family. The sons were Spencer, Robert, Richard, Thomas, William, George, and Fulke. Of the daughters, Constance married Sir William Spencer, of Yarnton, and afterwards Sir Edward Smith; Margaret died unmarried (see her epitaph in last chapter); Bridget married Sir Bryan Broughton; Anne, Sir William Underhill; Mary, Sir Matthew Herbert; and Elizabeth, Sir John Walcot. There was also a Theophila,born 1632, and buried 1638; and an Elizabeth, born 1633. Fulke was born in 1630, and William was buried in 1631.

Sir Thomas Lucy's will is in Somerset House. It had been drawn up on the 20th of September, 1639. In order "to advance his wife Dame Alice" and his children, he leaves to her, "all those my pastures and grounds inclosed, commonly known by the name of Fulbrook Grounds or Fulbrooke Parke, with appurtenances" for her life, and after her, first to Spencer Lucy, second to Robert Lucy, third to Richard Lucy, fourth to Thomas Lucy, fifth to George Lucy, sixth to Fulke Lucy.

"All the lands belonging to Fulbrooke, and not within the Parke, lately impaled, shall be liable for annuities. To my good friend, Mr. James Prescott .... that he may be assistant to my wife and family in their needs, an annuity of 40*l*. .... I give to Mr. Franchin, who is beyond the seas with my sons, if he bring them safe home again, an annuity of 30*l*. to himself and his assigns for three-score yeares. To my servant Launcelot Granger an annuity of 20 marks for life, 13*l*. *6s. %d.* To my servant William Lawrence the living he dwelleth in at Hampton for three-score years. To my servant William Matthews the living in Hampton he now. dwells in for three-score years. To my servant Robert Wootten the living he now holds at Hampton and 405. within three months. To all my servants double wages.

"I bequeath to my dear wife Alice all her jewels and plate, and the use of all the household stuff in Charlecote, to be there used and not elsewhere, and after to such of my sonnes as the house shall fall unto. I bequeath to my worthy cosen, Mr. John Hales, a diamond ring of fifty pounds price, which I would intreate him to weare in my remembrance, and one of my best mares he shall choose. To my most dear brother Sir Richard Lucy my bay ambling horse and one other of my mares he shall best like." "To Susanna Clarke, the wife of Thomas Clarke, immediately on decease of Thomas, for three-score years, the living now in tenure of Thomas Clarke in Hampton." "To my loving brother, Dr. Lucy my gray Barbary ambling horse." "The rest of my goods I leave to my dear wife, todistribute among my children at her discretion, my debts and funeral expenses being paid. Only I bequeath to Spencer Lucy all the stuff in the house of High Cleere, in Hampshire, and those two horses called the Hobby and Mingnon, with two colts and two mares. To my son Richard my bookes at Charlecote and two such of my great horses he shall like. To my son Robert all my household stuff in my house of Sutton in Worcester. I nominate my most deare wife, the Lady Alice Lucy, my worthy kinsman and friend, Mr. John Hales, of the Priory, in Coventry, and my approved and loving friend, Mr. James Prescott, executors, and I give unto every of them for their care 40*l*." This was proved by Dame Alice Lucy, John Hales, and James Prescot on the 18th February, 1640-41. At the margin is noted, "Received this 2gth day of August, 1657, the originall will of the sayd Sir Thomas Lucy deceased, by me, Richard Lucy, Esq., son of the said deceased, and one of the executors of the will of Dame Alice Lucy, relict, and one of the executors of the said Thomas Lucy." I have not been able to find the Inquisition Post-mortem at the London Public Record Office. It is probably in Warwick or Worcester. His funeral sermon was preached in 1640 by Robert Harris, B.D., pastor of the Church of Hanwell, Oxon., printed 1641, and dedicated to "the honourable and virtuous Lady Lucie of Charlcot." It is entitled "Abner's Funerall," and consists of a farfetched parallel between the death of Abner and David's mourning and the death of Sir Thomas Lucy, mourned by his country. We cannot explain the connection fully now, but we can note some special phrases in relation to Sir Thomas Lucy. " I have my hands andheart full with our present instance. Our friend Lazarus sleepes, and we cannot wake him. In this one bottom we have all our interests and suffer a wrecke. A noble lady hath lost, not an husband (as shee saith), but a father. Many children have lost, not a father, but a counsellor. An household have lost, not a master, but a physitian who made (as I am informed) their sickness his, and his physick and cost theirs. Townes full of tenants have lost a landlord that could both protect and direct them in their owne way. The whole neighbourhood have lost a light, the countie a leader, the country a patriot, to whom he was not wanting, till he was wanting to himselfe, in his former vigour and health."

For a short time after I read the will of Sir Thomas I hoped that I might find the beloved John Hales the same as the "ever-memorable" John Hales, of Eton, who appreciated Shakespeare; for Boase, in his Oxford Registers, gives only two "John Hales " in the century, both of Warwickshire, Armig. But I fear Boase is wrong, as Wood only speaks of the John Hales of Somerset, of the same colleges and dates. The Combes and the Lucys alike had wedded members of the Hales family. But I cannot prove the one point I started to investigate.

There was a John Harris, who had been appointed to the living of Cheriton by Sir Thomas Lucy, who had died this same year. His executors appointed in his place Christopher Smith. (See Dugdale's "Warwickshire," p. 589.) Probably this Robert was his brother, and interested in that way in the family.

His mourning wife raised a noble tomb for him, in which his effigy is represented half reclining. In the background to the right are shelves of books, to the left the representation of a barn, a river, and a gentleman on horseback, probably meant to illustrate his two chief tastes of reading and riding. The epitaph is in- Latin, and sounds very like the funeral sermon. A contemporary translation was printed.

Sir Thomas Lucye, Knight, one of this countie's greatest glories. An extract of a most Antient Familie. But a dis- esteemer of Birth in respect of worth. Wherin hee outshone the brightest of his noble ancestors. A singular and much honored Patriot. Witness the supreme Court of the Kingdom, whither he was frequently sent by the unanimous and fervent suffrages of his endeared countrie. His great estate none could either better manage or be less servant to. What Frugalitie laid up Liberalitie and Magnificence laid out. A loyal consort, a numerous offspring, and great abundance of Attendants were never blessed with a better governor. His servants' sick- nesse was his Sympathie, and their Recoverie his cost. Beeing thus a father in a master towards his servants, what must hee bee in a father toward his most lovelie children, and in a Husband toward his well-beloved Ladie? To his Table (which was always choisly sumptuous) all good men were ever mostwelcum; especially if Professor of either Sacred or Secular Learning. Wherein, though he were so rare prof1cient that hee was accounted a Living Librarie, yet was hee uncessantly acted with an impetuous desire after a greater height. His gate was no less propitious to the Poor; whose valediction to it was a Benediction, their farewel an heartie Praier for the master's welfare. Manie poore laborers hee daily employed, chiefly that they might not by doing nothing learn to do worse. Manie neighbor-towns hee yearly refreshed, sending unto them delightful provision. The great Horse was his great delight. Manie he had, as generous and elegant as anie were; which hee frequently backed with as much skill as anie could. Had hee not better known to moderate' his Horse then Himself (for from his Delight arose his disease), he in whom his Familie, Friends, Countie, Countrie were so happie and then whom none was more happier on earth, had not yet been most happie in heaven. Our happiness set, and his arose, Dec. 8, 1640, in the 56 yeer of his age.

This quaint translation is produced on broad black- bordered paperlone of the earliest examples of that sign of mourning that I have notedland occurs on signature H 2 of the funeral sermon of the Lady Alice, which was preached on August 1710, 1648, printed in 1649 by Mr. Thomas Dugard, and dedicated to Messrs. "Spencer, Robert, Richard,Thomas, Fulk Lucie, and to the Ladie Constance Spencer, Mrs. Briget Broughton, Mrs. Marie, Mrs. Alice, Mrs. Elizabeth Lucie, the remains of that Honourable Pair." The sermon is a general one upon " Death and the grave," closed by a special notice:l"Wee use to say to them that comming from London bring no news with them *they deserve to bee sent back again."* Many have said of her noble husband's epitaph, " It is true all that is said of him, everie word." " Much more might have been said there of

In the Warwickshire Visitation, 1682, the Rev. Thomas Dugard, of Barford, was among the Disclaimers, or one of those not entitled to bear arms. This appears in Sir Thomas Phillipps manuscript notes at the end of his index to visitations, f. 71.

him, but specially of her. But such was her modestie, that although in that magnificent monument which she erected for him she caused herself to bee layed by him in full proportion, yet shee would not suffer her epitaph to bear anie proportion with his. She conceived the most that could be said of him too little, and the least that could bee said of her too much." She was " a good wife for thirty years."

Her epitaph was added also in Latin, and this is translated in the black-bordered sheet at the end of Dugard's sermon asl

And Lady Alice his wife,

daughter and heir to Thomas Spencer, of Claverdon, Esquire, whose exquisite virtues are forbidden by her excessive modestie to appear in this marble. Nor can they be comprehended in it. She permitteth no more than this : that shee was most observant of her dearest husband while hee lived ; hath erected this monument for him being dead ; and through love and lamentation is herself (as you see) become marble.

We must with her close the notices of the Lucysthat were contemporary with Shakespeare. I believe

Only for local interest I may add that in Add. MS. 24, 121, is letter from a Lady Lucy at Charlecote, 24th March, 1746, to Thomas Wotton about the pedigree, which she notes as Dugdale does. The private letter accompanying it says:| " My dear nephew .... There is no pedigree preserved in ye family. Ye best account I know of ye family is in ye Baronetage, but it takes no notice of the Charlecote Arms, nor did I ever hear what they were. You know the present Baronet, Sir Berkeley Lucy, is collateral branch, and in him ye title will be extinct. Ye present Mr. Lucy is ye only heir male remaining yt th.it is directly descended from ye last Sir Thomas, to whom he is great grandson, as your friend observes. Spencer left no issue. Robert ye next brother left only a daughter Bridget, yt marryed Lord Mollineux, father to ye present Lord; she married to her second husband, Lord Arundel of Wardour. Richard ye next brother married Eli2abeth daughter of Thomas Uny, Esq., and had a son Thomas and a daughter Constance, yt married Sir Burgoine of Wroxhall, great grandfather to ye present Sir Roger. Ye son Thomas married Catherine daughter of Wheatley, Esq., of Bricknol, in Berks, and had only one daughter. Eli2abeth Lucy married first to Clement Throckmorton, of Haseley, in the county of Warwick, and having no male issue, the estate devolved upon Davenport Lucy, Esq., eldest son of Sir Foulke Lucy, (who married Isabella, sole daughter and heir of John Davenport, Esq., co. Chester) who was youngest son of Sir Thomas. He was killed at the siege of Limerick in Ireland, and his brother George succeeded. He had no issue, and the estate descended to William Lucy, Prebend of Wells and rector of Hampton Lucy, a living in the gift of the family. He died in his house at Red Lion Square, London,

that I have shown some reason for my opinion that
the relations between them and Shakespeare have been
misunderstood. It would be strange indeed that Sir
, Thomas Lucy the Third, with so many kindred tastes,
I should not have become acquainted with Shakespeare
in his latter days at New Place. But we do not know
! anything about this, and imagination must not run riot
i in critical studies of Shakespeare.

February 1gth, 1723-4, and was buried at Hampton Lucy without monument. He settled *his* estate upon Thomas the eldest son of Fiilkc Lucy, his youngest brother. He died 1744, and his estate came to George the present possessor, a bachelor, and it is entailed upon Sir Berkeley Lucy, of the Castle Cary family."

5

SECTION 5

CHAPTER V

John Somerville Of Edreston : 1560-1583.

We must turn from the busy and prosperous lives of the Lucys, who seem to have had no skeleton in their cupboard, and no sword hanging by the proverbial hair at their feasts, to the fortunes of another family, also ancient and honourable, whose escutcheon was stained with blood in the year that Shakespeare christened his first child.

The Somervilles were a family of the highest antiquity. Walter de Somerville came over with the Conqueror, and settled soon after the Conquest at Wichnour, in Staffordshire. A younger branch acquired the property of Aston Somerville, in Gloucestershire, before 45 Henry III., and on the failure of the elder branch of Wichnour, they became the chief English family of the name. In the time of Edward III. their coat of arms bore "Argent upon a fesse gules three Leopards' Heads Or, between three Annulets of the second."

Thomas Somerville, of Aston Somerville, had, in the reign of Henry VII., married Joanna, daughter and heir of the noble Warwickshire family of the Aylesburys, and settled with her at her family seat at Edreston or Edstone, in the parish of Wootton Wawen in the hundred of Barlichway, near Bearley- There he died in 16 Henry VII.

His son and heir, Robert, married Maria, daughter of John Greville, of Milcote (see Harl.MS., xii. f. 33), of whom I have hereafter something to say. Several of the family appear among the members of the Guild of Knowle. Robert died on the I3th December, 29 Henry VIII., and his son John succeeded, marrying Elizabeth, the daughter of William Corbet, of Lee. Some pedigrees state that she was his first wife, but I have been unable to find trace of any other. The State Papers mention that she was an invalid at the time of her son John's arraignment in

John Somerville, the elder, died on the 1st of April, 20 Eliz., and the registers of Wootton Wawen say that he was buried there on April 6th, 1 578. The Inquisition Post-mortem of his goods was taken at Warwick, 24th May, 20 Eliz., before Sir Thomas Lucy, Sir Fulke Greville, Edward Aglionby, Esquire, and Arthur Gregory. The jurors were Thomas Olney, gent., Christopher Knight, Thomas Allen, Thomas Saunders, Anthony Clements, John Burton, William Ives, Robert Weste, Roger Webbe, Robert Green, Hugerius Palmer, and John Barret.

John Somerville held Edreston or Edstone and Bere- ley, thirty messuages, a thousand and fifty acres ; 200 acres meadow, 1,000 acres pasture, 40 acres wood, and 20 arable in the messuages of Edstone, Wootton Wawen, Knoll, and Claredon ; one messuage in Halford, three messuages in Lapworth, and one tenement in Wydney super Bentley Heath. He had made an indenture on the 1 6th Oct., 10 Eliz., with Sir Fulke Greville, Sir Thomas Lucy, Thomas Blount, Esq., Ralph Sheldon, Esq., George Bromeley, Esq., William Sheldon, jun., Esq., that his property, after his decease should remain to his wife Elizabeth until the heir, John Somerville, or any other son that should become heir, should attain the age of twenty-four years ; that after the heirs male of John Somerville, it should descend to the heirs male ofWilliam Somerville, son to John Somerville, seniqr, then to the heirs male of Robert Somerville, then to the heirs male of Thomas Somerville, sons of John Somerville, senior, and Elizabeth his wife. There was no mention in this indenture of Elizabeth and Margaret, the daughters alluded to in the State Papers, yet they surely must have been born by that time. The Inquisition notes that some of the property was held under the Earl of Warwick, of the castle of Beaudesert; some under Robert, Earl of Leicester; the tenement in Hal- ford, of the heir of William Banwell; that in Lapworth of Sir William Catesby; a tenement in Wootton Wawen of Francis Smith; the tenements in Claredon directly of the Queen. The Inquisition, which is signed by Sir Thomas Lucy and Sir Fulke Greville, states that the heir, John Somerville, junior, was of the age of eighteen years and more at the date of the Inquisition.

It was a good thing for his family that he was not of age, because it saved the estates for his brother.

John Somerville had been educated at Hart Hall, then a favourite College for Catholics in Oxford. We hear nothing of his doings until he was dragged forth into the lurid light of a trial for high treason. He married, probably soon after his father's death, Margaret, second daughter of Edward Arden, of Park Hall. By the Harl. MS., xii., f. 33, we know that he had two little daughters: Elizabeth, who afterwards married Philip Warwick; and Alice, who married an Arden. Even had their father not been attainted, his lands, which came with a daughter, would not have gone to a daughter, through the terms of the grandfather's indenture, or entail in the male line.

By that same indenture, John Somerville, at the date of his death, had not yet become practically of age, nor had he fully entered intopossession at Edreston, though we see, from the State Papers, that his mother was both mentally and bodily incapable of enjoying her privileges.

Mr. French, in his " Shakespeareana Genealogica," says that half of the manor of Kingston belonged to young John Somerville, and at his attainder fell to the Crown and was bestowed on Mr. Abel Gower.

We nowadays can calmly consider alike the heresies and treasons of other ages, and can seek the causes of both. Very complex causes drove John Somerville the younger to his fate. The action of Henry VIII. lay at the root of all. Most of the Catholics, and even some of the Protestants, considered Elizabeth illegitimate, and disputed her right to reign, even under the will of a despotic father and the support of the majority of her subjects. But the majority was uncertain. Only about a third of her subjects were Protestants by conviction; another third were Catholics by faith, and the remaining third were of the religion, or no religion, of the strongest hand. But all preferred peace to war.

"The first blast of the Trumpet against the monstrous regiment of women," was published by John Knox abroad in 1558. It was directed against "that horrible monstre Jesabel of England a traitresse and a bastard." But it included all women. "To promote a woman to bear rule, superiority, dominion, or empire above any realme, nation, or citie, is repugnant to nature, contumely to God, a thing most contrarious to His revealed will and approved ordinance, and finally it is the subversion of good order, and of all equitie and justice." Though this was written against Mary, it came over in time to greet Elizabeth; and there is no doubt it affected much of the opinion of the country on both sides. John Aylmer answered it in a little book, "Ane Harborowe for the faithful, and trewe subjects, against the late blowne blaste, Strasburg, 1559"; for which he was afterwards made Bishop of London.

During the first twelve years of Elizabeth's reign, when she was consolidating her position and enjoying her life, as the Court-Lady describes it in "Leicester'sCommonwealth," there seems to have been comparatively little active repression of the Catholics. But the Pope's ill-omened Bull of February, 1569-70, had been translated into English, and had been fastened on the Bishop of London's gate on the I5th May, 1570. It was practically a declaration of war. Elizabeth, advised by Burghley, was forced to make reprisals. Elizabeth's relations to religion were more like those of her father than those of her sister. It was the passion for Catholicism in Mary's heart that kindled the fires of Smithfield for her heretics; it was jealousy of her political and religious supremacy that determined Elizabeth to despatch her heretics, not by fire but by the traitor's death. Anxieties abroad were kept alive by the attitude of Philip of Spain ; perplexities at home centred round the Scottish Queen, a prisoner in the sanctuary to which she fled.

The Parliament of 1581, in order to keep Elizabeth's subjects in due obedience, had added new penalties to the exercise of the Romish religion, and new terrors to the preaching thereof. Fines for nonconformity were increased. The penalty for saying mass was to be two hundred marks; for hearing it, one hundred marks and imprisonment. For neglecting to attend church, twenty pounds a month. Priests or persons practising to withdraw her subjects to the Romish religion were declared guilty of high treason; abettors, of misprision of treason. New powers were given to the justices of the peace in regard to checking recusants. Their houses might be searched upon the slightest suspicion, and the darkest construction put on all that might be found there. Spies and informers for the Privy Council were spread over the land.

The high-strung religious fervour in the hearts of those who clung to the proscribed religion was only deepened by fine and forfeiture. They prayed all themore earnestly from their purgatory on earth for the help of Mary, Mother in Heaven. Their chivalric instincts were stirred by the continued imprisonment among them of the Queen of Scots, a princess of their own faith, with stainless pedigree, the natural heir- apparent, at least, to the throne of England. Without thought of treason in any true sense the hearts of many Catholics turned to her, and their dreams pictured her on her accession reversing Elizabeth's policy as Mary Tudor had reversed her brother's.

And then Elizabeth took a more severe step. Archbishop Grindal died in 1582, blind, old, and in disgrace with his Queen for his incapacity to check nonconformity. To restore unity in the Church, the Queen appointed the sterner Whitgift as his successor, and gave him powers as great nearly as those of the notorious "Inquisition." A commission was appointed, with plenary jurisdiction over the kingdom, to reform all heresies, schisms, errors, vices, and sins, by fines and imprisonment at discretion. There were to be forty-four commissioners, of whom twelve were to be ecclesiastics. Sir Edward Coke pronounced this innovation as contrary to law. (See Sir James Mackintosh's "History of England," iii., p. 288.) The Commons mildly remonstrated against the tyrannical act, but Elizabeth thereby asserted her spiritual supremacy. The Commissioners administered oaths, dealt out fines and imprisonments to both Puritans and Catholics, though the latter bore the chief brunt of the attack. The Puritans were, after all, English subjects, and had no foreign Pope to stir them up into political action (though John Knox's book on "The Monstrous Regiment of Women" was not out of print). But the Catholics had a Pope ; and his emissaries, young priests, trained specially abroad for secret service in England, scorning martyrdom, swarmed through the land, and under the cloak of religiousguidance, often excited discontent with things as they were, and hopes that were disloyal to their excommunicated Queen.

In the midst of all this, an ever-increasing crop of slanders against the Queen arose on account of her injudicious partiality for the Earl of Leicester, whose known character was sufficient to foster them. Some of this floating gossip took shape in a letter purporting to be written by a Cambridge student to a friend, which, in 1584, was expanded and published as "Leicester's Commonwealth," popularly called " Father Parsons' Greenbacks " (from the colour of its binding and the leaf edging).

It openly speaks of Leicester's low origin, his vicious life, his frequent poisonings, and calls him " the chained bear, who had claws that can pierce and his bite is cureless." The Queen was indignant at its appearance, and the Lords of the Council sent a reprimand to the justices of the peace for Lancashire and Cheshire for allowing such a book to circulate, " both the Queen and they knowing the Earl of Leicester to be perfectly clear or the aspersions it contains," 20th June, 1585 (see Peck's "Desiderata Curiosa," i., 158). Sir Philip Sidney, the Earl of Leicester's nephew, answered the book with great indignation, especially against the derogation to the pedigree of the Dudley family. "Great honours it is true, came to the race by the mother, which had been allowed in all Ages, but the descent through

Father Parsons always denied its authorship and printed his denial in his preface to " Wamword to Sir Francis Hastings Wastword." There were many varying manuscript copies, some made possibly long before this date. The only clue to an author I have found is in one called " A Letter from a Cambridge Student to a friend in London," which is signed " R.F." (State Papers, Dom. Scr. Elir., Addenda xxviii., 113). The book was twice reprinted in 1641, in 410 and in 12mo, and was published as "The Secret Memoirs of the Earl of Leicester 1706," with a preface by Dr. James Drake. It was also printed in the "Harleian Miscellany," 1809 ; and in the "Collectanea Adamantaea," vol. xxiv., Edinburgh, 1887, where it is assumed that it had not been printed before.

the father was also honourable " (Collins' " Letters and Memorials of State," p. 64).

We must not forget the statements of this book in studying the causes that led up to John Somerville's fall. He had stayed from Christmas till Easter at Coventry, and a friend of his there, Harry Goodyere, with whom he had often conversed, had been talking romance to him about the captive Queen Mary of Scots, and had boasted of the souvenirs she had given him for his service and suffering for her sake. When he had been with his wife at Park Hall (the residence of his father- in-law), the priest, Hugh Hall, whom he met there, seems to have spoken to him not only of the views and doctrines of the Catholic Church, but of the society gossip of the day. He seems to have lent him books of an insidious and seditious character, and to have spoken approvingly of the attack of Jaureguy on the Prince of Orange, the account of which had been translated and published in 1582. Later, his wife repeated to him some things the priest had told her that concerned her Majesty much in honour.

Then a new book was put into his hands by his sister Elizabeth, a young woman of very decided views, who had been in a convent abroad without Royal leave, and had apparently returned to see her invalid mother. It was nearly a year and a half before the story of that book was fully discovered, and I took longer to learn its name.f

" A brief discourse of the assault committed upon the person of tl1e Most Noble Prince rif Orange by Juan Jauregui a Spaniard of Bilbao in Biscay 18th March 1582," translated and published in London by Thomas Dawson. It notes that the priest absolved him in advance for the deed, if he did not do it for mere gain, but only for the glory of God and 2eal for the Church.

| A mild and diminutive book called " Meditations" had been published at Douay in 1576. Another called " Certeyne Meditations and Prayers very necessary for a Christyane to read and meditate on," by F. Stacey, is preserved in manuscript in the British Museum (Add. MS. 33, 974). In 1582, "with privilege," but with no printer's name, appeared a little book by the Jesuit Cisoar Loartes, translated into English by Father Robert Parsons, called "The firr " ChriMirn Exercises pertaining to resolution." In none of these is the sedition very evident to the modern eye.

Edward Grant, son of Edward Grant of Northbrook, who had married Anne Somerville, John's aunt, was apparently also a Catholic. He had tried to get a certain "

Book of Meditations" from one Crowder, a prisoner in the Marshalsea, who had not a copy by him, but promised to send him one, and Grant had paid 55. *4[d.* in advance. It was duly delivered, and, when he was reading it in the park, his cousin Elizabeth joined him, read a little, and was very importunate that he should lend it to her. He refused, as he had not read it himself, but on his going home next day to his own house of " Kingswood, in the parish of Rownton in Warwickshire," Elizabeth found the hidden book, took it away, and showed it to her brother John. This he read, and it evidently impressed him profoundly. Several passages in the book make me think that Shakespeare had read it.

John Somerville did not have very much to occupy him ; he had good servants and abundant leisure. The energies of known Catholics were restrained within their own homes, public service was refused them,foreign travel denied them ; even kindred society was limited in various ways. Further, the fact that the exercise of their faith was prohibited added acute friction to their sense of repression. The thought seems to have risen in John Somerville's own excitable brain that one weak hand might set the country straight, deliver it from the thraldom of the illegitimate oppressor, restore the true faith, elevate the captive Catholic, the Queen of Scots, to the throne, and free from shame and tyranny thousands of his fellow-countrymen. And he dreamed that that hand might be his own. There was here no self-seeking, nothing save the natural desire of action and recognition, and the educated desire of an earned salvation through a meritorious act.

By the help of Professor Arber I at last found the book bought by Grant, borrowed by Eliiabeth Somerville, and read by John Somerville. It is " The Book of Prayers and Meditations," fourteen in number, written in Spanish by F. Lewis de Granada and translated into English by Michael Hopkins. It was published in Paris, 1582, dedicated to the Four Law Courts. This kindles the spirit which warms martyrs. "The Cross of Christ makes His followers seek a cross, and encourages and strengthens at this daye all holie Catholic men and women to suffer pains, in- justiie, wrongs, povertie, subjection, discipline, hunger, thirst, cold, nakedness and in shorte all the troubles, calamities, afflictions, persecutions, imprisonments, torments of the world."

For instance, in "The Meditation on the Grave," page 192, we find "but marveil to see unto how has a condition such a noble creature as man is now come; and to consider with whom he must keep companie there, even fellowe and fellowe, like who in his life-time had no fellowe or equal." About the death of a prince, p. 102, "Where in that royal behaviour and glorious magnificence? How quickly is all this gay pompe utterly overthrown and come to nothinge, as if it had been a mere dreame or a plaie on a stage that is despatched in an hour?" ... p. 104, "Is this the end of the glorie of the world? the ende of the Majestic of Princes' Sceptres and of Royall C'-ownes?" . . . "Then shall our earthly pleasures be our hangmen," *f"*

But it was the dream or a visionary, not of a politician or a warrior. There was no method in his arguments; there was no practical attention to a sound basis of action or any organisation of detail. He spoke of it to Sir John Conway, his wife's relative, to his wife and others ; but they either made no answer to his words, treating them as folly, or advised him to lay his fancies aside and go to sleep.

He sent for Hugh Hall, the priest, to come and confess him, but he feigned an excuse, knowing the man or fearing the risk. Therefore, the sense of loneliness seems to have weighed on his soul. He became unreasonably jealous of his wife. The times were out of joint for him. He, John Somerville, was standing alone in front of his whole generation of fellow-countrymen to do battle, single-handed, for the sake of the common weal, and he had not received absolution for what he wanted to do. The idea was enough to unsettle his feverish brain. He could not sleep at nights, his health failed, and apparently his reason gave way before the terrible strain.

Of the different accounts of his actions, all incomplete,we may say that Stow's was the most impartial. Speed uses very strong language of him, and traces his resolution to the instigations of his "wicked wife," without any foundation. Dugdale and Camden say what they can in his excuse. Miss Strickland is picturesque. Froude, who has taken some trouble to find the originals, does not take enough trouble to master their trying caligraphy; therefore, he is inexact in details, and directly wrong regarding the dates. He says that "at the beginning of October Somerville's plot exploded,'" whereas, had he read the papers, he would have seen that by some scribe the first paper of the series was dated in error the 6th October instead of the 26th, as it ought to have been.

On Tuesday, 22nd October, more gossip about Queen Elizabeth was added to Somerville's other causes of discontent. On Wednesday, the 23rd, he first thought of the plan of assassination. On the evening of Thursday, 24th October, he was apparently so excited that his wife- had fetched some of her relatives to see him in his bedroom. To them he disclosed his plan, but they advised him to lay aside these thoughts and go to sleep. He seems to have lain quiet after this, sleeping or simulating sleep. But early next morning, Friday, the 25th, he arose, and, with a single lad as attendant, insufficiently provided with funds, he set out for London without notice or farewells. He soon scared the boy away, and pursued his solitary way by devious paths, until he came to a village about four miles from Aynho-on-the- Hill, where he put up for the night. As soon as she knew of his departure, his wife pursued him along the London road as far as Aylesbury; but, hearing no news of him, she sent her servant on to London, and returned to her children. The servant soon brought back news of his arrest.

On that Frjday night, in the village inn, he must

evidently have been talking aloud to himself in bed, and thus have attracted attention, for again his room became filled with startled auditors of his frenzied exclamations that he was going to London to shoot the Queen through with his dagg or pistol, that she was a serpent and a viper, and he hoped to see her head set upon a pole.

No time seems to have been lost. A justice of the peace was summoned, he was apprehended, taken with much rough usage to Oxford, on Saturday, the 26th, and was committed to prison, where a preliminary examination was made of the sleepless and travel-worn youth, and he was sent on to London at once. On Sunday, the 2yth, he was at Uxbridge. On Monday, the 28th, the articles for his formal examination were drawn up; Tuesday, the 29th, and Wednesday, the 30th, he spent in the Gatehouse prison ; Thursday, the 31st, he was examined again, and committed to the Tower. The dates I find noted at the side of his examinations, probably by Burghley. He seems to have been treated from the first as mad by his captors, and yet the full blame was awarded him, as if he were a sane, free agent.

There was much care used in preventing his escape, as we may see from the charges for his bringing up. " To John Doyly, Esquire, upon the like warrant, dated at St. James, Primo November, 1583, for his chardges in coming up from Burester to Oxforde to apprehend John Somerfelde gent., and for bringing him from thence to the Courte at St. James, having in his company 12 men and 12 horses and for his attendance three days at Courte and so returning back againe, xiii/t. *vis.* viiu/." (Accounts of the Treasurer of theChamber, 1583.) Mad as he seemed to be, his words were eagerly received and acted on by sane men. Hasty meetings of the Privy Council had taken place. They sent down their secretary, Mr. Thomas Wilkes, with secret instructions to investigate the position of affairs in Somerville's neighbourhood. He was hospitably received at Charlecote by Sir Thomas Lucy, with whom he co-operated. Houses were searched, servants examined, books and writings seized, all relatives of Somerville were either apprehended or commanded to appear before the court. It is evident that Mr. Thomas Wilkes advised torture as a means to simplify his difficulties in finding the roots of the plot.

Mention is made of *a* picture found in the Catholic Earl of Arundel's trunk, of a hand bitten by a viper shaking it off into the fire, which, through a Biblical incident, was supposed to have a seditious meaning. This picture may have been the one that stimulated Somerville's imagination. (See Margrave's "State Trials," Vol. I. 166, "Trial of Philip, Earl of Arundel, 1589.")

Somehow or other, sufficient was discovered for the purpose. John Somerville and his wife, his father-in- law and mother-in-law the Ardens, of Park Hall, Mr. Francis Arden, of Pedmore, and Hugh Hall, the priest, were indicted at Warwick on 2nd December as traitors, and Elizabeth Somerville, his sister, as abettor of treason.- All were tried in London. Somerville and Arden, Mrs. Arden, and the priest were condemned on the 16th December. On the 1gth, John Somerville and his father-in-law were taken from the Tower to Newgate, in preparation for the execution next day, and were lodged in separate cells. Two hours later Somerville was found strangled, either by himself or by some friendly hand, and thus he escaped the horrors of a traitor's death. His head was set up on London Bridge ; but his body was buried in " the Moorfields, near to the Windmill." This Warwickshire traitor, first of the series, died at the age of twenty-three, leaving his baby girls homeless and destitute; for the Queen claimed his lands. They were fortunately settled on his mother until he came of age at twenty-four, so nothing was his own to forfeit, except the little estate ofWidenhay, which provided his private income. This was at once seized.

One point in the pedigree I ought to notice, as no one else has done so. His grandmother was a daughter of John Greville, of Milcote, whom Elizabeth Willoughby refused to marry. Some strain of homicidal madness seems to have run in the family, which John's other grandson Ludovic Greville displayed, and Ludovic was John Somerville's cousin.

That his madness was not denied in the highest quarters is amply proved, not only by the letter of Thomas Wilkes in the State Papers, but in that curious tract of Burghley's written to support the execution of Edmond Campion, but dated the day after Somerville's condemnation, and three days before the date fixed for his execution, "The execution of justice in England, for maintenance of publique and Christian peace, against certeine stirrers of sedition, and adherents to the tray- tors and enemies of the realme, without any persecution of them for questions of Religion, as is falsely reported and published by the fosterers of their treasons Iyth December, 1583." Lord Burghley says : "And where the seditious trumpeters of infamies and lies have sounded forth and entituled certain that have suffered for treason to be martyrs for religion, to this nomber they may, if they seek nombers, also adde a furious young man of Warwickshire, by name Somerville, to increase their Kalendar of yc Pope's martyrs, who of late was discovered and taken in his way, comming with a full intent to have killed her Majestie (whose life God always have in His custodie). The attempt, not denied by yc traitor himself, but confessed, and that he was moved thereto in his wicked spirit by inticements of certaine seditious and traitorous persons, his kinsmen and allyes, and also by often reading of sundry seditious vile books, lately published against her Majesty."

The pamphlet was answered next year by " A true,sincere, and modest defence of English Catholics that suffer for their faith, both at home and abroad, against a false, seditious, and slanderous libel entitled ' The Execution of Justice in England.' " "Therefore, when the adversarie chargeth D. Sanders and D. Bristowe with treason, for affirming such to be martirs in this sense, he sheweth himself to be ignorant as he is malitious in bidding us enroule Somerville in the number of our martirs, as perhaps before God he is, if he were distract of his wittes, or furious (as all men say, and the libeller confesseth), to whom can not be imputed whatsoever he did in alienation of mind; and to his enemies shall be imputed murther what so ever was done against him in that his state." " Unsound mind" would have been the verdict of posterity.

See *Note (ScJitious Bookt)* on p. 88.

The story of Somerville's "kinsmen and allyes " that were dragged down along with him in his fall throws even a stronger light on the various mysteries in the methods of examination and trial at the time.

The State Papers mention that Mrs. Somerville, his mother, was found very ill, " in the house of Hall, of Idlicote."

One of John Somerville's servants, John Purton, was imprisoned in the Marshalsea Prison for having told William Somerville that one of the clerks of the Privy Council was searching his brother's house. He petitioned Walsingham for release, as he did this in ignorance; and after confession of all he knew, he was pardoned.

The Council were not however satisfied that they had discovered the whole " plot." They therefore sent for William Somerville to answer questions; but he does not seem to have been severely dealt with, or even to have been imprisoned at all. In the Accounts of the Treasurer of the Chamber there appears the payment, " William Somerville, gent., upon the Counsell's Warrant, dated at Whitehall, xxii Dec., 1583, being sent for at her Majestie's commandement unto the Courte, and appointed to attend there, for his own diet and the charge of horsemeat, cxvlf." Another relative, probably an uncle, received a similar payment the next day, " To Edward Somerville, gent., upon the Counselrs warrant, dated at Whitehall xxiiird Dec., 1583, beinge by her Majestie's commandment sent for unto the Courte and appointed to attend for hir Majestie's service, viz., for his chardges and diet, Ixvu. viiu/."

This Edward was buried at Wootton Wawen, 22nd May, 1587. William, at some early date after the trial, succeeded to the chief properties. He married Elizabeth Ferrers, and had a son, William, baptised at Wootton Wawen, 25th September, 1588. The same registers also record the baptism of "Thomas Somerfield *[sic].* May I3th, 1599," and the burial of "Ferry Somerfield, June 24th, 1601."

The family kept quiet during the reign of Elizabeth; but William was knighted on 23rd July, 1603. He was appointed sheriff of the county in 8 James I., and was buried at Wootton Wawen, July 23rd, 1616.

He was the owner of what has been called " the Hilliard Portrait of Shakespeare." I do not believe in the attribution. It is much more likely to have been the likeness of one of the younger Somervilles. William was said to have been friendly with Shakespeare in his later years. Possibly he was. Had not John Shakespeare married an Arden, as John Somerville had done ? Many a time, probably, in later conversations, would they go over the terrible circumstances of the trial.

Fuller information regarding the case of John Somerville may be gleaned by comparing Speed's " Chronicle,"

In *Henry fl* Part III., Act v., sc. i. Sir John Somerville enters before the walls of Coventry, then supported by the Earl of Warwick, as a friend to King Henry VI. But I cannot find a "John" of that period (1471) among the militant Somerviltes.

ch. 24, p. 1155 (82) Stow's "Annals," p. 697 ; Bridge- water's " Concertatio," 1583, pt. 3, f. 409 ; Miss Strickland's "Lives of the Queens of England" (Elizabeth, p. 478); "A Thankful Remembrance of God's Mercies," by George Carleton, and ed., 1625, ch. 7, p. 67 ; Dug- dale's "Warwickshire," p. 907; Froude's "History of England," vol. xi., p. 609 ; Camden's "Annals of Elizabeth," p. 257 ; French's "Genealogica Shakespeareana," p. 450 ; " The Favourable Dealings of Her Majestie's Commissioners," by Lord Burleigh, 1583. But much more satisfactory than any of these, to those who have patience and skill to read them, are the State Papers themselves. See the Domestic Series, Elizabeth, clxvii. 4, 21-23, 26-28, 47-49, 53, 55, 70, 72, 78, 86, 180; clxxx. 59; the accounts for the Treasurer of the Chamber for 1583; and other papers at the Record Office.

I have lately discovered a Chancery case which throws a strange light on the family history, never before sug-

fested. The son and heir, William, who had been orn in 1588, had through some action unrecorded deeply offended his father shortly before his death in 1616. The transactions concerning the will made the heir perplexed and indignant. The trustees were Sir Thomas Lucy the Third, William Coles, Esq. (deceased), Sir Robert Lee, and Humphrey Coles. The chief family property of Edreston had been granted Lady Somerville for lifejand he had devised his Gloucestershire lands to the trustees for twenty-one years for the payment of his settlements, charges and debts. His daughter Grace was to have a portion of 1,500/., and until 600/. of this was paid and 200/. apiece to his younger sons Edward, Henry, John and Thomas, Grace was to have 60/. a year and the younger sons 20/. a year for their maintenance, William being only confirmed in a small portion of land until all were paid.

As he was twenty-eight, and apparently had visions of matrimony, he thought himself very hardly used. Blaming his mother and Humphrey Coles for sinister information which had roused his father to such bitter anger, he filed a bill against them in Chancery. He also filed a bill against the other executors, on the plea that his father died possessed of less property than when he drew up his will, and he considered it only fair that the other heirs should suffer in due proportion with himself. He was knighted in 1617 along with Sir Richard Lucy at Warwick, and his title is mentioned in the legal proceedings.

These Chancery proceedings become interesting because a good many Warwickshire names are mentioned. The case against his mother is preserved (Chancery Depositions, Eliz. to Charles I., Cat. v. 7, S. No. 12 [12]). William Chandler, mercer, of Stratford-upon-Avon, was called as a witness, who shewed that Lady Elizabeth Somerville had a mourning gown and other wares amounting to about 12/., and Mistress Grace Somerville had a mourning gown costing about *61.*; while Sir William had himself spent about 8/. 125. in his shop.

John Sheppard, of Warwick, yeoman, gave definite information concerning the amount of property which Lady Elizabeth had inherited from her husband. He also stated that he had paid Mr. Anthony Nash, of Stratford, 10f/., which was the debt of the late Sir William Somerville; another debt to Mr. Daniell Baker, of Stratford, 52/. Iq5. ; and a debt to Edward Sowter, of 405. more, and had brought the receipts to " Sir William Somerville that now is.'

William Lapwood, of Ryton-upon-Dunsmore, husbandman, gave details of Lady Elizabeth's croft.

Thomas Yates, of Wootton Wawen, knew the furniture left to Lady Elizabeth, with a coach and horses. He had been present when Sheppard paid the 105/. toMr. Anthony Nash, and, further, said that the present Sir William had promised to pay a further debt of his father to Mr. Thomas Combe, of Stratford.

William Whateley, of Henley, yeoman, spoke about the corn and the loss of the complainant. Mr. Edward Somerville and Mr. John had driven the cattle of their brother from the pasture, though he had offered rent for it.

Mr. Thomas Somerville, aged twenty-three, said that his mother only put the corn into her own barns until the Commissioners had decided upon it. Mr. John, aged twenty-five, was also examined.

Francis Sly, of Henley-in-Arden, yeoman, aged sixty, gave further information about the corn and about James Prescott, gent., of Warwick, who knew all the parties concerned, and knew that there had been two judgments of 200/. each against the late Sir William Somerville at the suit of John Brown, Esq.

The two suits against Sir Thomas Lucy and others are in Chancery Proceedings, Ser. II., Bundle 324, No. 16, and Bills and Answers, James I., Bundle S. 16, 30.

Sir William Somerville pled that the will was void because the third part, at least, of his father's property should come to him as heir, but the executors had taken upon them the sole power, and had filed a bill in Chancery on behalf of the younger sons. Sir Richard Verney, Sir Clement Throckmorton, and Roger Bur- goyne, Esq., had been appointed to consider his case last July, and he had agreed to allow the 20/. a year to his brothers.

The answer on 4th July, 1622, from Edward and Thomas Somerville, on behalf of their sister, Grace Somerville, *alias* Harrison, is that she did not wish her brothers to be vexed for her sake.

Sir Thomas Lucy and Humphrey Coles answered thatLady Elizabeth had her jointure in Edreston for life, and the younger sons from Cockbury; that Sir William Somerville the elder "had some displeasure with his son," which made him devise this will and settlement; but that the younger brothers had been reasonable. Sir William Somerville had only been debarred making a jointure until they all came of age and could join with him in doing so, and they had allowed him to enter the premises.

There had been already a Chancery case which had cost them eighty pounds. The cause of his father's displeasure is not revealed. Possibly the heir had refused a rich heiress of his father's choosing. Whether faulty or not, we cannot but sympathise somewhat with a young man thus cabin'd, cribb'd, confined. He apparently had been able to arrange a jointure with his brothers, because he married Cecilia, daughter and co-heir to Sir John Sturley, of Isfield, Sussex. But he did not live to succeed to his property or to see his only son and heir, William, who was born after his father's death in 1628.

After that, a long minority, and no younger brothers, allowed the property to develop again for the enjoyment of this third William, who made the old place lively enough, for by his marriage with Anne, daughter of Lord Tracey, of Tedington, he had a family of eleven sons and five daughters. He saw his grandson, William, the poet of the " Chase," before he died, and his memory is preserved by a tombstone in Wootton Wawen Church. He died 13th December, 1676, being forty-eight years of age.

Edreston has long since passed from the Somerville family.

Note.

Seditious Books.

On 1oth January, 1583-4, William Carter, printer, was indicted and condemned of high treason for printing the seditious book, "A Treatise on Schisme," and was the next morning taken from Newgate to Tyburn and there executed as a traitor. The author of the book was suspected but not discovered. See Camden's " Annals."

Lansdowne MS., xliii., 78, contains a list of "Traitorous and Popish Books intercepted 1584."

" A treatise of treasons against Queen Elizabeth and the Crown of England," printed January, 1572.

" Motives to the Catholic Faithe, by Richard Bristowe, priest, Licentiate in Divinitie, Antwerp, 1574."

" The Holy Sacrifice of the Masse, translated by Dr. Butler, Antwerp, 1570."

"The Hours of the Holy Virgin, Antwerp, 1572."

" The History of the Church of England by Bede, translated by Thomas Stapleton, 1565."

" A Fortresse of the Faith first planted amongst Englishmen, 1565."

" A Dialogue of Comfort against Tribulation, Sir Thomas More, Antwerp, 1573."

" A great number of Sheets of Miracles printed at Bruxelles,

IS73-"

Books found in the Recusant's Chamber in the gaol at

Winchester, 11th January, 1582.
" Gregory Martyn's Discouerye."
" Allen on Purgatory."
" A Booke Called Beware of Mr. Jewell."
" Smythe's Buckler of ye Catholique Faithe."
" Ric. Saunders on the Supper."

6

SECTION 6

CHAPTER VI

Edward Arden: 1533-1583.

Among Shakespeare's Warwickshire contemporaries, none touches our sympathy more powerfully than does Edward Arden, of Park Hall, the representative of the old Warwickshire family that traced its lineage back through Turchill de Arden to Guy of Warwick. He was connected by marriage and descent with many noble families.

In the *Atheneum* of August 10th, 1895, i "Mary Arden's Arms," opposing Mr. Nicholls's theories in the *Genealogist,* I think I proved his connection with Shakespeare, in a pedigree which I worked out more fully in my " Shakespeare's Family." The Walterf that married Eleanor Hampden had for heir his eldest son, John, and his second son was Thomas, of Wilmcote. The Thomas,J son of John Arden, of Park Hall, who died in 1563, would be cousin to the Robert Arden of Wilmcote, son of Thomas of that place. The William*of* Park Hall, who died before his father, would be half-cousin to Robert's seven daughters; and Edward would be a cousin removed by another degree to William Shakespeare. I think it necessary to be clear on this point as so much has been written to oppose it.

Among the entries of the Guild of Knowlc many concern the Ardens:| 1457. Walter Arden and Alianor hia wife. 1460. John Arden and Agnes his wife of Long Itchington.

1496. Robert Arderne, Master of Arts, Rector of Lapworth. 1504. Richard Arden and Margaret his wife, and for the souls of John and Johanna

their parents, of Long Itchington. I 506. For the soules of John Arderne and his wife.

Richard S.1Uv.iy and Estelle his wife, and for the soul of John Ardern. 1512. Alicia Ardern and for the soule of William Ardern, &c.

f See Note A, page 108.

j Among the Commissioners of the Peace for Warwickshire, 1539, were Thomas Arden, Edward Conway, John Grcville, Fulke Greville (Patents 31 Hen. VIII., p. 2, M. 4 a).

Edward's father, William, had married Elizabeth, the daughter of Sir Edward Conway, of Arrow. He made his will in "St. Brigydes' Parish, London," where he wished to be buried. It was proved by Sir John Conway, 14th April, 1546. (Somerset House. yAlen.) He left his young son on his death in 1545 to the care of Sir George Throgmorton or Throckmorton, of Cough ton, son of the Robert who appears in Mayowe's transfer to Thomas and Robert Arden of the land at Snitterfield, 16 Henry VII. (See " Mary Arden's Arms," referred to above.) Sir George had married the daughter of the first Lord Vaux of Harrowden, and in his home, near the seat of his mother's relatives at Arrow, young Edward was brought up in all the knightly exercises of the period, and in an enthusiastic love for the old faith, tempered with that loyalty to the Crown which had been the main point insisted on by Henry VIII. Sir George's eldest son and heir, Sir Robert, had married Muriel, daughter of Thomas Lord Berkeley, and it was his daughter, Mary Throckmorton, who was married to young Edward Arden. His grandfather, Thomas, died in 1563, and he succeeded to Park" Hall then, at thirty years of age. He was, therefore, about the same age as Leicester and Elizabeth and Sir Thomas Lucy.

During the first few years of Elizabeth's reign he seems to have led a happy and uneventful life. His uncle, Simon Arden, was sheriff of the county in 1569, the year the Pope issued his disastrous Bull against Elizabeth. But it did not seem to have brought much trouble to Park Hall, because in 1575, the year of the Kenilworth festivities, Edward was elected sheriff ofthe county. That the council selected him from the three gentlemen chosen by the shire that year is a strong proof that by that time at least he had done nothing to annoy the Queen or any of the Queen's courtiers. Possibly in what he considered the due exercise of his office that year, he first offended Leicester. Many men of high position in the county wore his livery to do him honour and to win his favour. Edward Arden scorned to wear the livery of a man," noble only in two descents, both of them stained by the block." His office, also, he might have thought, precluded him from wearing any other livery than that of his Sovereign. Therefore he did not cut a figure in Leicester's train on any of the famous seventeen days of the Kenilworth festivities. Had he contented himself with that slight it would have been better for him and his race.

But the Earl of Leicester's admiration was well-known for Lettice, the Countess of Essex, whose husband was then in Ireland. Leicester was said to have visited her at the house of George Digby and elsewhere. Arden's code of morality was different from that of the favourite, and he did not scruple to speak his mind freely of the great Earl.

Camden says that " he withstood Leicester in all that he could in the county," and that he further offended him " by refusing to sell some of his patrimony at his desire." The only action connected with land that I can find any trace of his being involved in, is one in which he made a Star Chamber affair of an attempt by some of his neighbours in Curdworth to make enclosures of some common lands (23 Elizabeth). Edward Arden was plaintiff against Raffe Rugeley, John Baskerville, gents., Thomas Feylde, Reginald Tuckey, Nicholas Pearson, Thomas Brookes, John Hill, John Johnson, and Edward Bucknam,defendants. It was a lengthy trial, and no decision is recorded in the State Papers. Probably the men wre creatures of Leicester. Doubtless the enclosers had their own way after Arden's fall, and no " decision" was ever necessary, for troubles of his own soon absorbed his attention. After the severe legislation of 1581 against Papists, Camden says in his "Memorials of the Reign of Elizabeth," p. 411, "that it was difficult for the most loyal and cautious to avoid the snares that were laid for their destruction." Hitherto Edward Arden had been able to steer himself and his family safely through the storm. But the Earl of Leicester never forgave or forgot, and opportunities come to those who have power to watch and wait. And all the more quickly to those who have power to create opportunities.

There is also a Chancery case (A. a. 9 Elir. 18, Edward Arden *contra* Joyce Massey) about deeds and evidences concerning the Manor of Berewood and Rectory of Curdworth, Warwickshire.

Edward Arden had married Robert, his son and heir, to Elizabeth Corbet, daughter of the Lord Chief Justice, some time before 1578, because in that year was christened " John Arden, son of Mr. Robert and Mrs. Elizabeth," in the Parish Church of Pedmore by Ped- more Hall, near Stourbridge, Worcester. (See my "Shakespeare's Family," p. 182.) Edward had married his eldest daughter Katherine to Sir Edward Devereux, nephew to Viscount Hereford; his third, Muriel, to William Charnells of Snarson in Leicestershire ; and his fourth, Elizabeth, to Simon, second son of Mr. Shuck- borough of Napton, Warwickshire. But for his second daughter, Margaret, he arranged a marriage that proved disastrous for her and fatal to himself. John Somerville (whose mother had been a Corbet) became the heir of Edreston at the age of eighteen in 1578, and seemed a suitable husband in all respects for his daughter. The causes that led this young man, even after he was a husband am' a father, to go forth as a Quixotic knight- errant and tilt against the troubles of his country and his time have been told in the last chapter.

But Arden's associations with his son-in-law and with the conspiracy Somerville was supposed to have initiated are worthy of more careful consideration than has as yet been paid them. In the first examination, October 26th, 1583, probably taken at Oxford, the frenzied Somerville was led by questions to say " Yl he hath hard his father-in-lawe saye y' the Queen would not suffar the Catholike Religion, and y she dothe execute all good Catholics."

The carefully-prepared questions administered to him, probably in the Gate-house at Westminster on 28th October, do not suggest Arden's name, and there is no mention of him in Somerville's replies.

New articles administered to the prisoner, probably under torture or threat of torture, on the 31st, elicited the fact that the idea of murdering the Queen first struck him after hearing his wife's report of what Hugh Hall, the priest, had said at Park Hall, in the presence of Edward Arden and Francis his brother," that touched her Majesty very greatly in honour."

The memoranda added to this State Paper note " To send for Arden, his wife, her daughter, and the two maydens, systers to Somervylle, and Joyce Hill, to apprehend suche as shall be any way in akin to all towcht, and to search their howses." The Council lost no time. Apparently Thomas Wilkes, their clerk, was sent at once to Sir Thomas Lucy, who rode off posthaste with him, to prove his loyalty, to Park Hall. On the yth of November Wilkes wrote to the Council and told the story. He had received their letter of the 2nd, when he was at Park Hall on the 3rd. " Over uppon my departyng from that place and the sending away of Arden to your honors, Sir Thomas Lucy, Mr. Griffin, the preacher, and myself took our voyage towards the house of Edward Grant, of Northbrookes, and Mr. Egliamby, accompanied with Mr. Burgoin, towards Hall's house

of Idlicote." " Although with all our travell here we cannot attaine to the depth of this treason, the whole discoverie of it will rest altogether in Somerville and Hall, and of the Bookes and the Agnus Dei, in Somer- ville's wife and sister."

This letter, open to all the members of the Council, was accompanied by a private one to Walsingham. " I have thought good never the les to signifie unto yr Honour that unless you can make Somerville, Arden, Hall the Priest, Somerville's wief and his syster to speke directly to those things which you desire to have discovered, that it will not be possible for us here to find out more than is found already, for that the Papists in this countye greatly do work uppon the advantage of clering their howses of all shews of suspition, and, therefore, onles you can charge them with mater from the mouths of your prisoners, looke not to wringe anythinge from them by finding mater of suspition in their howses." This earnest advice to make his prisoners speak, which is only the euphemistic method of naming torture, showed the weakness of the case.

Leicester had his private purpose to fulfil. Burghley was led to believe that there was a plot behind, and it was necessary to his peace to find it. Sir Thomas Lucy had his character as a vigilant justice of the peace to keep up under the new commission. Mr. Thomas Wilkes, Clerk of the Council, could best rise in office by finding what his superiors wanted to find. All these interests worked together, and by a travesty of justice Edward Arden was done to death.

Before the writing of this notable letter, on November 5th they passed a resolution for a commission of Oyer and Terminer, to send for William Somerville and "to examine Mrs. Somervylle, Arden, Hawle, and Elizabeth Somervylle." In examination, on the 5th, Mrs. Somerville was asked "whether she saw her father Arden, orreceived any message from him since the apprehension of her husband, and what is become of him." In Arden's examination the chief question was: "3. Whether did he make you privy to his repayre up to London and what was the cause thereof?" He was also asked " if Hall had married his daughter to Somervylle at a mass, and what were Hall's speeches about the Earl of Leicester ?"

It is probable that Edward Arden, for the convenience of Mr. Thomas Wilkes or Sir Thomas Lucy or his servants, was brought through Stratford-upon-Avon. on his journey from the moated park-surrounded hall of his ancestors, high set on the hill in the Hundred of Hemlingford, through southern valleys in hot haste to the Court of St. James, and thence to the traitors' cell in the Tower of London. He was lodged there by the yth November (see the Accounts of the Wardens of the Tower). By the 8th his captors were ready to return, and presented their bill. " To William Man, servaunte to Sir Thomas Lucie, upon a warrant signed as aforesaid, dated at St. James, viiith November, 1583, for the charges of himself and two others with four horses, in bringing a prisoner from Park hall, twentie miles beyonde Warwicke to the Courte of St. James, and for returning backe againe, xiii//. vi5. *vmd"*

The remainder of the month the prosecutors spent in attempting to find proof, the accused probably in prayer, for they knew no justice was possible ; no help or counsel was allowed them, nor were they allowed to confront accusers or witnesses, or plead their cause. " To Thomas Paynter, servaunte to Sir Thomas Lucie, Knight, by like warrant dated at St. James xviiith November, 1583, as well for his chardges and paines in bringing letters in poste, for her Majestie's affairs from Colsell, in the countie of Warwicke, from his said Mr- to the Lords of the Counsell, being at ye chardge of two horses for himself and a guide, and also attendingat the Courte for answers, and returning back again, iiii/r. *xs."* " To Henrie Rogers, gent., upon like warrant dated at St. James xxmo November, 1583, being lately imployed in the countie of Warwicke for her Majestie's service in searching sondrie houses and places for bookes and writinges dangerous to her Majestie and the State and so returninge to the Courte at St. James with answers and then returning againe to the saide Countie, bu."

The Stratford-upon-Avon accounts of the chamberlain about this date recordl" Paid for Mr. Rogers at the Beare, for dinner, and supper, and fyer, when he went to Sir John Hawbalke, Knight, 25.; more for his horse- meat, *is. 6d"* "To Sir John Browne, upon the like warrant, dated at St. James, xixth November, 1583, for the chardges and paines of himself, his guide, and two horses for ridinge in poste from the courte at St. James with letters to Mr. Wilkes, one of the Clerkes of her Majestie's Privy Council at Charlecot, in the Countie- of Warwicke, and for attendance there twoe daies and then returning, iiii//."

At last Thomas Wilkes' impatience to return to town was gratified. "To Thomas Wilkes, Esquier, Clerk to her Majestie's Privy Counsel!, upon the Counsell's warrant dated at St. James, 23rd November, who hath bene by her Majestie's speciall commandment im- ploied xv whole daies for her Majestie's service in the countie of Warwicke, with thre servaunts attending on him and two other persons from London to the said Countie, and also back againe xxx/." " To Edwarde Wingate, clerk of the Cheque of her Majestie's Guards, and Henrie Lanam, one of the yeomen of her Majestie's Chamber, upon awarrante signed by Mr. Vice-Chamberlain dated at St. James, xxviiith November, 1583, for the charges of themselves, their two men and horses being sent by order of her Majestie's Privy Counsellfrom the Court at St. James into Northamptonshire for the apprehension and bringing upp of one Hugh Hall and his man from thence to be examined at the Courte, concerninge her majestie's affaires, and for the chardges of the said Hall, his man and their horses, in their coming up, vi/z. xiii5. iiiu/." They seem to have been strangely delayed in finding out the whereabouts of Hugh Hall. Now they had got him to examine, and Wilkes to guide, things went on faster.

The examination of the servants, friends, and connections of the Ardens elicited nothing new. " The names of Somerfield's servants who came up with his wife Mrs. Somerfield and Mrs. Somerfield's sister, were Humphrey Morris, Richard Sheldon, Francis Emmes, William Thacker, Hugh Wright, servant to Sir John Conway." (State Papers, Dom. Ser. Eliz., clxiii., 72, 21 Nov.).

The articles administered to William Thacker and answered by him show that he had formerly been in Mr. Arden's service, "whose cloth he had worn aboute sixe yeares as a retainer," that he had entered Somer- ville's service at his own request, that he had served him about three years, and "that Mr. Sergeant Puckering and Mr. Cooke knowe him to have followed his master Somerfield's causes at law," that he knew no priests but Hall, that he had never heard of any masses or any conspiracy, and that he "went to service in the pub- lique church as it is now used, with the other servants."

Nicholas Wolf and others were also examined, December 6th, 1583, as to their participation in the late pretended mischief by Somerfield against her Majesty (clxiii., 78-86 and clxiv., 10), but though much interesting matter was collected, nothing of any importance to the examiners came out of this either.

There was also an "examination of Thomas Slye, of Bushwood, before Mr. Job Throckmorton and Robert Burgoyne, touching Popish plots." (State Papers.)

The examinations of Mr. Arden and his wife and daughter and of Hall the priest have not been preserved. Probably they were sent to satisfy the Earl of Leicester, and were never returned to the Clerk of Council. Possibly they were destroyed. It is generally said that Hall had turned informer, and had sacrificed the rest. (See Froude's "History," vol. xi., p. 609.) 1 cannot find any trace of this in the records, and a later allusion seems to tell the other way. But though the ordinary State Papers fail us at this critical point, more definite notices of the legal treatment of the case are preserved in the Baga de Secretis, Pouch xlv., mems. 9 and 10.

On the 2nd December, 1583, the prisoners, being in London, were indicted at Warwick. " Indictment found at Warwick against the said John Somervylle, Margaret Somervylle, and the said Edward Arden, late of Park Hall, aforesaid, gentleman, and Mary, his wife, Francis Arden, and the said Hugh Hall, for that on the 22nd October, 25 Eliz., at Edreston, they conspired to compass the death of the Queen, and change the pure religion established in the kingdom, as well as to subvert the Commonwealth, and in order to carry such their treasons into effect, the said Margaret Somervyle, Edward Arden, Mary Arden, Francis Arden, and Hugh Hall at Edreston, the 24th Oct., 25 Elizabeth, by divers ways and means incited John Somerville to kill the Queen, and thereupon the said John Somervyle traiterously said ' I will go up to the Court and shoot the Queen through with a pistol,' and on the following day he took a pistol, gunpowder, and bullets, and journeyed therewith from Edreston towards London, the Queen then being in her house called St. James, in the County of Middlesex, near the same city, in order to carry his treasons into effect."

On December 7th (Mem. 12), the Special Commission of Oyer and Terminer was issued to try those persons "sent forward by our faithful friends Thomas Meade, Justice of the Queen's Bench, Robert Shute, of the Exchequer, Sir Fulke Greville, Sir Thomas Lucy, George Digby, Edward Egliamby, Anthony Shuck- borough, Esq., Justices, along with others lately assigned to inquire into the state of religion in Warwickshire,"

&c. On the gth of December (Mem. n) appeared the Queen's writ of certiorari. The names of the jury are given, among whom are John Fulwood, of Tamworth, Richard Fulwood, of Tamworth, Thomas Astley, of Woolby, John Ensor, of Wilmcote, Roger Wigston, of Woolston, Robert Burgyn, of Wroxall, and Benedict Shuckborough, of Cubbington, who had agreed to the bill of indictment. The same day (Mem. 6 and 7) Sir Owen Hopton, Lieutenant of the Tower, was ordered to bring the prisoners before the justices at Guildhall on the 16th, the Warwickshire justices issuing a precept for the return of the jury for the trial. I give the names of those proposed and those selected, as they were all Shakespeare's Warwickshire contemporaries. Those selected were "Sir Walter Ashton, Sir Richard Dyghtley, Sir Francis Willoughby, Edward Boughton, Thomas Revyngton, Gabriel Poolteney, George Pudsey, Thomas Beoffoy, Timothy Lucye, John Bretton, Stephen Slaney, and Humphrey Davenport." The un- selected were "Anthony Cooke, Humphrey Ferrers, Thomas Andrews, William Leigh, Henry Dimocke, Christopher Wright, Thomas Wightman, William Porter, Bartholomew Hales, George Corbun, Edward Skaring, and Ralph Blunt."

The Record of the Sessions held at Guildhall on 16th December (Mems. 1-3) before the justices appointed to try the prisoners states that "John Somer- vyle, Edward Arden, Mary Arden, and Hugh Hall, being brought to the bar by the Lieutenant of the Tower,are severally arraigned. John Somervyle pleads guilty, Edward Arden, Mary Arden, and Hugh Hall plead not guilty. Venire from the county of Warwick awarded instanter. Verdict guilty. Judgment against the male prisoners and the female prisoner as is usual in cases of high treason. Execution on the 20th." The State Papers here continue the story, and give us interesting information regarding the way in which Edward Arden spent his time, and of his last supper with his wife. On this eventful Monday, the 16th December, the keeper Neve procured Sir Owen Hopton's permission, and the doomed pair were allowed to sup together. Arden's death was certain, but even then apparently there were expectations that his wife might be spared. He told her, if she lived, she must see Neve paid his twenty pounds for this meeting. The enfeoffment he had made for his wife's benefit would be all in vain, for she also had been proved a traitor, and a clause in the 1581 Act had been prepared to circumvent such "fraudulent conveyances," as they had been called.

On Thursday, the I9th, Edward Arden and John Somerville were delivered to the Sheriffs of London, taken to Newgate, and locked in separate cells in preparation for their execution on the following day. Had there been an opportunity of a farewell, and had Edward Arden tried to encourage the drooping soul and disordered brains of his son-in-law ? We know not, but we know that two hours later Somerville strangled himself or was strangled in his cell ; and Edward Arden went forth alone on the morrow to meet his horrible doom at Smithfield. He "suffered the full penalty of the law with his usual high spirit, protesting to the last his innocence of anything save of being a Catholic" (see Rishton's "Diary," Gillow's "Records of EnglishCatholics," vol. i.,p. 57). His head was set up on London Bridge among those of the other "traitors."

A "Secret advertisement from Exeter suggests that Somenrille was hanged by the Catholics to avoid greater evil." (State Papers, Dom. Ser. 1.'!.-.- 168, 24.)

Execution over, the servants of the Tower were examined, and certain secret letters were studied in hope of solving the mysteries of the plot that Burghley clung to.

One of these was to Arden's son, entreating him to pay the twenty pounds he had promised Neve, the only "debt of honour" which the confiscation of his goods on his condemnation made him unable to pay; another was about the affairs of his sister Barbara, married to Richard Neville, nephew of the deceased Lord Latimer, who claimed title and lands.

The examination of Neve showed that he had in his custody "seven or eight boxes of evidences of Edward Arden's, and a little bag of evidences" which Arden had sent him for to one Smallwood, a tailor without Temple Bar, and had asked him to give to his son or to his wife, but which yet remained in Arden's chamber. He had told the Lieutenant of the Tower of them, but they had not been used. The twenty pounds was due on account of a wager. Arden had said that if he and his wife should sup together before Christmas he would give Neve twenty pounds, and if they did not, Neve was to forfeit ten shillings. He had arranged the meeting by the Lieutenant's leave, and won the wager.

Arden said that his wife or his son would give him assurance of payment; "and *yesterday* when he was delivered to the sheriffs of London " he repeated this. Neve denied he had ever carried letters from Arden to his wife or son ; or that Arden and his wife had ever met until they were condemned. But he acknowledged that his comrade, John Kellam, had received a letter from Arden for his son the morning he was taken from the Tower to Newgate (the one referred to above). Arden himself had never told him of the contents of this letter; but about three days before his arraignmenthe asked Neve if he might trust him with a secret, and Neve agreed, if it was such as he should be trusted with. He said he had made certain conveyances of late for the benefit of his wife to " Mr. Atkinson and Mr. Sanford," which wanted nothing but the enrolment, which he wished Neve to tell his wife of and no one else. This he had done. But after they were condemned he had told Neve to say nothing about it.

Another examination of the priest Hall took place on December 31st, 1583, but very little was elicited from him. Burghley opened the new year by making a sum total of all the facts collected from the various examinations of the prisoners, and this is most important in determining the value of the evidence that had not been preserved in comparison with what we do possess. (State Papers, Dom. Ser. Eliz., clxvii., 59.)

John Neve had deposed what I have stated above, points about the wager, the letter, and the conveyance.

Robert Barrett had stated that he only knew Arden' by taking him his meat sometimes; that Arden had asked him to tell his wife not to repeat one speech he had made, or it would undo him. He had not delivered it, because Mrs. Arden would not hold speech with him, fearing he meant to undermine her, but she sometimes asked him to bring her word how her husband did, which he pretended to perform, but did not. Burghley also preserved an extract from Mary Arden's examination "That Barrett, Mr. Lieutenant's man, brought her a message from her husband that she should undo him if she uttered something. She was willed by her husband to be good to Neve, who had cheered him during his imprisonment." In an extract from Edward Arden's letter, it is noted," he doubteth not but his sonne will perform what he had promised to Neve. To see his writings and letters delivered with speed." And this is all that the great statesman with all his powers of discovering things could bring together!

Again they harrowed the feelings of the sorrowful widow on February 10th, 1583-4 (State Papers, Dom. Ser. Eliz., clxviii., ii.). This time they wished to understand another mystery about the communications between Mr. Neville and her late husband. She explained that Mr. Richard Neville had married her husband's sister Barbara, and that on the death of Lord Latimer, without heirs male, Richard Neville, his nephew, had sued for his title and some of his lands. Barbara had induced her brother Edward to assist them with the expenses, and Neville had given his bond to repay at the conclusion of the suit. She did not know or any conveyance to Neville's son beyond the sea. Thomas Wilkes conducted this examination, and Mary Arden added to it her initials, "M.A." All that the Inquisitors found told in favour of Edward Arden, who had been always provident and thoughtful for others.

Mary Arden is said to have been pardoned and released shortly after. But it was a poor pardon. She was always kept in poverty, because she was a recusant and a suspect. There is a letter, written 1st April, 1593, by the Privy Council to Thomas Bigge, John Harryson, and Henry Dingley,Esquires, thanking them for "searching the house of Thomas Throgmorton in Coughton Park, where Mistress Arden, wife of the traitour Arden that was executed doth dwell at this presente. Because it should seem by your letter to Mr. Topcliffe there was resistance offered at soche time as you did searche the house, and that they of the householde then did not carie themselves with that dutyfull course and obedience they ought to doo, and that divers superstitious things and furniture for masse was there found, and it was confessed that a seminary priest was harboured there, who was conveyed out of the way, or lieth hid in some secret place. Wee have thought good to requyre you to commit to pryson as well the saide Mistress Arden asthe rest of her servants . . . . to be proceeded withal, according to the qualities of their offences, which we refer to your discrecion." The Queen and Burghley settled "the lands growen unto her by the attainder of Arden and Somerville" (State Papers, Dom. Ser. Eliz., clxxi., 35) "upon the Darcies, but Edward's son, Robert, being a prudent person, and well versed in law, afterwards regained them," probably by legal advice, through an entail made at his marriage, and once more there were Ardens living at Park Hall. (See Dugdale's " Warwickshire," p. 931).

But he seems to have gone through much trouble after his father's death. In the search made in London in suspected houses, "in the house of John Spede in Powle's churchyarde were found 7 bokes tending unto papistry." "We found in the house of Gabriell Ca- wood, hymself, some men-servants, viz., Henry Kephor, Josias Parnell, John Snowden, and Robert Arden, who is committed" (State Papers, Dom. Ser. Eliz., clxxii., 102, 2yth August, 1584). On the same day, in the search made at Southampton House, was "Robert Arden, who had lykewise been lately ymprisoned."

In 1596 he was in prison again. His petition to Lord Burghley shows that he was a prisoner in the Fleet, and had been committed with his servant, William Frere, by the Court of Exchequer in Easter last for proceeding, contrary to a former decree, as was supposed, against Edward Darcy in an action of waste. He prays for release, "Mr. Darcy having answered to the charge and confessed that the petitioner had a remainder in tail for 21 acres of the land in question, yth March, 1596" (State Papers, Dom. Ser. Eliz., cclvi., 78). That was about the time of the petition of his uncle, Simon Arden, of

Longcroft, which clears up many knotty points. His great age made him an authority. (See my "Shakespeare's Family," Part II., p. 184.)

On May nth, 1599, there is a "Warrant to pay to Elizabeth and Mary Arden, daughters of Edward Arden, late convicted of High Treason, 40 marks a year each for life, out of revenue assured for life to their mother Mary Arden in lieu of dowry, and come by reason of her offence into Her Majesty's hands. This warrant was directed to the Late Lord Treasurer, 27 Eliz., and is now to pass the Privy Seal, directed to the Exchequer, as there is no warrant there to continue the annuities" (Acts of the Privy Council). Thus at the time John Shakespeare was applying for a grant to impale his wife's arms in his own new coat, the Arden family were not, as has been supposed, in very flourishing fortunes. The tide changed for them, as for others, in the next reign. Among the annuities granted by James I. we find"Robert Arden, 37*l. 1is.6d."* (Lansdowne MS., clvi., f. 113), which might, however, refer to another of the name).

Pedmore, Francis Arden's place, was given to Sir George Digby, but after the receiver's death Francis sued for it. (State Papers, Dom. Ser. Eliz., ccii., 40.) "Particulars by Richard Sutton of the state of the cause of Lady Digby and Richard, her son, against Francis Arderne, who sought to recover the lands of Pedmore and Whitmore, formerly leased to Sir George Digby, deceased." The accounts of the wardens of the Tower only mention Francis Arden's board until June 24th, 1585, when he was probably released. He could not, therefore, be the " Mr. Arden " who escaped with Father Gerard from the Tower on October 8th, 1597, by the assistance of John Lily and Richard Fulwood, unless he had been again imprisoned. Probably this Mr. Arden was one of Edward Arden's sons; not his brother.

The fate of Edward Arden excited universal sympathy. Leicester bore out his attitude towards him by the formation next year of "The Association for theProtection of the Queen's Person." In that same year there was printed abroad, and imported largely into this country, the little book called " Leicester s Commonwealth," in which the floating gossip of the period against Leicester was collected. Its date is verified by a slight allusion to this trial. "What say you to the device Leicester had of late to entrap his well-deserving friende Sir Christopher Hatton, in the matter of Hall his priest, whom he would have had Sir Christopher to send away and hide, being touched and detected in the case of Arden, thereby to have drawn in Sir Christopher himself? "(p. 166).

Burghley's relations to the case are very mysterious. In Somerville's story I have already noted that the day after the condemnation of Somerville and Arden, and three days before the date fixed for their execution, he published the strange pamphlet, "The Execution of Justice in England, &c.," lyth December, 1583. Though this was written to excuse the death of Campion, it was evidently intended to do double duty and support the execution of Arden, whose name is not mentioned therein, as is Somerville's. But it is found next year in the reply, "The true, sincere, and modest defence of the English Catholics," where a charge is made (p. 49), "of action for the prevention of the discoverie of certaine shameful practises about the condemnation and making away of the worshipful, valiant, and innocent gentleman, M. Arden .... which brought him to his most pitiful end, to the great regret of the whole nation."

In "The Rise and Growth of the Anglican Schisme, by Nicholas Sanders, D.D. ; with a continuation by Edward Rishton,"p. 221, after speaking of the Council, the writer adds, "But as it was impossible for them to destroy at once, every noble person who held the faith, in order to gratify the hate or the greed of upstartcourtiers, they assailed them, one after another, by lying accusations and falsehoods. Thus they shamefully put to death Edward Arden and others, men of the old religion and of ancient descent."

I have noted above that the chief examinations have disappeared, and that the sum total was insufficient to prove the justice of this recusant's execution. Dr. Nares, in his " Memoirs of Burghley," enters in the table of contents: "Case of Arden and his family," vol. Hi., cap. x., p. 183, but there is no allusion to the name in the text, as if it had been cut out. "The Letters and Memorials of Burghley," edited by Murdin, are silent on the subject; and the " Memorials of the Reigns of Mary and Elizabeth," a sort of political diary by Burghley, printed at the end of the volume, omit from the annals of this year all reference to this case, though much more trivial incidents are duly recorded. Altogether, the whole affair is so discreditable to all Edward Arden's judges and the methods of justice of his times that it is almost preferable that they should somehow or other have come to feel ashamed of their action, and try to hide it, probably after the Earl of Leicester's death.

Speed does not mention Arden. Dugdale openly expresses sympathy with him, and quotes Camden, who, in his ' Memoirs of Elizabeth," says, "The woefull end of this gentleman, who was drawne in by the cunning of the Priest, and cast by his testimony, was commonly imputed to Leicester's malice. For certaine it is that he had incurred Leicester's heavie displeasure, and not without cause, against whom he had rashly opposed himself in all he could, had reproached him as an adulterer, and detracted him as an upstart." (English translation, p. 257).

Every trait in the character of Edward Arden becomes doubly interesting to those who believe in the transmission of family characteristics, and who see in Edward Arden, the so-called traitor, the relative of William Shakespeare.

Note A. Walter Arden Of Park Hall (temp. Edward IV.).

Proceedings in Chancery, 6 Ed. IV., Easter term, Vol. I., bcxii. Walter Arden *contra* John Arden the Younger. To the Archbysshop of York and Chancellor of England.

Walter Arden complained that his brother John came to him and said piteously that he had nothing to live on like a gentleman, and, by mediation of Agnes Middlemore and her son Richard, he made estate of the Manor of Pedmore for life, to receive it only after Walter's death, and he delivered the deed to Agnes Middle- more, but she handed it on to John who had ever since been taking the profits during his (Walter's) lifetime.

The answer for John repeats what Walter had complained of, varying it only in so far as John was to receive the profits- of Pedmore during his life, but not to enter into possession of the estate and occupancy thereof, until after the death of Walter. He says that Walter's charge against him was not sufficient. If it had been true, Walter could have brought an action at the Common Law for "detynu" of the deed.

John himself says that for the good service he had done Walter in his household and divers other places for seven years and for the love Walter bare him, he enfeoffed him in the manor, and gave a letter to Thomas Hart to deliver seisin, which was openly done in the presence of more than sixty persons, which estate was made to the use and profit of John without any agreement being made that he should take no profits during the life of Walter. Nor was the deed delivered to Agnes Middle- more or her son in the way stated.

Replication.|That Walter out of pity did grant Pedmore to John, but it was faithfully agreed, that during his life Walter should have the profits and revenues thereof, the deed to remain meanwhile "in mean hand," supposing that neither could take the manor or profits contrary to agreement.

A commission was issued to the Abbot of Kenilworth, John Zerdeley, to examine witnesses.

On May 3, 6 Ed. IV., at Coventry, Walter Arden brought his servant William Levyng, who lived at Castle Bromwich, and his servant William Hart, "meniall servant at Pedmore," Worcestershire. They both agree with their master to a certain extent, but not very clearly.

The following Saturday John Arden brought two witnesses, William Berkeley, Squire, and Rafe Sydenale, gentilman, who deposed that they "were lettred," and they sealed a bill in John's defence, and the same day, Saturday, Agnes Middlemore, now called Lucy, being thirty miles *off* at Worcester ill, so that she could not appear, sent a bill in writing. John Arden offered other letters, which the Abbot advised to be sent on to Chancery. William Berkeley said that he had often spoken with Richard Middlemore, who said he had never heard of any such condition as Walter Arden now stated, and John Middlemore was at the delivery of the seisin of the said manor from Walter to John Arden, and he heard no such condition given either by Arden or Thomas Hart, his attorney, or from Thomas Gamell, who wrote the deed.

Agnes Lucy, formerly Middlemore, acknowledged receipt of letter of attorney and deed of the manor of "Peddmore in Wyrcestre," and that she delivered this by the will of Walter Arden to John Middlemore and to John Arden to deliver seisin, and after taking possession John Arden sent it back to her by John Middlemore her son (evidence 8th June).

On 6 Ed. IV., July, Friday next after St. Barnabas the Apostle, Ralph Sydenale said that Thomas Hart, bailiff of the lordship of Pedmore, said he never had heard speak of such a condition at the seisin, nor in the space of a year after.

Accord Made.|That Walter and John agreed that Agnes Middlemore of Edgebaston should keep the deed until Walter willed that she should give it to John Arden, until his death, when she should give it to John without delay.

Kl | !"| i$ J| iVJ 1"T' N O $jl w .,"3-s || B Ul J ? " Elizartr, *m.* Sir William Poolry of Bozstrar, co. Suffolk.i. Dorotry, r. of Basil Firlrirg.M'. Elizarrtr, Tron r. of Rrgiralr rrrt, J.R.P.ar .ry, F.r r. of Sir Rorrt ofPrr Trrockmortor. 3n. .ry r. of Sir Tromas Arrrrws of Crarwrltor. HN MAlicr, Trorr r. of Ricrarr (of Wilm B.crrrirgr of '"rgsrury. See t. Elizartr r. of Erwarr Co of Arrow. O f1- Xo | 5? ? P3 5-r, Simor, Gre rway ofLorgcroft. ,.'. at B1-IIii r ffl 0 "H0- 5; P f 3-L Q1.3.3 N ' 3 r w ?to § f 5 oa $1"3 3 H " ".ir 1 s:s si US. " ? ? 3 P o" 3 j&t. ifzMr d 13Fl s If I !- i-g? WE-3 fffl-g " |ijjy tx" S

X l3 flCT 5"rXN"""-' CJ O Ifji1. IBUl P 3 XU) 3 I??-P? 2.1""B3Bi tS M ,"O *Vf* 3 1 z Vl l 3 r a. 3P n' C3*f.* i If If- K g.' &t" sr u O r 3- 3. S l g 0 P f." rSz 5fl- $4 t/J0 1-3 3I 1 flit-a B Jo o E aB n –K$ll-rl-Cft00 t l5 j 00 !-s p. 1 Ml M 32 Ml 3B ?ls1 00 "' w S ' g ,S S-J " 1 1 1 II-' s'l " 3P- S'i- 31??- ? l c l 2 2 =" " 2,B3 S(A 4" -5 ?§ 3 Z'S-Jn G' TM " c lilt i l$? H0 2 jff-i? =" I i i"r ? S

7

SECTION 7

CHAPTER VII

Sir John Conway, Of Arrow: 1539?-!603.

One of the relatives of the Ardens mentioned in these examinations must have had some interest for Shakespeare, not only because he was well known in Warwickshire, but because he was a connection of the Ardens and had a story to stimulate the poet's imagination|Sir John Conway, of Arrow, a property lying a few miles from Stratford.

Sir Henry Conway had been knighted by Edward Mortimer, Earl of March, in the reign of Richard II. From him descended John. (See Harl. MS., 7189.)

In the fifteenth century, John Conway, of Portrethan (Flint), had two sons, of whom Sir Hugh, the elder, rose in the Court and service of Henry VII. He died in the last year of his reign. The younger, Edward, married Anne, sole daughter and heir of Richard Burdet, by whom he came into great Warwickshire estates. But his wife's cousins, the Burdets, waged legal war for many years, putting forward the claim of the heir male over that of the heir general for the inheritance. Many attempts at settlement had been made, the opinion of the times having commenced to veer towards the masculine claim. The contest was ended by the arbitration of Sir Anthony Fitzherbert and Sir William Shelley, Justices of the Common Pleas, who awarded half the manors, including Arrow and Lodington, to the Conways. Edward was gentleman usher to Henry VIII., and left a son, John, his heir, thirty-five years old, in 38 Hen. VIII.

This John had joined "the Guild of Knowle" the very year of its dissolution, 1535. He was knighted and afterwards made a banneret for active service in Scotland. Elizabeth, the daughter of Edward, and the sister of this John, married William Arden, heir apparent to Park Hall, and was mother of Edward Arden, whose life has just been told. Sir John Conway married Catherine, daughter of Sir Ralph Verney, (see Lipscombe's "Buckinghamshire," vol. i., p. 179), and he died 22nd July, 6 Ed. VI.

His son and heir, named also John, was in trouble at the close of Mary's reign, through being a Protestant. The Privy Council Journal (Harl. MS. 643) mentions him: "This gth September, 1558. To the Constable of the Tower, to suffer Knightley, Conwaye and Mallorye, presently prisoners in the Tower, to have the liberty of the Tower for the better recovery of their health, at the least until they be amended of their present desease." " 18th October. This day Knightley, Conwaye and Mallorye, having been for a good time prisoners in the Tower, beinge called before the Lords of the Councelle, it was ordered they should paye by waye of fyne for their offences theis summes following, viz., Knightly, 500/.; Conway, 300/.; and Mallorye, 100/.; and they returned to prison until further order should be taken with them for their said fynes." As this would be just a month before the accession of Elizabeth, matters would soon be changed. John Conway was knighted in 1559-60 (see Add. MS. 32, 102, fo. 122 a., and Metcalfe's "Book of Knights"). He married Eleanor, daughter of Sir Fulke Greville, of Beauchamps Court, and Elizabeth his wife, Baroness of Willoughby de Broke, and had four sons, Edward, Fulke, John, and Thomas, and four daughters, Elizabeth, Katherine, Mary, and Frances. His first literary publication seems to have been commendatory verses in praise of Geflray

Fenton's translation of "the Tragical Discourses; from French and Latin, 1567," dedicated to the Lady Mary Sidney. He writes in the style of William Hunnis and other writers in the "Paradise of Dainty Devices." In praise of this book there are also Latin verses by "M.H.," verses by George Turberville, and by Peter Beverley, who speak of it as a translation of Bandello. It is certain that Shakespeare read this book; and perhaps it may be as well to reproduce Conway's contribution.

Like as the slender Bee, by travell in her Kynde
Collects her fruite, the sugred sappe whereof wee dayly fynde,
So here my learned friend in nature lyke the Bee
Hath linkt his labour to his art and yeildes the fruit to thee.
In toung estraunged from us, whyles this succeeding worke
(As doth the honey in the flowre) by covert meane did lurke,
He labouring with effect, hath by his learned payne
Enforst a Frenchman tell his tale in English language playne
Not for hymselfe; thou knowest, it answered his delight
By skill to understande the tale, as did the author wryte,
But toyling for thy sake hath formed the hyve full fyne.
Take thou the Combe, the payne was his, the honey shall be

thyne:
Good reader yet beware, lest spyderlyke thou take
By cancred kynd a spiteful sting, whence he did honey make.
Let not in lieu of payne, a tounge compleat with spyght
Attempt to harme (though power shall want) the thing yl he

doth write,
For if thou dost the wise will feele thy festred kynde
And he to whom thou dost such wronge, shall so thy nature fynde.
No doubt our dayes are such as every man can see
And can at ease, and will perceyve the Spyder from the Bee.
Alowe hys labour then, and worke that well is done;
And thou shalt see, the golden race his muse pretends to runne.
Let Zoilus sucke the teate that Envy holdes in hell,
And say with mee God speed the pen that hath begun so well.
Thus hath hee his desire, thus shal thou live in rest,
Thus shall hys frendes have at thy handes the summe of their

request.

The Register of St. Dunstan's-in-the-West, London, records the baptism of "Frances daughter of Sir John Conway in May, 1569"; so it is probable that his town house was in that parish. In the parish of St. Clement Danes was buried on "May 11th, 1573, Edward Con- way, gent.," probably an uncle or a brother. On July 26th of that year Sir John had a license to travel for two years, about the Queen's affairs. (See State Papers, Dom. Sen Eli/., Addenda xxiii., 24.) He left John de Wyllam, Merchant Stranger of London, his agent. He is mentioned in the "list of gentlemen resident in Warwick, 1577-8," drawn up by Henry Ferrers, of Baddesley, and published in Nicholl's "Collectanea Genealogica," vol. viii., p. 298.

In January, 1578-9, Sir John Conway was nearly killed by Ludovic Greville, of Milcote. "Assassinations were not unheard of in these days. One or two such base acts of malice and violence were attempted against persons of quality in one day, as the Lord Talbot in his court news writ to the Earl his father in February that as the Lord

Rich was riding in the streets one Windham shot a dag at him. . . . The same day also, as Sir John Conway was going in the streets, Mr. Ludovic Grevil came suddenly upon him, and struck him on the head with a great cudgel and felled him, and being down, struck at him with a sword, and but for one of Sir John Conway's men, who warded the blow, he had cut off" his legs. Yet did he hurt him on both his shins. The council also sent for the said Grevil, and committed him to the Marshalsea" (Strype's "Annals," vol. ii., part 2, p. 207). It would have been better had he been kept there longer, to restrain his homicidal mania. The next thing we hear of Sir John was in connection with John Somerville's case. On October 31, 1583, in his examination, John Somerville was asked, "Whom did you make pryvye to thisintent?" And part of his reply ran thus, "He sayeth also that he made Sir John Conway privie unto the trouble of his mind about an intent he had to doe something for the benefitt of the Commonwealth, but did in noe sort acquaint him with his intent, and that Sir John Conway advised him to laye these conceipts aside." He did not forget Somerville's relation to the Grevilles in his reply. Young Mrs. Somerville had also consulted him in regard to the entail of Edreston. Burghley's note against these examinations was " to command Sir John Conway to repaire up" (State Papers, Dom. Ser. Eliz., clxiii., 26). Hugh Wright, his servant, was also examined. Apparently he was then imprisoned, for, even if he had done nothing, he was cousin of Edward Arden, though no biographer has taken notice of the fact. It will be remembered (see p. 76) that a certain book of "Meditations and Prayers," bought by Edward Grant, borrowed by Elizabeth Somerville, and lent to her unhappy brother, put the finishing touch to his insanity. The importance attached to it in the examinations must be borne in mind when attention is given to Sir John Conway's next literary venture, and the circumstances under which it was written. It is undated, and there is a literary puzzle connected with it. The title-page runs :|" Meditations and Praiers gathered out of the Sacred Letters, and Virtuous writers, disposed in fourme of the Alphabet of the Queene her most excellent Majesties name, whereunto are added comfortable consolations (drawen out of the Latin) to afflicted minds. Multae Tribulationes justorum et de omnibus liberabit eos Dominus. Psal. 34. The Neade of Vertue is the feare of God which goeth with the chosen wooman, and is knowen of the righteous and faithfull: She filleth the whole house with her ritche giftes, and the garners with her treasure. *Ecdes.* I. Imprinted at London in Fleete Street by Henry Wykes."

The two chief points to note are his extravagance of euphuistic compliment, such as was satirised by Shakespeare, and the suggestions for " The quality of mercy" in *The Merchant of Venice.* The work describes itself as "A posye of flowered prayers," each one beginning with a letter of the name of Elizabeth Regina, a Meditation on the Lord's Prayer, Consolation in Affliction, and the Authour's prayer:|

"Mine enemies have fortified rounde aboute mee and have enclosed me with torment and travell, my flesh and skinne are made olde, my boanes are bruised. They have hedged mee that I cannot geate out; and have laide heavie Linckes upon mee." "My innocence is trodden downe and my life subdewed with false surmises." "I am sequestered from all freedome and thou Lord knowest I am not giltie?" "I acknowledge my

faultes towards thy Celestial Seate But Lorde, if my

breaste ever harboured any unjust pretence or acte against thy servante Elizabeth my gratious Queene and Governoure, as a joyfull praie bestowe mee amongst mine eger enemies. To this daye from my birthe thou knowest Lorde, I have honored her with Loyal Love and served her with true hart and innocent handes. . . . Mine enemies swarm as Bees to the hive. . . . Wherefore Lord wash the understanding of my gratious gover- nesse with flowing springs of thy truth. ... As she is thy chosen Vessell, no usurping harte nor bloudy hande may ever have power over her."

One of the introductory " Flowered Prayers " runsl

E lecte by will of Mighty Jove in Royall Roumth to sitte
Livinge in Chaste Diana's Lawe, with sacred Saba's witte
J uno desmaide with stately Rule hath yeelded Heavenly mace,
Z enobia serves, wise Pallas sues, faire Venus seeks her grace,
Apollo with his heavenly Dome wants wisedome to define
Bounde if shee be to nature's Lawe, or if she be Divine,
Empiringe us unworthy wightes whose gratitude maie gaine
That our renowned Elizabeth
Here Nestor's yeares may rayne.

To the High puissant renowned Princesse of al Vertue ourmost redoubted Souereigne Lady Elizabeth of England, France, and Ireland, Queene, Defendour of the Christian Faith : Your majestie's trewe and loyall servant John Conwaye prayeth all things beseeming the Height of your Royall Desert, Imperiall Crowne, and dreadfull dignity.

On the following page he returns again to his Dedication "To the Queene," showing how, while "treading the weary march of this Loathsome Labyrinth" with all the weaknesses of" man's brickie body," he had been assailed by "The wicked serpent, Againste whose malignities the heavenly giftes of prudente skill and learninge are shrined in Royal seate of your unspotted life: associate with moste lovely nature, the true Victors of Regale Renowne, exercisinge eche vertue in proper kinde, that justly maie procure you everlastinge rewarde of undefiled Battaile : so under Bulwarke of those Angelical beauties, pearsinge the highest pointe of starry firmamente and mounte, I saie, of heavenly humilities, universally resounding all Europe, and making England specially blessed," &c. "The comfort . . . of prayer whereof holdeth backe my over feebled spirit, from her last steppe to that ugly Hell of Desperation, deeming there was never earst infelicitie in any degree equall to mine, whose foes by sinistre suggestions have not onely usurped the rewarde of my single intent and true service, but Zoylus hath stirred the ministers of your heavy wrathe against mee, to the abandoning of my desired libertie, suppression, with utter ruine of my poore sequell, and buried my halfe living carkas in the grave of deepe forgetful- nesse, where my voice is hoarsed with cryinges and my tongue fainted with uttering the griefe of my sorrowful mind . . . wherein I am wounded, maimed, wronged, and loste, it needeth a true confession, and not a false defence, in any thing by mee thought or done to the prejudice of your Royal person, crowne, state, or dig- nitie. I professe before the Almighty . . . that I am asinnocent as the child unborn. My whole studie, force, travell nor adventure shall ever be able to cancel the Recordes of your Princely thoughtes, touching my true loyalty which no antecedent of passed life can accuse, nor any poysoned tongue in true touch my present amaze. What more worthely beautifieth the maiestie of kingly rule ; advanceth wisedome to her highest steppe of glory, or can so sweetely make the chiere harmonie of al good gouernment, as againste the woefull afflicted to deliver clemencie, to each offender mercie, to the vertuous rewarde, and in cases doubtful to suspende judgment? Truely these are they which not onely satisfie the heavens and earth with a right aspecte of Divine justice, but are chief moovers, that the longe abandoned virgin Astrea hath resigned sacred seate to become your handmayde to highe glory." He asks the Queen to study his case, and "so wholy decipher my honest intent, true faithful fervent and dutifull care of your Royall person, Common Weale and happy gouernment." He wants means to publish this work, written where contagion of place oft annoys his senses. Sir John Conway seems eventually to have rebutted the charges and satisfied his enemieslperhaps his Flowered Prayers when they reached her, "written on his trencher with a leathy pencil of lead," moved his Sovereign. On 29th December, 1586, he was made Governor of Ostend, by Robert Earl of Leicester, then General of the English auxiliaries in the Low Countries (Thomas, Hist., Notes 1, 408,436). For some reason he was there made prisoner, as appears by an original letter from him at Ostend to Walsingham, 8th September, 1588. He gives advice how to act in the war, how to use spies, and surprise the towns opposed to the English, with no allusion to loss, disgrace, or change of position. (Harl. MS., 287,60.102.) The writer in the Dictionaryof National Biography, resting on the article in *Notes and Queries,* First Series, xi., 48, takes it for granted that he wrote his " Meditations" then, knowing nothing of the 1583-4 imprisonment, and not noting that the imprisonment at Ostend lasted only for a few days, when he was kept so strait that he could neither send nor write. He had been taken to the "Town House," seemingly by the inhabitants. Proceeding on this assumption, the biographer supposes he had been in the Tower then, and was allowed to return to Ostend in July, 1590. Murdin's " Burghley's State Papers," p. 794, tells simply that Sir John Conway, Governor of Ostend, was allowed to return; that it means to England from his governorship is implied, not only in the grammatical construction of the sentence, but by the fact that Sir Edward Norreys was then appointed Governor at Ostend.

But while the Dictionary article is evidently erroneous, my difficulty comes in here. No dated books of Henry Wykes appeared after 1571; he disappeared from the Stationers' Registers then, and is supposed to have died shortly afterwards. Ames mentions him as being in 1572 the servant of Sir Francis Knowles, but he had not found any book of his printed at so late a date. If Wykes were dead, it is impossible that Conway's book could have been published in 1583. Another edition was published by William How, who, however, went on printing till 1590. So either Wykes was alive, and able, by the connivance of Sir Francis Knowies, to print this in 1583, or it records an earlier unjust imprisonment of Sir John at a time when it is difficult to understand the use of the title " Meditations and Prayers." (See my paper in *Notes and Queries,* Eighth Series, x., Aug. I, 1896 ; and Harl. MS., 287, fo. 102.)

A marriage was planned between Sir John Conway'sson and Anthony Bourne's daughter, but Bourne seems to have got into money troubles, which hindered the marriage. (State Papers, Dom. Ser. Eliz., clviii., 49, Jan., 1583.) Perhaps Conway's own troubles had something to do with the difficulties.

Sir John Conway was enrolled as a member of "The Association for the protection of the Queen's person," founded by Leicester next year. In the Subsidy Roll, 35 Eliz., in the Hundred of Barlichway we find him assessed at Arrow 6/., for 30/. land.

On September 2 5th, 1588, Robert Cecil wrote to Lord Burghley from Ostend," Sir John Conway uses me with favour for your sake" (State Papers, Dom. Ser. Add. Eliz., xxx., 83). On 2yth December, 1588, the Butler- ship of the Port of London was granted to Thomas Conway.

The Privy Signet Bills, May, 1591, shew that a " pension of 20/. a day was granted to Captain Thomas Con- way in consideration of service done during my life."- The Register of St. Martin's-in-the-Fields records the Burial on 26th July, 1598, of "Thomas Conway, inter- fectus," who was probably his son.

Sir John Conway died 4th October, 1603. His daughter Elizabeth married Edward Conway, of Lough- ton. He was succeeded by his son Edward, who had been knighted by the Earl of Essex at the siege of Cadiz. Edward married Dorothy, daughter of Sir John Tracy, of Tedington, Gloucester. He sat as member for Penrhyn in the first Parliament of James I., and was appointed Governor of Brill in the Netherlands (see Chamberlain's Letters, p. 173). He there had a visit in 1616 from the voluble Lord Herbert of Cherbury (already referred to in connection with Sir Thomas Lucy the Third), who gives a lively picture of navigation at his time: "Winter now approaching, and nothing more to be done forthat year, I went to the Brill to take shipping for England. Sir Edward Conway, who was then Governor at that place, and afterwards Secretary of State, taking notice of my being there, came to me, and invited me every day to come to him, while I attended only for a wind; which serving at last for my journey, Sir Edward Conway conducted me to the ship, into which as soon as I was entered, he caused six pieces of ordnance to be discharged for my farewell. I was scarcely gone a league into the sea when the wind turned contrary, and forced me back again. Returning thus to Brill, Sir Edward Conway welcomed me as before; and now, after some three or four days, the wind serving, he again conducted me to the ship and bestowed six volleys of ordnance upon me. I was now half-way to England, when a most cruel storm arose, which tore our sails and spent our masts, insomuch as the master of our ship gave us all up for lost, as the wind was extreme high, and together contrary. We were carried at last, though with much difficulty, back to the Brill, where Sir Edward Conway did congratulate my escape, saying he believed certainly that (considering the weather) 1 must needs be cast away" ("Life of Lord Herbert of Cherbury," ed. S. Lee, p. 179). When Brill was delivered up to the Dutch in 1616, Sir Edward Conway received a pension of 500/. (Carew's Letters to Sir T. Roe, p. 35.)

On 30th January, 1622-3, he was made one of the principal Secretaries of State, and he was continued in that office by Charles I.; was returned member of Parliament for Evesham on 1gth February, 1623-4; and on 22nd March, 1624-5, was created Baron Conway of Ragley, in the county of Warwick, and sent ambassador to Prague. On 8th December, 1625, he was made Captain ofthe Isle of Wight. By Charles I. he was created Viscount Killultagh, of Killultagh, County Antrim, andon the 6th June, 1627, Viscount Conway, of Conway Castle, in Carnarvonshire, and was made Lord President of the Council; and died in St. Martin's-lane, London, 3rd January, 1630-1. By severance from the Arden connection this family throve.

In the Stratford Register of Burials we find :l"March 2nd, 1591, Catherine fili-i Edward! Conway"; "29th January, 1593, Johannesfilms Edwardi Conway, Esq."

From the Registers of St. Martin's-in-the-Fields we learn that on 4th April, 1620, there was buried "Richard us Conway." On Jth January, 1620-1, there i the baptism of "Anna Conway, filia Edwardi et Anna: uior cius." On 7th July, 1621, was buried "Anne Conway filia Edwardi et Anna; uxoris ejus"; and on 1gth August of the same year "Anna Conway uxor Edwardi." Bat it is not dear that this refers to Sir Edward's family.

Lady Dorothy Conway's letters to her husband, Sir Edward, on the 141TM and 23rd January, 1612-3, appear in Add. MS. 23,213, *ff. 1,* 3. His own letters from Brill are preserved in Harl. MS. —;- f. 42. Add. MS. 4,177. Warrants Add. MS. 5,753, f. 234. Add. MS. 4,106, f. 44.. Add. MS. 4,155, f. 36. Conway Papers Add. MS. 23, 228. Also Add. MS. 6,046 ; Harl. MS. 2,006, f. 97 and 107 ; Harl. 7,189, f. 17. The Honours of Sir Edward Conway, Harl. 1,137, f. i4;'; Harl. 7,187.

Concerning his son, the Rev. George Garrard, Master of the Charterhouse, writing to the Lord Deputy Stratford, March 15, 1635, says, "Your friend, my Lord Conway goes a Volunteer with my Lord Northumberland in his ship. He now is with his wife in Somersetshire, whom he hath not seen since Christmas was twelve months."

CHAPTER VIII

Edmund Neville.

The life of Edmund Neville is necessary to complete the story of the Ardens, of Park Hall. Barbara, daughter of William Arden and Elizabeth Conway his wife, and sister of Edward Arden, married Richard Neville, of Pedwyn, in Worcestershire, and of Wyke, in Warwickshire. Kings and kingmakers stood in the pedigrees of the Nevilles ; their intermarriages had been with the noblest of the land. Richard Neville was descended from George, third son of Ralph, first Earl of Westmoreland, by his second wife Joane, daughter of the famous "John of Gaunt"; George, created Lord Latimer, married Elizabeth Beauchamp, third daughter and coheir of Richard, Earl of Warwick. His only son, Sir Henry, died in his father's lifetime, leaving a son, Richard, to succeed him.

This Richard had two sons, John and William. John married first Dorothy Vere, daughter of the Earl of Oxford; and, second, Katharine Parr, who, after his death, became Henry VIII.'s last Queen (Harl. MS., 3882, f. 19).

John was succeeded by his son John, who married Lucy Somerset, daughter of the Earl of Worcester, and died 22nd April, 1577, leaving four daughtersl Catherine, married to Henry Percy, Earl of Northumberland ; Dorothy to Thomas Cecil, son of Lord Burgh- ley, afterwards Earl of Exeter; Lucy, to Sir John Cornwallis ; and Elizabeth to Sir John Danvers. The Latimer estates were divided among the four daughters, and the title was said to have fallen in abeyance among them.

William, the second son of Richard, Lord Latimer, had married Elizabeth, daughter of Sir Giles Greville, and had this son, Richard, who married Barbara Arden.

On the death of his cousin-german, Richard sued for the arms, the title, and for part of the lands as heir male of the Latimers. But powerful rivals, uncertain law, and an empty purse prevented his success. His elder son Thomas died young; his younger son Edmund, finding nothing to do at home, went abroad as a soldier of fortune.

A letter from Edmund is extant addressed to Secretary Walsingham from "The Camp,Gasbeek, near Brussels," dated 5th December, 1580, thanking him for the honour he had done him by the favour shown to his cousin Greville; begging him to remind her Majesty to raise the fortunes of his poor afflicted house ; expressing the utmost willingness to serve her Majesfy ; but explaining his inability (o leave the means he had in Belgium, unless the Queen restored him to the honours of his house, and to the lands to which he laid claim (State Papers, Add. MS. Eliz., xxvii.).

The "means" he speaks of were probably only his foreign commission and the use of the lands of his first wife, Jane de Martigny, Dame de Colombes, a native of Hainault, who died and was buried about this time in the church of St. Brise at Tournay. The family seemed always in difficulties.

We have seen (p. 103) that Richard Neville brought a lawsuit against the heirs of John Lord Latimer to recover some parts of the lands of Latimer. The suitwas unsuccessful, but he was allowed to bear the arms of the eldest branch of the family, a heraldic decision, important in relation to the discussion on Mary Arden's arms as Shakespeare quartered them, and personally important to Edmund Neville in relation to his later claims to the earldom of Westmoreland.

"John Lord Latimer died without issue male, leaving four daughters, who may quarter his arms. By the custom and usage of England, after the decease of John Lord Latimer, without issue male, Richard Neville, his cousin-german, may bear the arms of the family without distinction or difference" (State Papers,Dom. Ser. Eliz., clxxxv., 62). After this decision Richard Neville always wrote himself "Lord Latimer." Edward, or Edmund as he was more generally called, probably to distinguish him from his more fortunate cousin, Edward Neville, of Abergavenny, seems to have been staying for some time with the Catholic and seditious Nortons at Rouen. But we must remember that old Richard Norton had married Susanna the daughter of Richard, second Lord Latimer, and was thus connected ("Secret advertisement of Catholics on the Continent," State Papers, Dom. Ser. Eliz.,clxxv.). Edmund returned to England some time after the notorious Dr. Parry, who also claimed to be a cousin. Dr. Parry's mother was a Welsh Conway; Edmund Neville's mother was a Warwickshire Conway; yet the connection was ac- ; knowledged both by Sir John Conway and Neville.

The execution of Edward Arden had been the last 1 great horror of 1583. It had moved Europe and it moved Parry. Thomas Morgan in Paris urged him to free the country. Parry said he was willing to kill the greatest subject, meaning Leicester. "It is the Queen I mean," said Morgan.

It is difficult to know which side to believe in the various accounts of the events that followed. Parrywent to the Queen at Greenwich, told her there was a conspiracy against her, and asked as the price of information the Mastership of St. Katherine by the Tower. Refused any reward or benefice, he went discontented to London, and there received from Paris Cardinal Allen's reply to Burghley's pamphlet on the "Execution of Justice in England."

This confused his moral perceptions, and made him feel assassination no crime, though he was still unwilling to do the deed himself. He confessed afterwards that his cousin Neville had come to his house in August and had said, "Cousin, let us do something, since we can have nothing." Neville's notion was that he might deliver the Queen of Scots, presuming upon his credit and kindred in the north. Parry thought it dangerous to her, and impossible to men of their fortunes. Then Neville spoke of the taking of Berwick. Parry said that he had a greater enterprise in hand, more honourable and profitable to the Catholic Commonwealth, and lent Neville Allen's new book.

Parry, however, resolved to try other means first. He had himself returned as member for Queenborough, Kent, to the Parliament that met on 23rd November, 1584, to legislate against the Catholics. The terrible bill against Jesuits and seminary priests was being rushed through the House on 1yth December, the same day that the private bill for the assurance of certain lands to Sir Thomas Lucy passed. It had reached its third reading, and was about to be passed by acclamation, when, to the surprise of all, a solitary member rose and spoke against it, denouncing it as "full of blood, danger, and despair to English subjects." A speech worthy of Hampden at a later day roused the wrath of that Parliament. The audacious member was sent to ward, but released next day. D'Ewes says in his journal, "This zealous man had better have heldhis peace," because in six weeks he was accused of a plot.

Edmund Neville's conscience had never been easy about Parry's doctrine of " killing no murder." When he found him, wrathful after his defeat on honest and manly lines, concentrating his ideas on the darker plot, he first remonstrated with him, then warned him, and, finding him fixed, informed a member of the Council on 8th February. After hurr1ed consultations, he signed a formal deposition on 10th February.

Parry was meanwhile lodged in the house of the friendly Walsingham, where he was given opportunities or explanation, but was finally removed to the Tower, where confessions and letters followed each other on nth, I3th, and I4th February (see State Papers and Strype's "Annals," vol. iii., pt. 2, f. 557). He naturally accused Edmund Neville of deeper complicity than was suspected, and he also was lodged in the Tower. The truth is hard to find; confessions, retractations, rapidly followed each other. Parry said in a private letter to Elizabeth, "I beseech Christ that my death and example may satisfy your Majesty and the world. . . . Give some ease to your Catholic subjects, and you shall find that God will bless you, foreign princes esteem you, and your subjects obey you." The House of Commons was in a ferment. On 23rd February Sir Thomas Lucy moved that some especially severe death be found for the villain Parry, though one would have thought the traitor's death would have glutted even the taste for horrors of the Englishmen of his day (D'Ewes's "Journal," 341-364, and Parl. Hist., 824).

The trial took place on the 25th February. Parry's confession was read. In it he gave a new colour to Edmund Neville's actions. He said he often came to his house, and was most familiar with him; that it wassurprising he did not reveal till February a treason he knew to have been conceived in August. " If it cost him not an ambitious head let him never trust me," because he thought Edmund Neville's hearing of the death of his cous1n Charles, Earl of Westmoreland, of whose lands and titles he assured himself, "had bred belike this conscience in him." But if this rumour had gone abroad, it was an error, as may be seen. Parry protested that his confession had been extorted from him under torture and was false, but he was condemned, and on the 2nd of March,

1584-5, was drawn on a hurdle to the Palace Yard at Westminster, and there, probably in the presence of his fellow-members, with much delay, he was executed, denying he had ever meant to kill the Queen, and summoning her to answer for his blood before God. ("Baga de Secretis," Pouch xlvi.)

Edmund Neville seems to have been in the Tower for some years, though there is reason to believe he was at times liberated and re-committed. I find among . the Coke MS., Hist. Man. Com., June, 1585: "A pardon granted to Edmund Nevell, Esquier, of all treasons and offences by him committed, by reason of his confederacie with one William Parry, lately attainted of high treason, with proviso that if the said Nevell shall at any time hereafter during his lyfe conspyre, attempt, or take in hand eyther within her Majesties dominions or without, anything against her Majestys person, or to the disturbance of the State of the Realme, that then this pardon to be voyd."

"June 1585. An annuity of 100//, a year for life, granted Edmund Neville, Esquire, to begin from Chistmas last."

On 25th September, 1585, he wrote both to Leicester and Walsingham desiring the liberty of the Tower on account of railing health, and denying the truth of the accusations against him (State Papers, Dom. Ser. Eliz., clxxxii).

Several other of his letters are preserved among the State Papers. On 8th October, 1586, he wrote a long letter to the Lord High Treasurer, "from his undesired and undeserved lodging in the Tower." He had then lost his living abroad, because his wife had died, through mourning for his absence. His second wife, the date of whose marriage I have not yet found, was Jane, daughter of Richard Smith, son and heir of Sir Walter Smith, of Shelford, in the county of Warwick. It was probably during his imprisonment that the event occurred recorded in his collection of Heraldic MSS., Harl. 853. Through some severity of the sheriffs of London, Skinner and Catcher, probably during a search for recusants, his wife gave premature birth to a child, Ralph, who died a few days after and was buried in Hoggesdon Churchyard, Middlesex, 8th July, 1588. The distracted and helpless father, disappointed in his hopes of an heir to his empty titles, charged in poetry the sheriffs with having murdered his only son, and imperilled the life of his wife.

Richard Neville seems to have died in 1590, because on 1yth September of that year Edmund was granted administration of his effects. His unfortunate cousin, Charles Neville, Earl of Westmoreland (attainted for his rising in the north in 1569, in favour of Mary Queen of Scots) died in deep poverty and distress at Brussels on 16th November, 1601. He had married, in 1564, Jane, the daughter of the famous poet, Henry Howard, Earl of Surrey, and left four daughtersl Catherine, married to Sir Thomas Grey; Eleanor, who died unmarried; Margaret, who married Sir Nicholas Pudsey; and Anne, who married David, brother of Sir William Ingleby, of Ripley. Edmund Neville, again male heir in front of four female cousins, tried to claim the Westmoreland title and estates, but his claim was disregarded. He had no money to win favour at Court or justice at law.

For after John's decease, my uncle's sonne
On whom that line of Latimer did fall,

And I to shew my father's height begonne,
Who shoulde succeed him as his heire male,
His daughters' matches did so much prevaile

By reason of their great authoritie
As forced me leave at once both lands and countrie.

Again in James's reign he applied, with higher hopes, as he had not only sympathised with the Scottish Queen, but had been on friendly terms with the Scottish King himself, who had indeed promised to make him Earl of Westmoreland when he was King of England. But the court decided that though he was heir male of the first degree, yet in cases of high treason the offender forfeited all estate of inheritance, as his cousin Charles had done (Reported by Coke, Rep. 7, Mich. 7, Jac. I.). A new creation might remedy this. On 3rd April, 1605, he wrote a touching personal letter to James, urging his claims and pleading the royal promise to reinstate him (Harl. MS., 787). His enemies tried to implicate him in the Gunpowder Plot, but he seems to have cleared himself, and shortly afterwards made an offer to the King of fifty thousand pounds for the Earldom of Westmoreland and the present rents (State Papers, Dom. Ser. James I., xvi., 72).

A statement of Neville's claim, with notes by Salisbury, is preserved in the State Papers, Dom. Ser. James I., xxiv., 70. Pending the settlement the King

granted him various allowances and a pension of six undred pounds a year, which was all absorbed by claims of creditors, from whom he had borrowed money to press his suit (Lansdowne MS., xlvi., 22). On 25th November, 1611, he had a grant of the fines due on alienation of land, but the expense of collection came to more than the profit. There was buried in St. Clement's Danes on 2nd January, 1612, "Mounseer Nevyll, oneof the Palsgrave's gents." I know not whether this refers to a member of his family or not.

A life of sorrow, anxiety, ever-recurring disappointment, was his, though no "treason" was ever proved against him. On yth February, 1617, from Dunkirk, he wrote again to try to touch the heart of the King, recounting his services on his behalf, and reminding him of his promises. He had now one foot in the grave, and begged that he might not die in a strange land, but "reaching the happy land of promise, might sing his *Nunc Dimittis* in peace " (State Papers, Dom. Ser. James I., App. xc., 51).

He must have died very shortly afterwards, though whether abroad, and besieged with creditors, or in England, in the arms of his family, I know not. But in Eastham Church in Essex, in the chancel, behind the communion table, is a handsome mural monument of marble with the effigies of Edmund Neville and his lady|"In memory of the Right Honourable Edmond Neville, Lord Latimer, Earl of Westmoreland, and Dame Jane his wife, with the memorials of their seven' children; which Edmond was lineally descended from the honourable blood of Kings and Princes, and y yth Earle of Westmoreland of the name of Neville."

"Ralph, Catherine, Ralph, Dorothy, Jane, Margaret, Anne,
By God's great power (who doth command all powers),

To us these seven children were for blessings given,
Some do survive, as images of ouers,

And some are gone from whence they came to heaven:
Birth, blood, and beauty, like to flowers still fade,
Death turns each living substance to a shade."

The arms of a dozen noble families are blazoned above, and the motto, "Virtus cum sanguine crevit." In front of the monument is an elevated tombstone to the "right vertuous, fair, and noble ladie Katharine Neville, first daughter of Edmond Earl of Westmoreland, and Jane his wife, who died a virgin the fifth of Dec., 1613, being of the age of 23 years."

Of the other children one only could long have survived him. Among the State Papers, believed to be of the date of 1618, is a petition from Dorothy the wife of Arthur Hill to the Lords of the Treasury. She is daughter and sole heir of Edmund Neville, Lord Lati- mer, late reputed Earl of Westmoreland, whose estates were escheated to the Crown. She prays that her annuity of one hundred pounds, which is in arrears, be paid her. Edmund Neville's widow made her will as Dame Jane Latimer, Countess of Westmoreland, 22nd January, 1645-6, and it was proved 25th February, 1645-6, and on 13th July, 1646, Thomas Ferrour, cousin of her late husband, was permitted to administer her effects (Surtees' "Durham," iv., 162-164).

Among the heraldic collections which Edmund Neville made to establish his claim we find the best pedigree of his mother's family, the Ardens of Park Hall, which concludes "Here endeth the descent of the heirs male of Sir Guy Arden, Baron of Wallingford and Earl of Warwick, and followeth the heirs general, with whom the Earldom went with favour of the Conqueror " (Harl. 853 and 113).

Upon the evidences collected by Edmund the title was restored to his cousin, Edward Neville, in 1624. It is because he wrote his own life in this measure and manner, that I consider him the author of the "Poetical Life of Sir Nicholas Throckmorton," already referred to. He might have called him *uncle,* a degree removed, both by the father's and the mother's side. One verse runs thus:

"This custom is good, Baldwin, as I trowe
To write their fates which are unfortunate
Within this vale by fortune's overthrowe,

Amongst which heape my most unhappie state
I may complain, and in my life relate
Contrary to the course of all the reste,
In which respecte I holde them three times bleste.

Wherefore I pray thee, lend thine eares awhile
To heare my crimes, although not magistrate.

Upon whose house fortune did laugh and smile, Thou knowest once, though nowe she frown and hate

Both it and me, borne to no less estate Than anie one of those which were before But rather should of right enjoy much more."

CHAPTER IX

The Throck.mortons

The Throckmortons became owners of Coughton through the marriage of John, son of Thomas Throck- morton, of Fladbury, county Wigorn, to Eleanor, daughter and co-heir of Guy de la Spine. Their eldest son was Thomas Throckmorton, who died 12 Edward IV., and his son, Robert, then aged 21, succeeded. One of Robert's sisters was Elizabeth, the last Abbess of Denny, whose memory is still preserved by the brass plate in Coughton Church. She died 10 Henry VIII. (1547). Another sister was Mrs. Margery Middle- more. His brothers were Richard, and William the Doctor of Laws. The "Visitation of Huntingdon" traces the Throckmortons of that county to Richard, whose children were : John, Raphael, Gabriell, Anthony, Simon, Goditha, Jane, Margaret, Catherine. The son of John was Sir George, Serjeant of the Hawks to Queen Elizabeth, who became father of Raphael and George.

Robert Throckmorton made the park at Coughton 2 Henry VII., and enclosed with it a certain common ground called Wykewood. He was that "Robert Throckmorton arm.," who on 16th May, 1501, was associated with Thomas and Robert Arden of Wilmcote in Mayowe's transfer of the lands at Snitterfield farmedby the Shakespeares,lin a manner which witnesses to great intimacy, and goes far to prove the relationship of Thomas Arden or Wilmcote to the Ardens of Park Hall, for whom this same Robert Throckmorton was also trustee. He married Catherine, daughter of William Marrow, Alderman of London, and he and his wife were brother and sister of the Guild of Knowle. He was summoned to be knighted in 10 Henry VII., but Dugdale does not find the title attributed to him until 17 Henry VII. Having made his will in 1518, he set out on a pilgrimage to the Holy Land, but died on the way, 1520, and his body was never placed in the beautiful tomb he had prepared for it at Coughton. His daughters were Elizabeth, married to Sir Thomas Englefield, and Mary, the wife of Thomas Burdet of Bromscot. His sons were Sir George, his heir, Anthony, and Michael. He desired that the goods he had sent before him to Florence should be divided between his two younger sons. Anthony was slain at Pavia, and Michael became the trusted follower, secretary, and friend of Cardinal Reginald Pole.

Sec my "Shakespeare's Family."

Henry's wrath at the position Pole took against his divorce forced Michael to stay abroad during his reign, but on the accession of Mary he was welcomed in England, and she granted him many Warwickshire manors of the attainted John Duke of Northumberland. Among these was Haseley, which he handed over to his nephew Clement next year. He died at Mantua 1st November, 1558. His son Francis succeeded to his estates, and lived at Ullenhall in the parish of Wootton Wawen, where his tomb commemorates him as "The son of Michael, born at Coughton Court, Warwick, and brother to Sir George Throgmorton. After the sayd Michael had lived many years in Italy in good and great reputation with bountifull hospitality, entertayn- ing most of the noblemen and gentlemen of Englandthat had occasion to come that way, did returne into the Realme of England in the beginning of the Rayne of Queen Marie, and received of her gift the manors of Haseley, Blackwell, Parkhurst, Winderton, and Ullen- hall, and after went into Italy again, where he departed this life and lies buried in St. Martin's Church in the said city of Mantua under a faire tomb. The said Francis married Judith, daughter of Richard Tracie, of Stanway, and Barbara Lucy, of Charlecote, and had six children, Francis, Michael, Judith, John, Michael, Judith." The last three were alive at the Visitation, 1619.

Sir George, the heir of Coughton, was present at the coronation of Anne Boleyn, and was sheriff of the county in 35 Henry VIII. He built the great gatehouse at Coughton, and the tomb for himself and his wife, Catherine, daughter of Nicholas, first Lord Vaux. They were brother and sister of the Guild of Knowle, 1526. He was made Keeper of the House of the Lady Anne of Cleves, to have the government thereof. His life is best illustrated in the career of his large family of eight sons and eleven daughters. His sons, whom we must take in their order, seem to have been all capable men.

1. Sir Robert, who married first Muriel, daughter of Lord Berkeley, and second, Elizabeth, daughter of John, Lord Hussey, and widow of John Lord Hungerford. By the first he had his heir, Thomas, who married Margaret, the daughter of William Whorwood, Attorney-General to Henry VIII.; Mary, who married Edward Arden, of Park Hall; Emma, who married Ralph Sheldon, of Beoley; and other children. By his second wife, he had, among others, George, and Anne, who married Sir William Catesby, of Leger's Ashby. Among the State Papers, 2nd June, 1580, is preserved

See Acts of the Privy Council, 26th May, 1553.

an indenture between Sir William Catesby and Sir Robert Throckmorton, about the jointure of Dame Anne. The eldest son of Thomas was John, who died before his father, leaving Sir Robert heir, who married first Dorothea, daughter of Francis Fortescue, and second Maria, daughter of Francis Smith, Esq., of Wootton Wawen. There are various notices or this family in the State Papers, but nothing very special.

2. Sir George's second son was Killome or Kenelm, of whom nothing remarkable is recorded, except that, objecting to the old family names for his children, he gave them outlandish ones, such as Octavian, Marpol- lian, Theodorus, Constantine, Mymsbrey, &c. The certificate of levy for the hundred of Dunmow, Essex, is signed by him, 1593.

3. Clement, the third son, was a cupbearer in the Queen's Household 17 Henry VIII. (see Harl. MS., 642). On 14 April, 7 Edward VI., he assessed the value of the College of Stratford-upon-Avon (see the Book of Fees and Annuities, No. 69, P.R.O.) and he had a life annuity from its income. He drew up also the plan of Birmingham in 1553, lately translated and published by Mr. W. B. Bickley. On him, probably on account of his literary tastes, his Catholic uncle Michael settled Haseley next year. He was justice of the peace, and is often noted in the records. He was one of the members forming the Russia or Muscovy Company in 1555. (See State Papers, Dom. Ser. Addenda, Mary, VII.) Clement married Katherine Neville, eldest daughter of Sir Edward Neville, the sister of Lord Abergavenny, and had seven daughters and six sons, of whom the eldest Job succeeded. At the Inquisition Post-mortem of Clement's property, 1st April, 1575, it is stated that he had extensive lands at Claverdon and elsewhere in Warwickshire ; that Haseley had been settled on himself and his wife for life, then on his sonJob and his heirs male, then on his other sons, failing whom, on

his brothers in the following order: Anthony, Kenelm, George, John, Sir Nicholas, Sir Robert, or their heirs male.

Job was a learned man, but over-zealous in his Protestantism and loyalty. He was in the Commission at the time of the Somerville-Arden trial, and on 21st January, 1583-4, writes from Haseley to Mr. Ralph Warcupp, that he had apprehended William Skinner, searched his house, examined witnesses, and considered there was enough to bring him within the statutes, as he believes in toleration for Catholics, insists that the Queen of Scots is heir-apparent, and shelters Jesuits. "If certain men near me were well *wrung* there might happen to be *wrung* from them some evident matter for the servyce of her Majistie in the full discoverie of Skynner and his adherents. Their names are thesel Thomas Hunte of Busshewood, Thomas Attwood of Rowington, Sir William the priest at Batsley, John Cooper of Rowington, and Dorothy his wife, Henry Hudsford schoolmaster of Solihull, with his father and elder brother. . . . We leave Mr. Skinner to the Councell to wring from him what they can. . . . The Lord turn his heart or cut him off speedilie." Christopher Kirkland, B.D., minister of Rowington, said the Skinners did not come to church; Thomas Slye, of Bushwood, yeoman, fifty-four years old, said that he remembered that Mr. Skinner said once within seven years "that a Protestant doctor of their own syde did defende that a woman could not be supreme Heade;" and John Fairfax, parish clerk of Rowington, said Mr. Skinner "hoped that religion would turn, or that there would be a decree that all men might believe as they list."

The payment for the messenger carrying this correspondence is recorded :l"To Jeames Darwin, upon theCouncill's warrant, dated at Whitehall, 1yth Jan., 1583, for bringing letters in post for her Majestie's affairs from Mr. Job Throgmorton at his house at Haseley in the countie of Warwick to the Courte of Whitehall, and for his charges back again, *vili"* (Account of Treas. of Chamber.)

Job went too far in his zeal, and became entangled in the Martin Marprelate controversy.

Seeing that this was a hanging matter then, he published in 1594 a small volume entitled "The defence of Job Throckmorton against the slanders of Master Sutcliffe, who had said that he was a party to the Martin Marprelate Tracts," though elsewhere the same writer had stated that the noble " Martin " was John Penry, John Udall, and John Field, all Johns. He had nothing to do with it. Camden uses rather strong language concerning him. He married Dorothy Vernon, the sister of Elizabeth Vernon, Countess or Southampton, and it is curious to imagine the possible relations between the two sisters, and their strongly contrasted husbands. Job's son was another Clement, a man learned and eloquent, who served in several Parliaments along with Sir Thomas Lucy.

4. Of Sir Nicholas, the fourth son, we know more, both from printed history, from the State Papers, and from that very curious poem, after the manner of Churchyard, professing to be dictated by his ghost to his nephew. It is preserved in the Harl. MS., 6353, which once belonged to Anne Fortescue, a connection. Peck imagines the nephew to have been Sir Thomas, but there are no grounds for his opinion. Sir Thomas spent much of his life in prison for the old faith, and would not call it "superstition," or speak of "spiteful Papists." The editor, John Gough Nichols, suggests that it might

have been by Job Throckmorton ; or by John, son of Anthony Throckmorton, of Castleton, youngest brother of Sir Nicholas. But I think it is much more likely to have been by Edmund Neville for reasons that I have given fully in Chapter VIII.

There are many inexactitudes in the dates, but the main incidents in the story are evidently founded on family tradition. The ghost relates that being a fourth brother and far from hope of land, his parents sent him as a page to the Duke of Richmond, Henry VIII.'s natural son, whom he served patiently, dreading his blows when he was in his rage. He lived most carelessly with him in France, and learned to speak the language, though not readily. He tells how his uncle Michael, in Reginald Pole's service, went against the divorce, and the risks he ran thereby; of the number of noblemen brought to the block about that time; and how his father's roc s clapped him in the Tower, and hoped to "joint his neck." Among his foes were "the Grevilles." By the Duke of Richmond's death Nicholas was left without a master. Everything seemed to go. wrong.

Our sun eclipsed, a long time did not shine,
No joys approached near unto Coughton House ;
My sisters they did nothing else but whyne,
My mother lookt much like a drowned mouse.

No butter then would stick upon our bread,
Wee all did fear the loss of father's head.

Then his mother sent him to her brother, the Lord Parr, who kept him out of charity. This connection is rather difficult to work out, but is important in the story of the family. Elizabeth, one of the co-heiresses of Lord Fitz-Hugh and Alice, daughter of Ralph Neville, Earl of Westmoreland, married first Sir William Parr, of Kendal, by whom she had a son Thomas, and other children. She married second, Nicholas, the first Lord Vaux, by whom she had three daughters, theeldest of whom, Catherine, married Sir George Throck- morton. Lord Vaux's second wife was Anne, daughter and co-heir of Sir Thomas Green, of Greensnorton, whose other daughter, Maud or Matilda, married Sir Thomas Parr, of Kendal. By Maud Sir Thomas had one son, William, and two daughters. Catherine the elder married first, Edward Borough; second, John Neville Lord Latimer; third, Henry VIII.; fourth, Thomas Lord Seymour. Anne the younger married Sir William Herbert, afterwards created Earl of Pembroke by Edward VI. William became Marquis of Northampton at the same time. Hereby the story of the poem is made clear:l

Oh luckie looks that fawned on Catherine Parr
A woman rare, her like but seldom seene,

To Burrough first, next unto Latimer
She widow was and then became a Queen.
My mother prayed her niece with watery eyes
To ridd both her and hers from endless cryes.

Catherine Parr was apparently kind and sympathetic to her aunt and family :l

With wooing time denials disagree
She spake and sped, my Father was set free.

Nicholas then went cheerfully back to the Court with his brothers Clement and George (the latter not mentioned by Dugdale). Clement was made cupbearer to the King, Nicholas sewer to the King, and George a gentleman pensioner. Three of the brothers followed the King to Boulogne, the fourth waited on Viscount Lisle (afterwards the Duke of Northumberland).

Nicholas received an annuity, and thereupon married Anne, the daughter of Sir Nicholas Carew. Sir William Herbert and Lord Parr were very friendly and attentive to the Throckmortons, therefore the other nobleswere friendly. They all feared trouble at the death of the King, but it passed. Nicholas still served Katharine after her marriage to Lord Seymour, and then served Edward VI., with whom he was a great favourite. The young King wanted to make him a knight against his will, and he ran out of the room and hid in a corner in the passage, but the King found him and knighted him there.

On going to pay a visit to his father at Coughton, he was not very well received, and when he found that the cause of the displeasure was that he should have been knighted before his elder brother, Nicholas went back to Court with Robert and John, where Robert was knighted. John became the King's man, and Sir Nicholas received the manor of Paulersbury.

In childish cradle of securitie
I rocked myself asleep, devoid of fear.
For why ? I was the King's familiar.

On the death of the King their joy was changed into sorrow for their loss, and anxiety for their future. Sir Nicholas accepted the claim of Mary, and went to announce to her, her brother's death. But when Wyatt rose against the Spanish marriage, Nicholas was suspected of complicity, was sent to the Tower, and arraigned at Guildhall, where his wife, mother, and brethren came to see him in tears. His skilful replies during a ten hours' trial convinced the jury of his innocence, and he was acquitted.

But the jurymen were all fined, and he was kept in the Tower for a year. When he was set free on 18th January, 1554-5, he fled at once to France, but his brother and other friends having interceded for him, he was brought home and reconciled to the Queen. Hewent to fight at St. Quentin, fell sick, returned to England, and visited Elizabeth by stealth, who said she would never believe in her sister's death until she received the black enamelled ring given by Philip to Mary on her betrothal. When Mary died he waited to receive this from a kinswoman of his, who was in the service of Mary, and fled with it to Elizabeth, but was mortified to find that she had not only already believed in her inheritance, but had bestowed all the places in her gift, except that of the Chief Butler, which he was fain to accept. Sir Nicholas, however, received later many honours from the new Queen. He was sent over as ambassador to France to remonstrate with Francis II. and Mary Stuart when they assumed the arms of England. The State Papers, September 9, 1561, tell us, "Mr. Thomas Cecil has been ill of ague in Paris. Sir Nicholas Throckmorton has been kind as a father to him. Sir Nicholas wishes to be recalled." The Volumes of the Hardwicke MS. (Add. MSS. 35,830; 35,831; 35,832), contain his correspondence. He is the only one of the family who may be called a public man, and his life is a part of the history of his time. He was sent to Scotland when Mary Stuart was in trouble with her own people, and supported her cause. Leicester suspected him of being against his marriage with the Queen. He died (supposed by some to be poisoned) after eating a "salad at supper" in the house of the Earl of Leicester, in spite of the royal doctors being sent to his aid. Camden says it was at the house or Lord Burleigh. Sir Francis Walsingham, then at Paris, deplored his loss in a letter to Leicester: " Be it spoken without offence to any, for counsel in peace, and conduct in war, he hath not left, of like sufficiency, his successor, that I know of" (Collins's Peerage, vi., 578). Camden calls him, "A man of large experience, piercing judgement, and singular prudence." Nicholas Throckmorton'salabaster tomb is on the south side of the chancel in St. Katharine's, Creechurch, near Aldgate, London. "Here lyeth the body of Sir Nicholas Throckmorton, Knt., the fourth son of Sir George Throckmorton, Knt., the which Sir Nicholas was Chief Butler of England, one of the Chamberlains of the Exchequer, and Ambassador Leiger to the Queen's Majesty, Queen Elizabeth, in France. And after his return into England, he was sent again into France, and twice into Scotland. He married Anne, daughter to Sir Nicholas Carew, Knight, and he got of her two sons and three daughters. He died the 12th day of February, A.d. 1570, aged 57 years." His son Arthur succeeded him. His daughter Elizabeth married Sir Walter Raleigh. His widow Anne married Mr. Adrian Stokes. Many of her letters are preserved among Brit. Mus. MSS.

This is evidently a literary reference to the conception of the early play, "The Cradle of Security." See Willis's "Mount Tabor," 1639.

5. Apparently Thomas was the fifth son, of whom I can find little record. In Henry Dudley's trial, 1556, the Council makes a memorandum to inquire if Sir- Nicholas Throckmorton or Thomas was concerned (Mary, VII, 60). On March 18th, 1570, the justices of Warwickshire wrote to the Council saying that they all had subscribed to the Articles of Uniformity for Common Prayer except Sir Robert Throckmorton and Thomas Throckmorton.

6. George, the sixth son, is mentioned in the Legend of Sir Nicholas as having gone to the siege of Boulogne with Henry VIII. He was wounded and taken prisoner, and the French wanted a thousand pounds for his ransom, as they heard he was of the King's kindred. Henry exchanged three Frenchmen for him, and always jested about his high value. He appears in the Throckmorton Pedigree, Harl. MS. 1100, f. 68-70, Harl. MS. 1393, f. 87. A strange story is recorded of him in 1559. His wife, Frances, daughter of Sir John Bridges, Lord Chandos, seemed to have been fond of resorting tothose that used palmistry and enchantments. He said she was wishing to poison and destroy him. He accused her himself, and bullied the witnesses, threatening them with prison and rack if they did not confess just what he told them. Lady Elizabeth Chandos wrote to Lord Robert Dudley complaining that her daughter, wife of Sir George Throckmorton, was kept a close prisoner in the Fleet; being with child, it was a great risk to her. The charge was witchcraft and sorcery, but the accused protests her innocence. Sir George brings forward some witnesses, poor people of no credit, who speak of things said to have happened seven years ago, but she denies them (Add. MS. 32, 091, f. 176).

Lady Elizabeth also wrote to Cecil on 20th August, 1559, asking him to favour her daughter, Frances Throckmorton, whose innocence will be apparent if she has impartial judges. A new set of judges had up the old witnesses before them, and unravelled the truth. The second judgment was that the lady was overmuch given to fantastical practices of palmistry and suchlike devices, but that she had made no attempt to poison her husband. On the contrary, her efforts had only been initiated to win his perfect love (see State Papers, Dom. Ser. Eliz., vi. 24, and vii. 42). Sir George left two sons, Nicholas and John, and three daughters, Elizabeth, Sara, and Jane.

7. John, mentioned frequently by Nicholas, though reckoned the fifth son in the visitation of Warwickshire, 1619, is evidently the seventh son. Dugdale's assertion of this is supported by his tomb in Coughton church, a stately edifice, with the effigies of Sir John and his wife clasping hands. The epitaph gives the main facts of his life. "Here lieth interred the bodie of Sir John Throgmorton, of Feckenham, the yth son of Sir George Throckmorton, Knyght of Coughton, sometime Master of the Requests unto Queen Marie

of happie memorie, who, in respect of his faithfull service, bestowed upon him the office of Justice of Chester and of her Counsel in the Marches of Wales, in which roome he continued xviii. yeares, and supplied within the same time the place of Vice Presidente the space of iii. yeares. He had to wife Margerie Puttenham, daughter of Robert Puttenham, esq., by whom he had issue 5 sons and four daughters. He departed this life the 22nd of May, 1580. His wife survived who lived and died his widow, and is here interred, on whose soules God have mercy." His name is recorded in connection with several Warwickshire transfers, with many law cases, and various State Papers.

In " East Cheshire," vol. i., p. 59, among the judges of Chester, Ormerod notes, 1558: "John Throckmorton, Esq., from 6 Mary to 21 Elizabeth; *i.e.,* 1558-1579. Edward Hassall his deputy in 13 Elizabeth; Simon Thelwall his deputy 18 Elizabeth. In 1579 there were two judges, John Throckmorton and Henry Townshend lSimon Thelwall their deputy."

The children of Sir John Throckmorton were Francis, Thomas, John, George, Edward, Joan, Mary, another Mary, and Anne.

It is said that he died from mortification at the slights and wrongs put on him by the Earl of Leicester.

Sir John Throckmorton's brother-in-law was George Puttenham, of a double literary interest. Sir Thomas Elyot, who wrote " The Praise of Women," also wrote a little book on "The Education of Children," dedicated "to his only entirely beloved syster, Margaret Puttenham, 27th November, 1535." In it he gives her advice how to bring up his young nephews in the rule of virtue. One of these was George Puttenham. A niece, born later, was Margery Puttenham, Lady Throckmorton. George Puttenham seems to have been born about 1532, to have been a scholar atOxford, a gentleman pensioner of Elizabeth, a traveller, and a literary man. But he was somewhat combative. There were difficulties between him and his wife, Lady Windsor; there was discord between him and his brother Richard. Sir John Throckmorton had himself to appear before the Privy Council, and help to put matters right among his relatives.

George Puttenham is generally believed to have written about 1585 his "Art of Poesy," in which he mentions the Epitaph he had written "to the honourable memorie or a deere friend, Sir John Throgmorton, Knight, Justice of Chester, and a man of many commendable virtues" (Book III., Chap. 17). This book was published at first anonymously by Richard Field in 1586, with a prose dedication to Lord Burghley written by Field himself, as was noticed in the first chapter of this book.

8. An eighth son of Sir George Throckmorton was Anthony, of whom Dugdale gives no clear account. This is all the more confusing because there was a cousin Anthony of the Huntingdonshire branch, who also married a Katherine.

One thing is clearlthat he married Katherine, one of the seven daughters of William Willington of Bar- cheston. On April 5th, 1555, William Willington made a grant to Sir Robert Throckmorton, Robert Myddlemore, and Humphrey Underhill, of his lands in Hawford, Wilmington,Burmington andHonnington, and other lands in the counties of Oxford, Worcester, Gloucester, in trust, for his own use for life, and then to the use of Anthony, one of the sons of Sir George Throckmorton, and of Katherine, his wife, one of the seven daughters and heirs of Willington ; and then to the use ofthe heirs of the said Katherine by William Catesby, son of Richard Catesby, her late husband (State Papers, Dom. Ser., Addenda, Mary, VII. 38).

They seem to have settled at Chastleton, co. Oxford, and to have had a large family. Anthony makes a great show in the visitation of Oxford, for he had all his ancestors' arms, empaled and quartered, blazoned in his house, which is described. Katherine, his wife, died on 6th January, 1582, and her tomb was carefully preserved.

In 1558 Queen Mary granted the manor of Brinckley to Sir Robert Lane and Anthony Throckmorton, who aliened it in the same year to William Dawes.

James Cruce, of Kenilworth, gent., had on 1st March, 1556, passed Milbourn Grange to Anthony Throckmorton, citizen and mercer of London, who, on 1st May, 1563, sold it to Sir Thomas Leigh, citizen and Alderman of London. This may refer to Anthony, son of Sir George, or Anthony, son of Sir George's second brother, Richard, who settled in Huntingdon.

Katherine, the widow of John Butler, citizen of London, alienated the manor of Pipe, near Erdington,' and afterwards married Anthony Throckmorton. From the State Papers we know that this Anthony was the brother of John Throckmorton, the only brave man of the Dudley Conspiracy in Mary's reign, who was executed as a traitor on 24th April, 1556. Katherine Butler, alias Throckmorton, the wife of Anthony, was called to prove that John was her husband's brother, and resided in their house, but that she knew nothing of his conspiracy. No pedigree gives a John, the brother of Anthony, "attinctus," but it is possible he was a second "John," and therefore naturally dropped out. John, son of Richard, and the recognised brother of an Anthony, was father of Sir George, Serjeant of the Hawks to Queen Elizabeth.

A quaint little contemporary quarto volume tells the story of a Robert Throckmorton, who was " born of an honourable, ancient, and worthy family, a younger son,his native countrie being in the very heart and bowels of our land." He was tempted to risk highway robbery, through the difficulty of earning an honest livelihood. He was tried and executed with two others in South- wark, London, on 26th February, 1608, after sincere repentance of his sin. From which branch of the family this young man sprang I have been unable to learn.

Sir Thomas Heneage had some cause of dispute with one of the Throckmortons, which had been settled in his favour, but Throckmorton would not yield. Heneage writes to Lord Burghley three years afterwards, on 8th May, 1591 : "He still keeps possession, and he hath, since the issue, spoiled all the woods. I desire no whit of favour, only justice of my own." Throckmorton had brought in a "writ of error"; so on 3rd June, 1591, Heneage asks Lord Burghley to publish the judges' decision, adding "I have deserved as well as Mr. Throckmorton in the state of my calling" (Lansdowne MS., Ixviii. 2, 7).

In the Register of St. Clement's Danes, London, are the following entries: Marriages, "Sir George Throckmorton and Dorytic Walson,

May 8th, 1605." "Sir George Throckmorton and Mistress Anne Wright,

a5th June, 1630." Burials, "Lady Anne Throckmorton, wife of Sir George Throckmorton,

Knight, 29 Nov., 1632."

"George Throckmorton, son of Sir George Throckmorton and Dame Anne, deceased Dec. n, 1632."

8

SECTION 8

CHAPTER X
Franc1s Throckmorton.

I Would like to dwell for a little on the sad story of Francis Throckmorton, the eldest son of Sir John Throckmorton, of Feckenham. On the 3rd June, 1571, there was a marriage contract drawn up at Worcester between Francis Throckmorton, son and heir of Sir John Throckmorton, and Anne Sutton, alias Dudley, one of the heirs of Sir Edward Sutton, Lord of Dudley,- and a license granted them to marry in any church, chapel, oratory, or other consecrated place after the publication of the banns. Her pedigree is worth noting here, because there has been much confusion about it. Dugdale mentions the story, but from Twamley's "Dudley Castle" we get fuller details. The Suttons belonged to the old nobility. The unfortunate John, Baron of Dudley in 1501 had married Cecily, daughter of Thomas Grey, Marquis of Dorset.

John (afterwards Duke of Northumberland), the ambitious son of the notorious Edmund Dudley, was determined to prove his descent from this ancient stock, and is said to have written out a pedigree with his own hand, which no contemporary genealogist would accept.

Finding this Baron John was weak, extravagant, and unfortunate in money matters, through bonds, mortgages, and moneylenders, Northumberland bought up his debts, took possession of his estates, and ousted him from his castle. John spent the remainder of his life in paying visits to his friends, and was popularly called "Lord Quondam." His wife was left to the support of her own friends. His son Edward, Baron Dudley, married first Catharine, daughter of John Bridges, Lord Chandos, Maid of Honour to Queen Mary. After the fall of Northumberland he was reinstated in his Warwickshire estate. His only daughter by this marriage was this Anne, who married Francis Throckmorton. Edward Lord Dudley married second, Joan, daughter of Edward Lord Stanley, and had a son Edward. He married third, Mary, the daughter of Lord Effingham. It is curious that in the chief plot of Mary's reign, Anne's uncle, Henry Dudley, and John Throckmorton, a relative of Francis, had been among the prime movers.

After the contract of marriage, Francis Throckmorton went in 1572, along with his brother Thomas, to Hart Hall, a favourite College for Catholics in Oxford ; and his brother George joined him there in 1573. Francis was "attainted in 26 Elizabeth, *i.e.* 1583, for treason laid to his charge, as having conspired, God knows what, on behalf of the Queen of Scots," says Camden. It was so easy in those days to slip unconsciously into treason through sentiment and faith, before prudential reason had calculated worldly peril. We can only understand it by putting ourselves back in the period. Treason depended on whether Elizabeth Tudor or Mary Stuart lived the longer. Francis was one of the Throckmortons who clung to the old faith. He was young, chivalrous, romantic, and discontented with the treatment of his father, his house, and his co-religionists. It is evident that he had personal interviews with the Queen of Scots, and that herwonderful charm and afflicted condition had won his chivalrous devotion. To restore her to freedom, and to win liberty of conscience for all, were the two aims of his action. A modest and honourable programme enough, one would think. Unfortunately the ties of faith drew him towards others whose ways were dark. Away in Rome was the Pope, still powerful in the hearts of faithful Catholics; still urging, as a holy mission, the destruction of the heretic usurper Elizabeth, and the restoration of the country by force to the old faith. On the one side was the temporal arm of the King of Spain, on the other of the King of France, united only in religion and in the desire to circumvent the free action of England. The emissaries sent into the country were legion.

Burghley was more than a match for them all. He had spies everywhere. He soon knew all about the Throckmortons. He knew that Thomas, the second son of Sir John, was abroad under suspicious circum-. stances; that George, a younger son, had served the Prince of Parma, and had returned to London on the 26th January, 1582-3. He knew that Francis went much abroad, frequented disloyal company, and that he was in the habit of carrying letters to the Scotch Queen. He had him stealthily watched for six months, his letters intercepted, his ciphers translated, his companions followed.

Even in Carleton's "Thankful Remembrance of God's Mercies," p. 68, it has been suggested that "cunning was practised and counterfeit letters scattered." When Burghley had found sufficient proof somehow, about the middle of November, he sent two gentlemen to Francis Throckmorton's house at Lewisham, and other two at the same time to his house in London, by St. Paul's Wharf. At his town house they found him. He was in the act of ciphering a message to the Scotch Queen,and he rushed upstairs, destroying the letter as he went. He managed to secrete a certain mysterious green casket, full of letters, afterwards sent to Mendoza, the Spanish Ambassador, in spite of Burghley's care. One of the emissaries marched *off* with the captive to the Tower, and the other remained to search his chamber and take possession of all papers.

The State Papers necessarily go back on previous events in the record of the examinations. Oh gth October, 1583, Lady Margery Throckmorton, their mother, had written to her sons suggesting they should go to Lady Arundel at Arundel Castle, who, having a ship of her own, would pass them over safely to France (State Papers, Dom. Ser. Eliz., clxiii., 8). Some spy was examined, in the same month, about the communications of the Spanish Ambassador with Francis Throckmorton, Charles Arundel, Lord Paget, and others.

John Somerville, it may be remembered, was arrested on October 25th, and examined on the 28th ; but he said nothing that incriminated these young men. On 10th November Richard Poulet petitioned the Council that Francis Throckmorton, son and heir of Sir John Throckmorton, deceased, should reassure him in the Manor of Herierd and the farm of Upton Bernard, co. Southampton (State Papers, Dom. Ser. Eliz., clxiii., 60). This suggests that he was then free. The exact date of his arrest is not given in the accounts printed, but on 18th November Sir Francis Walsingham wrote from theCourt to Thomas Wilkes, who had just returned from his inquiry atCharlecote into the Somerville-Arden case, "You shall do well to give Mr. Norton warning this night or to-morrow in the morning early to meet you at the Tower at such houre as by you shall be thought meet. I have seen as resolute men as Throckmorton stoop, notwithstanding the great shew he hathmade of a Romish resolution. I suppose the grief of the last torture will suffice, without anye extremity of racking, to make him more conformable than he hath hitherto showed himself" (State Papers, Dom. Ser. Eli/,., clxii., 65).

The opinion of Walsingham was correct. Throck- morton confessed to his intimacy with Sir Francis Englefield, owner of Fulwood Park, seven or eight years before in Liege. (They were cousins, it may be remembered.) He confessed that he meant to aid the Duke of Guise to deliver the Scotch Queen, to ensure tolerance in religion, and if Queen Elizabeth resisted their demands, to remove her from the throne. He allowed that the Queen of Scots was privy to the enterprise, and that he knew of the list of safe havens drawn up for strangers landing in England.

He was offered a free pardon if he would disclose the whole story (a false offer). He said that he had already confessed all, to the utter ruin of his house and family,- "and I have disclosed the secrets of her who was the dearest thing unto me in the world [meaning the Queen of Scots], and whom I thought no torment should have drawn me so much to have prejudiced as I have done by my confession. I see no cause why I should spare any, and since I have failed of my faith towards her I care not if I were hanged." Thereupon, removing from the place where he sat beside the rack, he used this proverb in Italian, "Chi a perso la fede, a perso 1'honore." (State Papers, Dom. Ser. Eliz., clxiii.)

Froude is very scornful of his cowardice. But the enthusiastic youth, to whom the world shone fair, blest with a loving wife and a devoted mother, started, for the sake of the captive princess, with heroic courage, the unequal battle with the torturers and examiners. It was only after he was weakened by continued imprisonment, unnerved by repeated racking, that he spoke. Itwas hard to face the grim engine of agony again, knowing what it could do, and be deaf to the specious words of promise, that ensured at least a temporary relief if he would only confess.

It must not be forgotten that they who scrupled not to torture his body would not scruple to torture his words. When news went abroad that he had "spoken" there was an exodus from the kingdom of Catholics in any way "touched," which threw more suspicion on Francis Throckmorton (State Papers, Dom. Ser. Eliz., clxiv., 5). The intercepted letters that passed between Lady Margery Throckmorton and her steward Vaughan, on the 16th, 24th, and 2gth November show the great pecuniary straits to which the family was then reduced. Vaughan was in extremity for money to supply his wants. Lady Margery wrote to him that she could not help him, as her son was a close prisoner in the Tower, " for what I hear not, nor cannot guess, wherefore, to make your own supply, sell what you can, and how you can, of that which is his, and rather let Warwick men and others have a reasonable bargain at your hands than in any wise you should yourself take any loss or discredit. I hope in time he will prove himself the honest man, whatever be conceived of him at this present" (State Papers, Dom. Ser. Eliz., clxiv.). On 5th December the lady herself was examined as to reasons for suggesting that her sons should go abroad by Arundel Castle. She said she had been riding in her coach from London to Lewisham, and she asked Owen where Thomas might have the surest passage over, for she heard that the ports were straightly searched. Her son, George, offering to pass not long before, was stayed, and his apparel and other things were taken from him, of which he could never receive restitution. She "wished Thomas to pass safe with such money, plate, apparel, and other things that he was to carry over with him forhis own provision" (State Papers, Dom. Ser. Eliz., clxiv., 9).

The day after, Ambrose Cowper, from Coleshill, Warwickshire, wrote to Mrs. Elizabeth Throckmorton (apparently a cousin left in charge at Feckenham), saying that there was "glass" belonging to his master at Bridgnorth, about which he had written to Mr. Vaughan. He thought it ought to be conveyed to Feckenham, because there " if the worst do befal, my Lady is to have it by Patent, as I take it, for that all felons', and I think traitors' goods, are granted thereby to my Lady." He also added that he heard that Lady Throckmorton had not yet received "the last Lady-day's rent of Crab- Tree-Field, in Coventry, which the tenant said he hath paid to my cousin Kemp. Pray learn the truth and certify me, as I mean to ride towards London on Wensday next." On the same day he wrote to William Bell, Deputy Clerk of the Peace in the County of Worcester, apologising for his long silence, the cause of which he dare not reveal. He mentioned, however, that the Ardens had been indicted at Warwick last Monday, and were to be tried next Monday in London. "My master is in great fault by the judgment of common opinion, which now I rather believe than before, for that I hear my Lord Paget, Mr. Sheldon, and others are lately fled beyond seas" (State Papers, Dom. Ser. Eliz., clxvii., 35). On nth December this same William Bell was interrogated as to the connection of Parsons the Jesuit, Lady Throckmorton, and her sons Francis and Thomas. AHad he taken any letters or books from Parsons to Mr. Francis Throckmorton's wife, namely, the booke called Christian Exercise ? Was the declension of the noun ' heretic' in the beginning of the book of his own doing?"

The replies are written too faintly to be read (State Papers, Dom. Ser. Eliz., clxiv., 19, 20). On 12thDecember they screwed another confession out of Francis as to his dealings with the secretary of the banished Duke of Lennox in the gallery of the French Ambassador (State Papers, Dom. Ser. Eliz., clxiv., 22).

Mistress Cicely Hopton, the daughter of the Lieutenant of the Tower, here becomes associated with the plot in a romantic manner. She had fallen in love with Mr. Stonor, a Catholic prisoner in the Tower, had been converted to his faith, and did what she could to help his fellow prisoners. She had been discovered, and on 14th December was examined as to her dealings with George Throckmorton. She confessed to having spoken to him three or four times in his chambers, and he "moved her for some device to have his brother Francis out of the Tower." This was about a week after he had been arrested. He offered her a reward, which she neither accepted nor told her father of. George Throckmorton had also asked her to bring up a man he saw walking in the yard to speak to him, and she brought him to the chamber door, where he spoke to Mr. George Throckmorton through the keyhole. She did not know how long they spoke, nor what they said, as she had gone into Mrs. Somerville's chamber. This was four or five days ago. The examiner thought the man's name must have been "Douglas" (State Papers, Dom. Ser. Eliz., clxiv., 27).

Next day, I5th December, a more serious examination took place of John Throckmorton, a servant in Throckmorton House, as to the letter said to have been written by Francis to his wife, and brought by a little boy with long hair. This John confessed that the day of his master's arrest Elizabeth Cooke, the lady's maid, brought him the green velvet casket, and told him to take it to a place of safety. He first took it to a tailor's called Russems, and then Meredith asked him to bring it to the house of another tailor, called Haddocke, in St. Paul's Churchyard," where Meredith gave it to a man of the Spanish Ambassador with long hair " (State Papers, Dom. Ser. Eliz., clxiv., 29).

That same day Thomas Wilkes and Mr. Norton wrote to Walsingham from the "Gilt Key" that they could not find the letter, but had found the boy, and had sent him to Bridewell. They suggested an order to Mrs. Cooke to search Mrs. Throckmorton and her sister for the letter, and asked to be excused further, as they had not eaten nor drunk the whole day (State Papers, Dom. Ser. Eliz., clxiv., 32).

On 1 yth December the Earl of Northumberland was examined as to his knowledge of Francis Throckmorton and Lord Paget; and on the 18th Mrs. Francis Throckmorton and her sister were examined about the letter, which seems only to have been a request for linen and bedding. Both on the 18th and 20th December George More was examined as to his knowledge of Francis Throckmorton and his relations to Lord Paget. On' this latter date a friend, signing " F.V.F.K.," writes to Charles Paget, telling him that his mother's house had been searched, and he and his brother were shortly to be indicted; that Edward Arden had been condemned; "and it is said that Throckmorton shall be arraigned to-morrow. He hath been often racked, but they say he confesses nothing" (State Papers, Dom. Ser. Eliz., clxiv., 47).

This was the very day of Edward Arden's execution, the news of which was, doubtless, carried to his unhappy cousin Throckmorton, still kept uncharged in his cell. On the 3 1st, Hugh Hall, the priest, was re-examined. He knew Sir Thomas Cornwallis and Sir Thomas Kidston, had said Mass in Mr. Ralph Sheldon's house, had stayed with Mr. John Talbot, Sir John Throckmorton, Lord Windsor, and Mr. Sheldon, as well as with Edward Arden. But he had no intimacy withFrancis Throckmorton (State Papers, Dom. Ser. Eliz., clxiv., 77).

Then the Attorney-General added up the result of the information he had gained through the examination of all these prisoners, taking notes from the letters of Sir Francis Englefield (State Papers, Dom. Ser. Eliz., clxv., 10). More arrests ensued. Mendoza calculated that by the middle of winter there were eleven thousand people in prison. On 10th January, 1583-4, William Carter, a London printer, was indicted for having printed a seditious book called "The Treatise of Schisme," condemned at once, and next morning was taken from Newgate to Tyburn and there executed as a traitor. The author or the book was suspected, but not discovered. Others were brought to the block; but it was not until 21st May that Francis Throckmorton was really brought to trial in Guildhall. He was found guilty. The next day the Earl of Leicester wrote the Queen a letter from Kenilworth, clearly advising her to make an end of Mary Stuart as well as her friends (State Papers, Dom. Ser. Eliz., clxx., 88).

On 1st June, Sir Owen Hopton tells the Council that he had admitted Lady Throckmorton to see her son Francis; that she had given him good motherly advice to deal plainly with the Queen. He had given him ink and paper, and enclosed the letter the poor prisoner had written imploring her Majesty to "forgive the inconsiderate rashness of unbridled youth" (State Papers, Dom. Ser. Eliz., clxxi., 1).

He was allowed to see his wife, and he was being tempted by fair promises. Life was still sweet to him, and his hopes revived. The Attorney-General meanwhile was drawing up a treatise showing the justice of his condemnation (State Papers, Dom. Ser. Eliz., clxxi., 79, 85, 86). Dr. Allen and other Catholics abroad prayed God to comfort his soul. He had need ofcomfort. On 10th July, 1584, he was taken from the Tower to Blackfriars by water, thence dragged to Tyburn, and executed as a traitor. Both at the arraignment and on the scaffold he denied the truth of his confession, charged her Majesty with cruelty and the Council with untruth (State Papers, Dom. Ser. Eliz., clxxi., 86).

The fate of Francis Throckmorton must have been common talk in Stratford-upon-Avon during that year, and following upon the death of Edward Arden, must have deeply impressed the youthful mind of Shakespeare.

Lady Margery Throckmorton's troubles were not over when her son died. On 25th September, Joane Morley, alias Mathew, prisoner on suspicion of felony in Chester Castle, was found to have been formerly her servant, was carefully examined, and gave information about the Catholic proclivities of her mistress, her interest in Morgan the priest, and her consent that her son Thomas should be made a priest. Margery, daughter to Hugh Throckmorton, was about to be made a religious woman abroad. All which things told against Lady Margery (State Papers, Dom. Ser. Eliz., clxxiii). But ere long she found some one to lay her at peace by the side of her beloved husband, Sir John, at Coughton. Anne Sutton, alias Dudley, the young widow of Francis Throckmorton, afterwards married Mr. Thomas Wilmer, councillor-at-law.

CHAPTER XI

The Grevilles And Lord Brooke.

The original home of the Grevilles was at Drayton in Oxfordshire. "The first notable increase in their possessions happened when Lewis Greville married Philippa, the daughter and heir of Sir Giles Arden," of the same family as the Ardens of Park Hall. "The grandson of Lewis married the daughter and heir of the Corbets, and his son the daughter and heir of Pointz" (Add. MS. 5937, f. 88).

Many of the Grevilles were members of the Guild of Knowle. One of this family, Sir Edward Greville, of Milcote, Warwickshire, in the reign of Henry VIII., married the daughter of Thomas Denton. He had the wardship of an heiress, Elizabeth Willoughby, to whom he offered his eldest son, John. She said she preferred Fulke the second. His father said "that he had no estate of land to maintain her, that he was in the king's service of war beyond the seas, and his return was doubtful." She replied that "she had an estate sufficient for both; that she would pray for his safety and wait for his return," which she did. Her great grandfather, Richard Beauchamp, in the time of Henry VI., had three daughters, the eldest of whom married Robert Willoughby Lord Brooke. He had one son Edward, who married Margaret, daughter of Richard Neville, Lord Latimer, and died before his father, leaving three daughters. One of these died early; the third married Francis Dawtrey, and left no children; and the eldest was this Elizabeth, who brought Beauchamp's Court and broad lands in Warwickshire to the younger Greville.

Her race had reason to bless her choice. Sir John, the elder brother, who had been proposed to her, got into trouble. Among the Acts or the Privy Council, 26th October, 33 Henry VIII., 1541, it is noted, "Upon an informacion gyven that John Grevell of Milcott in the County of Warwyke, should misuse his owne daughter, and shot at one of his servants with a crossebow, it was decreed that the said John Grevell should be sent for to appear immediately before the Counsell. Whereupon Burner Sergeant at Armes went for him and the same day was a letter directed to Streteley of Oxfordshire his brother-in-law to appear likewise to testify against him." He appeared, but the court was too busy to attend to his case, and he was bound in 500*l*. to appear every day until he was dismissed. He died in 2 Edward VI., leaving his son, Sir Edward, to succeed him, who married Margaret, the fifth daughter of William Willington, a London merchant of the Staple. (He bought lands in Warwickshire and depopulated and enclosed Barcheston, having no sons but seven daughters, in whose favour he made his will in 1555.) Sir Edward died in 2 Elizabeth, and his son Ludovic, then twenty-two years of age, became head of the family. He married Thomasine Petre. Even in early years he was eccentric, passionate, and wrong-headed. The Council wrote to Sir Thomas Lucy, Thomas Smyth and John Hyckford, desiring them to hear the complaints of the tenants of Wellford, in Gloucestershire, against Ludovic Greville, 18th March, 1576 (State Papers, Dom. Ser. Eliz., cvii., 89). In January, 1578-9, he felled Sir John Conway in thestreets of London, and would have killed him had not his servants interfered (Strype's Annals, vol. ii., pt. 2, p. 209). He was sent to the Marshalsea for this, but through interest he must soon have been liberated.

When his two sons were practising archery, Edward the younger shot from his long bow an arrow straight upwards. It fell on his elder brother's head and killed him. Ludovic, his father, treated the matter lightly, and made a jest of it, telling the boy " it was the best shot he had ever shot in his life" (Dugdale's "Warwickshire," p. 711). Nowadays they would, doubtless, have treated him for homicidal mania; then he was allowed to run free, and at last he suffered a terrible penalty.

He obtained permission to build a new manor house on the top of the hill near the old one, and his ambitious plans ran him short of funds. He coveted the possessions of one Webbe, an elderly bachelor, who had been his servant, and was now his tenant at Drayton. He inveigled Webbe to his house at a festival, strangled him in bed, sent for a clergyman, made one of his servants personate his victim in bed, and dictate a will in his master's favour. Webbe was supposed to die shortly afterwards, and was openly buried, without suspicions.

One of the servants, however, at a drinking-match at Stratford-upon-Avon, boasted that he knew what would hang his master. Greville then instigated his other accomplice to kill his fellow. Being discovered, the murderer confessed the whole plot. Both master and man were tried at Westminster; the servant was hanged, but Mr. Greville, to save his lands for his family, which would be forfeited should he die a felon's death, refused either to defend himself or answer questions. The penalty of being pressed to death for contempt of courtwas decreed him, but this carried no confiscation with it. He died thus on the 14th of November, 1589.

It has not been noted that he was a cousin of John Somerville by the mother's side.

Ludovic's son Edward succeeded, and took his natural place in the family. He was sheriff of the county, 37 Elizabeth, 1595. In a list of "the gentlemen of account living in London," made on 28th November, 1595, there is included " Edward Greville, of the County of Warwick,-Esq., in Bread Street Ward" (Lansdowne MS., 67). He was knighted in 1603. His name is frequently mentioned in the Stratford-upon-Avon Records. Dugdale thinks it a judgment on him that he had no male heirs, and that his debts were so great that at his death his estates had to be sold and scattered.

The Fulke Greville that Elizabeth Willoughby chose was knighted, received from Henry VIII. in 1541 the site of Alcester monastery, and became one of the largest landowners in the county. He was Sheriff in 1543 and 1548, Member of Parliament in 1547 and in 1554, the year of his grandson's birth. He died on 10th November, 1559, and was buried in Alcester Church, leaving two sons, Fulke and Robert. Fulke was knighted in 1565, being then twenty-nine years of age. In 1570 he became a justice of the peace, and his name is frequently mentioned in association with Sir Thomas Lucy's, both in the State Papers and in the Stratford-upon-Avon Records. He was Member of Parliament in 1586 and in 1588, and died in 1606. "A man no less esteemed for the sweetness of his temper than the dignity of his station," says Camden in his "Britannia." He married Anne Neville, daughter of Ralph, Earl of Westmoreland. Their only daughter, Margaret, married Sir Richard Verney, of Compton Mordack, Warwickshire, and their only son and heir was Fulke the third. The life of this third Sir Fulke has been written by Dr. A. B. Grosart, in the "Fuller Worthies Series," and it is almost unnecessary for me totake it up, except to complete the group of Shakespeare's Warwickshire contemporaries that I have selected.

Fulke Greville was born at Beauchamp's Court in 1554, the same year as Sir Philip Sidney. The year before his birth Edward VI. founded the Grammar School at Shrewsbury, to which Sir Henry Sidney (doubtless because of its proximity to Wales) sent his son Philip in 1564. The very next entry recorded after that of Master Philip Sidney was "Foulkus Gryvell, films et haeres Foulke Gryvell armigeri de Beauchampe Courte in Comitatu Varvici. xvi Cal. Nov. 1564." Dr. Grosart had this entry from the books of the school.

Probably the ties of far-off relationship, of equality in station and in age, founded the friendship thus early, afterwards so firmly cemented by mutual esteem and similarity of tastes. The boys studied there together for four years, but were afterwards sent to different universities. Sidney went to Christ Church, Oxford, while Fulke Greville went to Jesus College, Cambridge, as the matriculation books prove. Some have supposed that he studied at Trinity Hall, because his arms appear in the eastern oriel window there (probably on account of some benefaction). His separation from Philip did not cause estrangement. They probably visited each other, and read together occasionally in each other's colleges. Greville was made Master of Arts of Oxford in 1588. They received to their mutual friendship a youth called Edward Dyer. These three were members of the literary society formed by Gabriel Harvey, called "Areopagus," whose chief object was to introduce classical rules into English literature. Two pastorals, written by Sir Philip Sidney," upon his meeting with his two true worthy friends and fellow poets, Sir Edward Dier and Maister Fulke Greville," are preserved in Davison's "Poetical Rapsody," 1602.

Sir Henry Sidney, Lord President of Wales, had appointed young Fulke to a small office under him in 1576. Having the reversion of two better offices promised him, he resigned this and went in 1577 to Court, along with Sir Philip Sidney, where he at once attracted the Queen's notice. He possessed many qualifications to retain her favour, being young, brave, handsome, and independent in means. But frequent frictions at Court were caused by his passionate desire for foreign travel and active service. Elizabeth would not grant him permission to go abroad, but he sometimes went without leave. In 1577, when Sidney was sent to Heidelberg to convey the Queen's condolences to Lewis and John Casimir on the death of their father, the Elector Palatine, Fulke Greville accompanied his friend.

In 1578 he went to Dover to embark for service in the Low Countries, but Sir Edward Dyer was sent with a Royal mandate to stay him. He managed to accompany Walsingham on a diplomatic mission a month or two later, but on his return was forbidden the Queen's presence. Nevertheless, in 1579 he accompanied Lan- guet (the tutor and friend of Sidney) on his return to Germany, and on his way home had an interview with William the Silent, Prince of Orange, in which the conversation ran on the merits of Sir Philip Sidney.

When the French nobles came over in 1581 to negotiate a marriage between Elizabeth and the Duke of Anjou, Philip Earl of Arundel, Frederick Lord Windsor, Sir Philip Sidney, and Fulke Greville gave a costly entertainment on Whit Monday, 15th May, 1581, in which were martial exercises, tilts, and tournaments, these gentlemen being challengers to all comers. Fulke Greville won special fame for valour, and was appointed to attend the Duke of Anjou to Brussels.

A letter to Walsingham about that time representshis estate as a poor one, but it must only have been a temporary difficulty and comparative poverty.

In April, 1583, Greville was made Secretary for the Principality of Wales, with a salary of 2,000/., but the duties do not seem to have required constant residence.

In that year Giordano Bruno came to England, and Greville received him with enthusiasm; and in his house in London, Bruno held several of those disputations which he recorded in "La Cena de la Ceneri" (Frith, "Life of Giordano Bruno," 1887, p. 227, &c.).

Meanwhile the hearts of the two young friends had been fired by the discoveries of Magellan and Frobisher. They had read together Hakluyt's First Folio, then just appearing, and dedicated to Sir Philip Sidney. Fulke Greville himself describes how, in 1585, Sir Philip had planned great schemes of conquest and colonisation in the West Indies with Sir Francis Drake, Sidney finding the funds, and Drake taking the public responsibility. It was a dangerous but delightful secret to all concerned. Fulke Greville, with pardonable pride, narrates how Sidney "chose him out of all England to be his loving and beloved Achates in this journey."

They had stolen together down to Plymouth, and were waiting there secretly for a favourable wind to start with the fleet. Some one, quite possibly Drake himself, gave information at Court. A royal mandate was sent to stay them. Sir Philip, with some disguised soldiers, stole it from the messenger, so that it was not formally delivered. It was, however, soon confirmed by urgent letters. The wind changed too late, Drake set sail without them, and the youths went sadly back to Court. Possibly had they then had their will the whole history of the American settlement would have been different, and Sir Philip might have shewn the fruition of his riper manhood to the world. Sir PhilipSidney was allowed, however, to go to serve under his uncle Leicester in the Low Countries, only to show his wonderful powers in the field and in the Council, and then to lose his life, after twenty days' suffering, from the effects of a random shot at Zutphen. Leicester had begged that Greville might be granted-permission to accompany his nephew, but in vain. On the day when all England mourned her national loss, Fulke Greville had a private and peculiar woe, not unmixed with bitterness. Had be been permitted, he would have been by his friend's side until the end, might have nursed him, might even, he thought, by love and care, have saved him. Sidney left his books to his two friends, Greville and Dyer. Greville was one of the pall bearers at the great burial in St. Paul's, 16th February, 1587, and wrote an Elegy on his friend, which appeared later in the "Phoenix Nest" (1593). He also wrote a prose "Life of Sidney," in which he showed an almost idolatrous love.

When war threatened in 1591 between Henry III. and Henry of Navarre, he shipped over to France without telling anyone but his friend the Earl of Essex, and was six months in disgrace on his return. In December, *159St* ne was charged with certain abuses and "waste" in Packwood in Warwickshire, before the Lord Treasurer and Sir John Fortescue, but the case was decided in his favour.

In 1597 the Earl of Essex wished him to join the "Island Voyage," but again Elizabeth refused permission, and he had to learn that " it was sufficient for the plant to grow where its Sovereign's hand had planted it." In March of that year he became Treasurer of the Wars, and the following year Treasurer of the Navy. Notwithstanding the warmth of his friendship with his cousin the Earl of Essex, he was one of the party selected to arrest .the favourite on Sunday, 8thFebruary, 1600-1, and he did what he could to advise and save him.

Elizabeth granted Greville the Manor of Wedgnock in 1602-3, and in J604 James granted him the Manor and Park of Knowle and the ruined Castle of Warwick, with a tenement called the Vineyard House, and an orchard and gardens adjoining (Privy Seal, July, 1604), on which he spent 20,000/. He later purchased land of the Town of Warwick worth 1,000/. His inheritance on his father's death in 1606, added to his own possessions, made him very powerful in Warwickshire.

He was Member of Parliament for Warwickshire in 1592-3, 1601,and 1620. Among the smaller offices he held was that of the Recordership of Stratford-upon- Avon, and his name frequently appears in the Corporation Records. On James's accession he was made Knight of the Bath, and his Secretaryship confirmed for life. But higher preferment was denied him through the adverse influence of Robert Cecil, Earl of Salisbury. The great work he designed, and for which he was specially fitted, was a history of the reign of Elizabeth, but Cecil jealously refused him access to the State Papers.

On the death of Cecil (1612) Greville was made Chancellor of the Exchequer, Privy Councillor and Gentleman of the Bedchamber, and in January, 1620, he was created Lord Brooke of Beauchamp's Court, with limitation of the title to his favourite cousin Robert and his heirs. He was less active in politics after this time, and seems to have spent his time chiefly in revising his poems, which he left in charge of a friend. His end was tragic.

He had omitted to mention in his will an old servant, Ralph Haywood, who, in revenge, stabbed him in bed one morning, went to his own room, and committed suicide. Lord Brooke lingered for a month, died onthe 3oth of September, 1628, in Brooke House, Hoi- born, and was buried in the tomb he had raised for himself in St. Mary's Church, Warwick. The simple yet striking epitaph runs : "Fulke Greville, servant to Queen Elizabeth, Councillor to King James, and friend to Sir Philip Sidney, Trophaeum Peccati." The meaning of the last phrase is doubtful.

There was widespread lamentation for his loss. Martin Peerson, in his " Mottects or Grave-Chamber Musique" (1630), writes:

"For thy losse, worthiest lord, no mourning eye,
Has flood enough; no muse nor elegie
Enough expression to thy worth can lend,
No, though thy Sidney had survived his friend."

Yet someone wrote a scurrilous and profane elegy on him, printed in Huth's " Inedited Tracts." His biographer thinks the same hand wrote the tractate called "The Patron," in Add. MS., 4839, fol. 131. I do not- think so. The elegy is too openly false to be considered, and confuses him with Ludovic and Edward Greville. The article philosophises on the evils of patronage and dependency, and points out Lord Brooke's case as an example. It is not amiable, but represents a view of the case possible to Haywood's friends.

The kind deeds of Lord Brooke were many. No courtier was ever so ready to use his influence for others, or so chary of using it for himself. In 1594 he spoke to Elizabeth in favour of Francis Bacon, and when James I. sent him the "Life of Henry VII." to read, he returned it with high commendations. He boldly defended Bacon against the slanders of Maynham in 1618, and was faithful to him to the last. The story of the fallen man being refused beer at Brooke House may safely be discarded, says Spedding. His exertions procured Camden leisure to follow his literary pursuits;and John Speed, the chronicler, acknowledges a similar debt of gratitude. Samuel Daniel writes that this generous patron " drew him forth from close obscurity." Dr. John Overall, Sir John Coke, Bishop Corbet, had all their thanks to express. He took William Davenant into his service when a youth, and one can see his influence in "Gondibert." The University of Cambridge expressed its gratitude for the help of Secretary Naunton and Sir Fulke Greville in the contest about the navigation of the Cam in a letter written by George Herbert, the poet, then public orator. The cordial words of Naunton in his "Fragmenta Regalia" show the estimate in which his fellow officials held Fulke Greville. The thirty-fifth sonnet of Henry Lok (1597) addresses Greville thus: " Who can of learning treat, and you forget ? Who may of vertue talke, and you neglect?"

He never married ; the extraordinary continuance of Elizabeth's favour is doubtless partly owing to that; but the tenderness of his heart, formal though the expression may be, is shown in "Coelica," a series of a hundred and nine sonnets. Quotations from his works appear in Bodenham's " Belvedere," and two of his poems are in "England's Helicon," 1600. The tragedy of *Mus- tapha* was surreptitiously published in 1609, and evidently appreciated by his learned contemporaries. Other poems appeared after his death, and also the tragedy, *Alaham.* A third tragedy he had written on *Antony and Cleopatra* but he destroyed that. He wrote in prose "Advice to an Honourable Lady," supposed to be Lady Rich; "A Letter of Travel," and "The Life of Sidney," with an autobiography.

It is always considered strange that such a man should not have mentioned Shakespeare. We must not forget that his poems were chiefly written in his youth, before Shakespeare was known ; that he was a leader in theclassical school, and therefore more likely to be associated with Ben Jonson than with the Romanticists; and, further, that the absence of notice is no evidence of the lack of interest in the poet.

But I do not think that it is absolutely certain there is no trace of association between the two. The " Song of Old Meliboeus" certainly alludes to the story of Venus and Adonis ; some of the sonnets give suggestions of Shakespeare's, and may we not imagine that one

i cause of the destruction of the tragedy of *Antony and Cleopatra* was the vision of what his fellow-countryman had done on the same subject ? The character of Rossa

i in *Mustapha* is akin to that of Lady Macbeth.

We know that he befriended Giordano Bruno, whose works were published by Vautrollier and Field, and read by Shakespeare. We know that he protected the young Davenant, and it may be permitted us to imagine that he did so, for the sake of Davenant's godfather, the friend of the Earl of Southampton, the royal player and national poet, who had delighted the two sovereigns with whom Fulke Greville's life was so closely associated.

9

SECTION 9

CHAPTER XII
Dr. John Hall.

There is such complete uncertainty regarding the early days of the poet's elder son-in-law that it is wise to group all the suggestions that have been made. He cannot have been the son of Dr. John Hall, of Maid- stone, Kent, whose translation of Lanfranc's "Chirur- gerie," with portrait of the translator, appeared in 1565. The Maidstone practitioner would have been an eminently suitable father, distinguished in his art, and the author also of "The Court of Virtue" and many metrical Biblical translations. But he died in 1566, apparently not over thirty-six, and the Stratford Dr. John Hall was born in 1575.

In Halliwell-Phillipps's "Outlines," followed in the notice of Hall's Life in the Dictionary of National Biography, it is supposed that he was connected with the Halls of Acton, Middlesex, though not born there, because he left to his only daughter "his house in Acton." A John Hall was married at Acton on 1gth September, 1574, to Margaret Archer. But he had christened a daughter, Elizabeth Hall, on 5th June, 1575, about which date our John Hall must have been born. We have either, then, to imagine that the evidence on his tombstone as to the date of his birth is erroneous or that his relation to the Halls of Acton was further off than filial. Hall is too common a name to be definiteabout; the arms on the tombstone are borne, with a difference, by many branches of the family.

I have a strong impression, which may be confirmed later by researches in registers and wills that he was connected with Idlicote, in Kineton Hundred. My reasons are the following: There was a family called Hall residing there at that date. It is not mentioned by Dugdale, who only speaks of the Underhills and states that the village contained sixteen houses; but in "A Catalogue of all the noblemen and gentlemen resident in Warwick, 1577-8, by Henry Ferrers, of Baddesley," published in Nichols's " Collectanea Topo- graphica et Genealogica," vol. vii., p. 298, I find mentioned Richard Hall of Idlicote. There is only one interesting association with this name which I have found in the Public Records. At the same time as the search was being made by Sir Thomas Lucy and Thomas Wilkes in the house of Edward Grant, of Northbrookes, a search was made of " Hall's House of. Idlicote," as if something suspicious were expected to be found there.f Wilkes said they found nothing there but the mother of Somerville, who was so ill in body and mind as to be past remembrance. This proves a considerable intimacy with the Somerville family of Edreston, a probable connection with Hugh Hall, the priest, and a certainty of Catholicism, which would give a natural reason for the foreign education and travel of John Hall. No record exists of his having been at an English university, yet he called himself Master of Arts. He would not have done so had henot taken his degree, possibly in Paris or in Leyden. This would quite accord with his turning up in Stratford, after the death of Elizabeth. His Warwickshire origin may account for the degree of intimacy he seems to have had with the county families, both Puritan and Catholic, when he began to act as a physician.

The Rector of Idlicote, the Rev. Mr. Cotterel, has kindly searched the registers for me, but the name of John does not appear at the proper date. An Edmund Hatl and his wife $mma sold the Henley Street property to John Shakespeare in William's early days. There were Halls in Worcester and in Rowington, and a John Hall supplanted Richard Shakespeare as bailiff of the Priory of Wroxall, the last year of its existence.

| The day after the apprehension of Edward Arden, of Park Hall. See State Papers, Dom. Ser. h'i.-., J.xiii., 55.

We know unfortunately nothing of his life before his marriage to Susanna Shake- speare on the 5th of June, 1607, he being then thirty-two and she twenty-five. But it is perfectly allowable to believe that his early attentions were paid to the illustrious father, only thirteen years older than himself, so similar in many of his tastes, and that, like Othello, he would often come and describe his travels to him, while Susanna, like Des- demona, listened, and fell in love.

Dr. Hall resided in a house in Old Town, in the road leading from the Church to the Chapel. His only daughter, Elizabeth, was baptised at Stratford-upon- Avon on the 21st of February, 1607-8. His name occurs in the Town Records in 1611 among the supporters to a Highway Bill; and in 1612, when he leased from the Corporation a small piece of wooded land on the outskirts of the town.

Doubtless he began early to build up the practice that afterwards became so ex- tensive, but we have no account of what he did until 1616. He must have remained on friendly terms with his father-in-law, because he and his wife, Susanna, were left residuary legatees and executors of Shakespeare's will. In June, 1616, he proved the will in London in the Archbishop of Canterbury's Registry. He shortly afterwards removed to New Place beside his mother-in-law, where the vestry notes of the 3rd of February, 1617-18, record him as resident.

He was elected a burgess of Stratford-upon-Avon in 1617 and again in 1623, but was excused from takingoffice on account of his professional engagements. In that year his mother-in-law died, the love of Shakespeare's youth. The touching ideas of her epitaph were doubtless his wife's, put into his Latin, but they go far to repel the unpleasant suggestions so many writers on Shakespeare have made on Anne Hathaway. "Thou my mother gavest me life, thy breast and milk ; alas, for such great bounty to me I shall give thee a stone; how much rather I would entreat the good angel to move the stone, so that thy figure might come forth, as did the Body of Christ. But my prayers avail nothing. Come quickly, O Christ. My mother lies closed in the tomb; she will rise again and seek the stars."

Among his other benefactions Hall gave the church a costly new pulpit. In 1628 he was appointed a borough churchwarden, in 1629 a sidesman, and in 1632 he was compelled to become a burgess, and was soon afterwards fined for non-attendance at the Council meetings. It must have been difficult for a popular- physician to be a regular attendant at such meetings, and at times distressing to his patients. There is a letter extant from Sidney Davenport, urging Dr. Hall to come and see him as he was in a dangerous state, and objecting to the excuse that he had been summoned to the Town Hall, and would be fined if he did not go. Davenport thought it was wrong that any physician should be incorporated, as the lives of his patients might thereby be endangered.

In 1633 he was made the vicar's warden, and in that year the vicar, the Rev. Thomas Wilson, against whom the Corporation had complained to the bishop, induced him to join a Chancery action against the town. Hall was already in trouble with his fellow-councillors, who, in October, 1633, expelled him from their body for his "breach of orders, sundry other misdemeanours, and for his continual disturbances at our Halles."

Evidently Dr. Hall had opinions of his own, and the courage to express them, whether they pleased the Corporation or not. Probably the vicar was the special subject of contention at the time.

It would appear, however, that the church at Stratford was well filled, uncomfortably so, because there is a petition preserved among the Stratford " Miscellaneous Documents" from the Corporation of Stratford, that their wives might have one of Dr. Hall's pews to sit in (1635). It seems there were two pews, one on each side of the church, occupied in common by Dr. Hall and his wife, and his son-in-law and his wife; that is, there was a pew for the Halls and a pew for the Nashes. But the townspeople thought they could do with one between them. They acknowledged that Dr. Hall had been a great benefactor to the church, and that the bishop of the diocese had specially appointed him his pew. But as there was not room for the burgesses' wives to sit and kneel in, he was asked which of his large pews he would prefer to keep, along with Mrs. Woodward and Mrs. Lane, and let the aldermen's wives have the other. I do not know how they settled this difficulty.

On the 25th of November of the same year (1635) John Hall died, and was buried the next day in the chancel of the Parish Church, though he had in 1625 disposed of the lease of the tithes purchased by his father-in-law. The burial register describes him as " Medicus Peritissimus." He must have been a great loss to his county as well as to his town, for he was undoubtedly far in advance of his contemporaries in skill, and added sympathy and good-will to his knowledge and experience.

He has been supposed to have shown Puritan tendencies in later life, but if so, it was a Puritanism that did not eschew Catholicism. He was a deeply religious

man, who felt the constant presence of an ever-living God, and so ruled his life with a direct reference to the Unseen. But probably he did not trouble himself with dogma. He faithfully attended Catholics, Protestants, and Puritans alike, with a devotion that seems to have undermined his health. The direct cause of his death is not recorded.

We do not know who wrote his epitaph. Did his devoted wife give the ideas, and were they latinised by his vicar, his son-in-law, or Mr. Boles?

"Here lyeth the body of John Hall, gent. He married Susanna daughter and co-heir of William Shakespeare, gent., and deceased Nov. 25, anno 1635, aged 60 years.

Hallius hic situs est, medica celeberrimus arte,

Expectans regni gaudia Iseta Dei;

Dignus erat mentis qui Nestora vinceret annis,

In tern's omnes sed rapit aequa dies;

Ne tumulo quid desit adest fidissima conjux,

Et vitae comitem nunc quoq : mortis habet."

This may be rendered :

" Here is interred Hall, most famed in medical art, awaiting the glorious joys of the kingdom of God. Worthy was he by his deserts to surpass Nestor in years; but impartial Time snatches away all men on earth. Lest anything be wanting to the tomb, his most faithful spouse is there: and he has the companion of life now also in death."

(See Dugdale's "Warwickshire," first edition, 1656, p. 518.)

It has been thought that the last couplet implies that the epitaph was not put up until after his wife's death. We need not accept this interpretation. Possibly she was so overwhelmed with grief that death seemed very near to her, and I think she chose the words herself. It was a custom not uncommon at that time to write one's own epitaph.

By a nuncupative will John Hall left a house in

London to his wife, a house and a meadow in Acton to his daughter Elizabeth, and his study of books to his son-in-law, Thomas Nash. The manuscripts he would have given to Mr. Boles had he been present, but Nash might keep them or burn them as he pleased. Were any of these manuscripts Shakespeare's work ? Did the legatee burn them, or was it by a later heir that they were destroyed ? Probably among the " Manuscripts" left to Nash, were the two note-books written by John Hall himself, from which James Cooke selected the materials for the little book entitled " Select Observations on English bodies, or cures both Empericall and Historicall, performed on very eminent persons in desperate diseases." We learn many things from that volume concerning the physician's contemporaries, his relatives, and himself, and something of the methods of medicine at the time. The title-page assures us it was "First written in Latine by Mr. John Hall, Physician living at Stratford-on-Avon, in Warwickshire, where he was very famous, as also in the counties adjacent, as appears by these observations, drawn out of severall hundreds of his as choycest, now put into English for common benefit by James Cooke, practitioner in Physick and Chirurgery," 1657.

It is no slight compliment to a physician for his cures to be recorded twenty-two years after his death, and pass through more than one edition. The manner in which Mr. James Cooke became possessed of them is interestingly told in his preface. "Being in my art attendant to parts of some regiments to keep the pass at the Bridge of Stratford-on-Avon, there being then with me a mate allyed to the gentleman that writ the following observations in Latin, he invited me to thehouse of Mrs. Hall, wife to the deceased, to see the books left by Mr. Hall. After a view of them she told me that she had some books left by one that professed Physick with her husband for some money. I told her, if I liked them, I would give her the money again. She brought them forth, amongst which there was this *[i.e.,* "The Cures"] with another of the author's, both intended for the press. I being acquainted with Mr. Hall's hand told her that one or two of them were her husband's and showed them to her. She denied, I affirmed, till I perceived she began to be offended. At last I returned her the money." Thus it was a stranger who accidentally bought Hall's "Observations." This has often been used as a support to the argument that Mrs. Hall could not read. 1 do not see the force of it. I have no doubt that even now the wife of many a London physician, who had been quite able to read his English love-letters and his domestic notes, would be confused as to her husband's handwriting in closely- written pages of contracted Latin. These had been placed also, either by intention of her husband, or by mistake of others, in the packet of books left by some wandering son of Esculapius for money. Had they also been manuscript, and had Dr. John Hall intended to have published the entire collection ? We can quite well see how confusion arose in Mrs. Hall's mind when, from the dusty, well-known bundle, Mr. Cooke disinterred two, and said, "These are your husband's." To her mistake then, we owe the book now.

Who was this Mr. Boles ? Was he the eccentric Richard Boles, rector of Whitnash, near Stratford, who wrote epitaph, and set his own up in his church while he yet lived ? (See *Notes and Quiria,* fifth scr.- 187.) Or was he the Mr. Boles who lived just opposite, in the house that afterwards became the Falcon Inn ? (See "Stratford Town Records," Title Deeds, Mr. Joseph Boles, 1640.)

This interview probably occurred in the summer of 1643, when Queen Henrietta Maria came to Stratford to meet Prince Rupert, who awaited her with his reinforcements. She held her Court for three days in New Place, as the largest house in the town, and left it with Prince Rupert on 1jth July to meet King Charles I. at Edgehil"

After the "Observations" had become his own, Mr. Cooke, aware of the fame of Dr. John Hall, used them as guides in similar cases, and found them so valuable that he sent them to an able London doctor to see if they should be published. The doctor replied that "the Latin was so abbreviated or false that it would require the like pains as to write a new book." Mr. Cooke, however, found time to edit the notes, translate the Latin, and expand the abbreviations of Hall's handwriting, "being somewhat acquainted with its conciseness, especially in the Receipts, having some acquaintance with his apothecary." (From the "Observations" themselves we know the apothecary to have been Mr. Court.) Cooke mentions that " Mr. John Hall had the happiness (if I may so style it) to lead the way to that practice almost generally used now by the most knowing, of mixing scorbutics to most remedies. It was then, and I know for some time after, thought so strange that it was cast as a reproach upon him by those most famous in the profession." It is to Cooke we owe the information regarding Hall's education abroad, and that he practised physic for many years, and was in great fame for his skill far and near among high and low; that a relative of his, also a physician, was Cooke's companion, and on terms of intimacy with Mrs. Hall; and that there was another book of Dr. John Hall, also prepared for the press. We wonder what that contained.

Hall's book begins with the significant remark, "Health is from the Lord." The "Observations" record the symptoms, treatment, and cure in each interesting case. What I noticed chiefly is severity of treatment, complexity of ingredients, and the use of such horrors as worms and spiders. External applications were even more revolting. We only hear the stories of those who are saved, and feel inclined to echothe old question," Where are they that be drowned ?" Doubtless he had attended his father-in-law in his mortal illness, but even with the aid of the antiscorbutics, his skill and affection were not sufficient to save him. His notes were of his cures, not his failures. It was the great failure of his life that he let this patient slip through his hands into the grave at an age comparatively early. And because of his failure then we do not know of the symptoms shown by the poet, after the merry-making with Ben Jonson and Drayton, when later gossips said he drank too hard. Is it too much to imagine that the illness of Drayton, recorded in "Obs. xxii.," occurred at the same time, when he was in Warwickshire, and likely to be attended by Dr. John Hall ? " Mr. Drayton an excellent poet, labouring of a Tertian, was cured by the following treatment." There is no date, but let us imagine it was in April, 1616, and that Shakespeare suffered from a similar cause, or something like influenza, which made the going out to the merry-making prove fatal to him. The earliest case given dated is that of Lord Compton in March, 1617.

In "Obs. xix." he mentions an illness of his wife, Mrs. Hall, without date. "Obs. xxxiv." concerns his only daughter, and supports the opinion that I have long held, that Anne Hathaway was of an extremely delicate constitution. I always imagine she looked young for her years, and Shakespeare old for his; that she was fair and clinging and dependent; he, bold and masterful; and so the difference in age passed unnoticed. The loss of his only son, the early extinction of his direct descendants, points to delicacy somewhere; and it is not insignificant that Anne Hathaway's grandchild should have been vexed by "tortura oris," or convulsions of the mouth, and ophthalmia. She was cured of one attack on the 5th of January, 1624. In the beginning of April she went to London, and on returning on the 22nd of the same month she took cold and fell into the same distemper, which affected the other side of her face. This second time "by the blessing of God she was also cured in sixteen days." In the same year, on the 24th of May, she was afflicted with an erratic fever. Sometimes she was hot, by-and-by sweating, again cold, all in the space of half-an-hour. Her father's treatment again healed her; "the symptoms remitted daily till she was well; thus was she delivered from death and deadly diseases, and was well for many years." She married Thomas Nash in April, 1626.

Hall was frequently called to attend on the Earl and Countess of Northampton, at Ludlow Castle, more than forty miles away. Many another familiar name is mentioned in the course of this little volume: Mrs. Queeny, Mrs. Smith, Mr. Wilson, Mrs. Throckmorton, Mrs. Sheldon, Mrs. Green, John Nason, the Under- hills, Mrs. Baker of Stratford-upon-Avon, Mrs. Combs, Katharine Sturley, Mrs. Grace Court ("wife to my apothecary"), Dr. Thornbery, Bishop of Worcester, aged 86 on 1st February. This bishop is the young student who in his college days at Oxford," spent no time in studies, but only," said Dr. Simon Forman," to hunt the deer and other game in forbidden parks." In Case Ixiv. Hall speaks of "the only son of Mr. Holy- oake, which framed the dictionary." Case Ixxxii. of Book ii. records the restoration from the gates of the grave of " Mr. John Trap, minister, in piety and learning second to none." Case Ix. of Book ii. gives an account of Hall's own severe illness in 1632. It begins "Thou, O Lord, which hast the power of life and death, and drawest from the gates of death, I confesse without any art or counsell of man, but only from thy goodness and clemency, thou hast saved me from the bitter and deadly symptoms of a deadly fever beyond the expectations of all about me, restoring me, as it were, from the very jaws of death to former health, for which I praise thy name, oh most merciful God, and father of our Lord Jesus Christ." About the fifty-seventh year of his age, from the 2yth of August, 1632, to the 2gth of September, he was far from well, yet always going to various patients, riding when he was not fit to do so, and beside other trouble, he " fell into a most cruel torture of his teeth and then into a deadly burning fever, which then raged very much, killing almost all that it did affect." He treated himself at first, but his alarmed wife sent for two physicians, who prescribed for him satisfactorily, and he became perfectly well, and praised God for it. We must not forget this was the period of his quarrel with the Corporation. When he died three years afterwards, on the 25th of November, 1635, his disease is not recorded.

His son-in-law, Thomas Nash went after Dr. Hall's death to reside in New Place, and took the position of. head of the house. Indeed, in one of his letters he speaks of" Mrs. Hall, my mother-in-law, who lives with me." But the house really belonged to Mrs. Hall, and everything but the study of books above mentioned.

Thomas Nash died at New Place on the 4th of April, 1647, and considerable trouble arose about his will, for he had treated New Place as his own, and left it to his nephew Edward Nash. But his mother-in-law and his widow satisfactorily proved their claim in court. Mrs. Elizabeth Nash remained with her mother there until the 5th of June, 1649, when she married Mr. John (afterwards Sir John) Barnard, of Abington, at Billesley, a village four miles from Stratford. Why did she go there to be married? It is unfortunate the registers cannot answer that question, as they are not extant. The manor had been sold by Mr. Thomas Trussell before 1619 to Sir Robert Lee.

Whether her marriage weakened her mother's health, or whether the state ofner mother's health had hastened the marriage, we know not, but a month later, on the nth of July, 1649, her mother died, and was buried beside her husband on the 16th. The Latin scholars of the family were gone. Is it too much to suppose that Elizabeth herself, Shakespeare's grandchild, composed her mother's epitaph, so suggestive to Shakespeare students of hereditary traits ?

"Witty above her sex, but that's not all,
Wise to Salvation was good Mistress Hall.
Something of Shakespeare was in that, but this
Wholy of Him with whom she's now in bliss.
Then passenger hast ne'er a teare

To weep with her, that wept with all ?
That wept, yet set herself to chere

Them up with comforts cordiall.
Her love shall live, her mercy spread,
When thou hast ne'er a tear to shed."

I think this second epitaph shows that the earlier notice on her husband's tomb was only a sign that Susanna Shakespeare was determined to be buried by him whom she had loved so faithfully through life. This also is a striking witness to the virtues of both the favourite daughter and the distinguished father.

In the early part of last century these verses were erased to make space for the record of the death of Richard Watts, who owned some of the tithes, and had the right to be buried in the chancel. Fortunately they had been preserved in Dugdale's "Warwickshire," and in 1844 the Watts epitaph was removed, and Mrs. Hall's was restored.

Her daughter Elizabeth died before her husband, Sir John Barnard, and was buried on the ryth of February, 1669-70, at Abington. She made a will leaving him everything for life, and fully disposedof all her property thereafter to the Harts, the Hatha- ways, and her own friends and relatives. Her second husband did not put up any tombstone to her memory, and on his death in 1674, his children by his first wife, in recording his epitaph, did nothing to commemorate the only daughter of the distinguished Dr. Hall, and the grandchild and last descendant of the much more distinguished William Shakespeare.

A brass plate has been lately placed in Abington Church by Stanley Cooper, Esq., of Oxford, in remembrance of her.

10

SECTION 10

CHAPTER XIII
Michael Drayton, 1563-1631.

Michael Drayton was in spirit more nearly akin to Shakespeare than any other of his Warwickshire contemporaries, and though his life has been often told, it must be told again to recal many interesting associations.

Dugdale says that he was born at Hartshill, near Atherstone, in the parish of Mancetter. The Register does not begin early enough to record his birth, but it begins before the date of his brother Edmund *(b.* *i*579, to whom the administration of Michael's effects was granted in 1631). Edmund was the son of William, the grandson of Christopher Drayton, and he had several brothers and sisters. Aubrey says of Drayton, as he had said of Shakespeare, that he was the son of a butcher, but there is no clear proof of this. The family seems to have been of the respectable yeoman class, and may have descended from the noble old family of the name, but more likely from the Draytons of Fenny Drayton. (See Burton's "Description of Leicestershire.")

Drayton says of himself in "The Owl," 1604, that "he was nobly bred, and well allyed." His "breedlng" he received through the kindness of Sir Henry Goodere of

Polesworth, who took him into his family as page, about the age often. It was rarely that a good family admitted as page anyone below the rank of a gentleman. According to the heralds, "a duke's son serveda king, an earl's a duke," and so on, each "servant" being selected from the class just below that of the master. The selection of Michael as page, therefore, supports his assertion that he was well allied. It also suggests that he had already shown some special signs of capability or character which commended themselves to his noble patron. There was no grammar school for Drayton as there was for Shakespeare. The free school of Atherstone was founded in 15 Eliz. *(i.e.,* 1573) by Sir William Devereux, knt., then residing at Merivale; and the school for boys and girls at Polesworth by Sir Henry Goodere's grand-daughter long after that date. So there was all the more need of private training, and Polesworth gave to Drayton of its best. He was very fortunate in his tutor, who won his confidence, and taught him so as to make him love learning, guiding him even into the paths of poetry. In an epistle to his friend Henry Reynolds, "Of Poets and Poesy," published in 1627, Drayton states that about the age of ten he had come to his tutor and asked him to make him a poet. The tutor read to the pupil Mantuan, Virgil's "Eclogues," and other classic poems, with satisfactory explanations.

"I scorned your ballett then though it were done,
And had for *Finis* William Elderton."

It would have been comforting to us to have had as much authoritative autobiography of Shakespeare as we have of Michael Drayton. The latter was very communicative about himself, he had many friends and patrons, he showered dedications among these broadcast, and from the dedications we learn much about his circumstances and ambitions. In the dedication to Henry Goodere the younger, of" Mary the French Queen to Brandon," he acknowledged that he had been indebted to Sir Henry Goodere for the most of hiseducation. Though no definite record is preserved, it is quite possible that Goodere sent him to the university. Sir Aston Cokaine in his " Remedy for Love," 1658, refers to the poet as "my old friend Drayton," a phrase which implies some degree of intimacy; and speaking of the colleges which had produced poets, he says in the same poem :

"Oxford, our other Academy, you
Full worthy must acknowledge of your view :
Here smooth-tongued Drayton was inspired by
Mnemosyne's manifold Progenie."

Sir Henry Goodere wrote to Lord Cecil to further a suit to the King on July I2th (no year, but endorsed 1605 ; Cecil Papers, 190-131). He wrote again to him as Earl of Salisbury asking his furtherance in his request. He has been suing the King for the Escheat of one John King, one Bennett and others, who have lately slain a man at Stepney. He has had no benefit of former grants of escheats and recusants. "His chargeable service to the King (being thereby 5000/. worse than he was) has brought his poor estate so low as almost nothing can add to his misery now, but to be neglected by Salisbury." Undated, but endorsed 1st February, 1609 (Cecil Papers, 195-99).

After the death of Sir Henry Goodere he was protected by Sir John and Lady Harington and by their daughter Lucy, who, on the 12th of December, 1594, was married to Edward Russell, third Earl of Bedford. In a dedication to that nobleman Drayton writes that he had been " bequeathed to the protection of that noble lady your countess by that learned and accomplished gentleman, Sir Henry Goodere of Polesworth (not long since deceased) whose I was, whilst he was, whose patience pleased to beare with the imperfections of my heedless and unstayed youth. That excellent and matchless gentleman was the first cherisher of my muse,which had been by his death left a poor orphan to. the world, had he not before bequeathed it to that lady, whom he so derely loved," referring to the countess.

With all this definite encouragement, Drayton's muse was late in development. He brought out nothing worth naming poetry until he was thirty years of age. He seems to have at least visited London before that time, for in his Sixth Pastoral he tells us that he had been kindly regarded by Sidney. Nicholas Baxter says:

"O Noble Drayton well didst thou rehearse
Our damages in dryrie sable verse,"

i.e., on the death of Sir Philip; but this may have been written at a later date than 1587.

He dedicated from London in 1591, to Lady Jane Devereux of Merivale, his first publication, "The Harmony of the Church," dull rhymed translations of parts of the Bible after the manner of the metrical' psalmists. Strangely enough, the Stationers' Registers show that this book was seized by public order, though, for some unexplained reason, the Archbishop saved forty copies. None of these are known to exist except the one in the British Museum.

Spenser, "the prime pastoralist of England," inspired him in his first real poetic work, a series of Pastorals, called "Idea, or the Shepherd's Garland, Rowland's Sacrifice to the Nine Muses," in which he writes of himself as Rowland. This was entered in Stationers'. Registers on the 23rd of April, 1593, and dedicated to the Noble and Valorous gentleman Master Robert Dudley, enriched with all Virtues of the mind, and worthy of all honourable desert by your most affectionate and devoted Michael Drayton." It is interesting to note that Dray- ton was thus early befriended. by the brilliant and unfortunate son of the Earl of Leicester. The "Legendof Piers Gaveston " followed in the same year, dedicated to Master Henry Cavendish; and " Matilda the fair and chaste" was dedicated, in 1594, to Lucy, daughter of Sir John Harington, afterwards Countess of Bedford. In this poem Drayton is generally supposed to refer to Shakespeare's " Rape of Lucrece," published the same year. This is not absolutely certain, because if the whole stanza is read, instead or the first two lines alone, it will be seen to refer to a drama, not to a poem.

" Lucrece of whom proud Rome hath boasted long
Lately revived to live another age
And here arrived to tell of Tarquin's wrong,
Her chaste deniall and the tyrant's rage.

Acting her passions on our stately stage
Shee is remembered, all forgetting mee,
Yet I as fair and chaste as ere was shee."

This appeared again in the edition of 1596, but was afterwards withdrawn.

" Endymion and Phoebe" is entered in the Stationers' Registers on the 12th of April, 1594, and was doubtless printed that year. In it Drayton praises Spenser, Daniel and Lodge. It was not reprinted, but some passages reappear in "The Man in the Moon," 1606.

In his "Idea" he had said, "Now I will make a myrror of my dolors," and he fulfilled that promise next year. " Idea's Mirrour, Amours in Quatorzains," appeared in June, 1594, containing fifty-one "Amours," and a sonnet dedicatory to Anthony Cooke, "my ever- kind Mecasnas." These poems openly imitate the sonnets of the French school, yet are undoubtedly based on personal experience. They are the impassioned reflections of his fits of despair and gleams of hope in his efforts to win the lady who was so soon by marriage to put herself out of his reach.

The student of Shakespeare's Sonnets must expressly study Drayton's, so much may be learned through thecomparison. In Drayton's case we have the advantage, or the disadvantage, of possessing many editions. He was constantly revising his works, and frequently altered, added, or subtracted poems in later editions. Unfortunately he did not always excise his worst, and sometimes threw aside poems worth retaining. Twenty-two of his earlier sonnets were never reprinted, but he replaced them by others, adding also to the number. His changes seem to show Shakespeare's influence on his thought and language. The most notable parallel is, "An evil spirit, your beauty, haunts me still."

In 1596 he published "The Tragical Legend of Robert of Normandy," with the legends of Matilda and of Piers Gaveston dedicated to the Countess of Bedford. Following the dedication is a sonnet "To the Lady Anne Harington," an address to the reader, and a complaint of the sinister dealings of publishers, who had apparently already begun to trouble the poet.

" Mortimeriados," published in the same year, was also dedicated to the Countess of Bedford. It is clear that by this time he was supported by the Harington and Bedford families.

" England's Heroical Epistles," Drayton's most popular work, appeared in 1597, "printed by I.R. for N. Ling." The first poems, "The epistle of Rosamond to King Henry" and his reply, were dedicated to the Countess of Bedford; but the second pair of epistles was inscribed to Lord Mounteagle. He spread his compliments over a large circle of friends, for the following poems are dedicated to Lady Anne Harington, the Earl of Bedford, Lord Henry Howard, Mistress Elizabeth Tanfield, Sir Thomas Mounson, Henry Goodere, Esq., and " Mistress Fraunces Goodere." Another "enlarged" edition came out in 1598, "printed by P.S. for N. Ling." Here wehave a strange illustration of Drayton's method of compliment. His dedications are not intended to be " in perpetuity," but are only guaranteed for an edition. Thus, in the 1598 edition, the Countess of Bedford retains her position, but Lord Mounteagle drops out, leaving the epistles of "King John to Matilda" and " Matilda to King John," without a dedication, perhaps as a supplement to the Countess of Bedford's portion. Lady Anne Harington retains the epistles of "Queen Isabel to Mortimer" and "Mortimer to Isabel," after which follows, undedicated, the new poem, "Edward the Black Prince to the Countess of Salisbury," with her reply.

The sole known copy is in the Bodleian Library.

The Earl of Bedford retains the epistles of " Queen Isabel" and "Richard II.," but "Queen Katherine to Owen Tudor," and "Owen Tudor to Queen Katherine," which had been dedicated to Lord Henry Howard, are now left without his protection, and along with the new poem "Elinor Cobham to Duke Humfrey" and "Duke Humfrey to Elinor Cobham" are undedicated. Mistress Elizabeth Tanfield retains "William de la Pole Duke of Suffolk to Queen Margaret" and her reply, and Sir Thomas Mounson still holds "Edward IV. to Shore's wife," with her reply. Henry Goodere still presides over " Mary the French Queen to Charles Brandon" and Brandon's reply; but a new patron is introduced in Master Henry Lucas, for a new poem," Henry Howard Earl of Surrey to Geraldine," her reply not being given. Mistress Frances Goodere is still graced with the patronage of "The Lady Jane Gray to Lord Guilford Dudley," and " Dudley to Lady Jane." In the third edition of 1599, also in the British Museum, there is a new dedication to Master James Huish of the undedicated poem "Elinor Cobham to Duke Humfrey"; and the reply of " Geraldine to Henry Howard Earl of Surrey " is added. At the end appears "Idea" with no separate title or dedication.

The Fourth Edition, 1600, is not in the British Museum. The Fifth Edition, 1602, has the "Epistle of Edward the Black Prince to the Countess of Salisbury," and of the "Countess of Salisbury to Edward the Black Prince," dedicated to " Maister Walter Aston." Henry Goodere, Esq., has by this time become Sir Henry, and his wife is addressed as "The Lady Fraun- ces Goodere." Amid all these changes it may be seen how the dedications help to supply the biography, not only of the poet, but of his friends. While not obsequious, Drayton laid himself out to please, and was not ashamed to eat the bread of what was then thought an honourable dependence. In the number of his patrons he was different from Shakespeare, whose dedications were "to one, of one, still such, and ever so" (Sonnet cv.). But, in spite of all his patrons, at the time of the publication of the "Heroical Epistles" Drayton had been compelled to take to writing for the stage. He evidently utilised his historical reading in selecting and working out his plays. Henslowe's "Diary" preserves many entries concerning him between 1597 and 1602, generally in association with Chettle, Dekker, and Munday. *Mother Redcap* is referred to as his and Mun- day's in 1597. *Henry L, Earl Godwin, Piers of Exton, Richard Cordelion's Funeral, Piers of Winchester, Cardinal Wolsey, The Civil Wars in France,* were partly written by him. On the 20th of January, 1598-9, two pounds were given to him in earnest of his play, *William Longberd,* as Henslow has it. Drayton signed the receipt for the money, naming the play *William Longsword.* In 1599 the first part of *Sir John Oldcastle* was acted, in which Wilson, Hathway, and Munday were his collaborators. It is probable that it was only the printer who made the fraudulent suggestion of Shakespeare's authorship. In 1602 Drayton wrote in conjunction with Dekker, Middleton, Webster and Munday a play that appears

to have been called *The Two Shapes*; and in the same year he was engaged with Webster and Middleton on *Cesar's Fall.* The names of other lost plays in which he had a hand will be found in the "Diary." His "Heroical Epistles" suggest some association with *Henry VI.*

Richard Barnfield, in his "Poems written in divers humours," has"a remembrance of some English poets," wherein he names Drayton beside Spenser, Daniel, and Shakespeare:

"And Drayton, whose well-written tragedies,
And sweet epistles, soare thy fame to skies."

This does not necessarily imply that Barnfield praised Drayton as a dramatist, for the word "tragedies" might refer to his "Legends" and other tragical poems; but in 1598 Meres classes him among "those by whom the English tongue is mightily enriched," under many heads, and among these as a dramatist. In 1603 he re-issued " Mortimeriados," which had been dedicated to the Countess of Bedford in 1596, with the new title of "The Barons' Wars," and a new dedication to Sir Walter Aston. It has seemed to many that this implies that he had been dropped by the Bedford family; that he resented the slight bitterly, and had expressed his temporary anger in the only invective he was ever known to write, "To the Lady Selena," in the Eighth Eclogue of "Poemes, Lyrick and Pastorall," 1606. There is a good deal to be said for and against the theory; but it seems that Drayton, like Shakespeare, had a heartache over some rival poet, and, thinking that Selena had transferred her patronage to the deceitful "Cerberon," wanted to speak his mind.

On the other hand, the Earl and Countess of Bedford were apparently supporting him when he brought out "The Heroical Epistles." They might have thoughthe minimised his gratitude and vulgarised their names by only including them amid a herd of lesser friends. The invective was soon dropped, but the sonnet to the Countess of Bedford always retained its place.

Drayton, however, got into trouble in higher quarters. He had differed from Shakespeare in lavishly praising Elizabeth while she lived; but he resembled him in omitting to sing of her glories after her death. In 1603 he brought out a gratulatory poem to King James, and "fled to the happy north," only to be disgraced. In r 604 he wrote "a poem triumphal" for the Goldsmiths' Company on the King's entry into London. His royal panegyrics did him no good. Indeed, he always implied that a cloud had fallen over his fortunes when the new king came in. Chettle, indeed, says to him in 1603 :

"Think 'twas a fault to have thy verses seen,
Praising the King ere thou hadst mourned the Queen."

Among his numerous dedicatees, none seemed powerful enough, or enthusiastic enough, to protect him effectually at this juncture save Walter Aston, to whom he dedicated much of his future work. This patron was the son of Sir Edward Aston of Tixhall, who had married first, Mary, daughter of Sir John Spencer of Althorpe, and second, Anne, daughter of Sir Thomas Lucy of Charlecote. Sir Walter Aston chose Drayton for his Esquire when he was made Knight of the Bath at the King's coronation, and the poet ever afterwards styled himself "Esquire" in the chivalric sense.

In 1604 Drayton wrote "Moyses, a map of his miracles"; and in 1605 he brought out another selection of his poems, dedicated to Sir Walter Aston, in which he included " The Barons' Wars," " England's Heroical Epistles," " Idea," " Certaine other Sonnets to great and Worthy Personages," and three " Legends." To 1606 belongs the undated "Poemes Lyrick and Pastorall."Here is found (under the title of "To my friends the Camber-britons and theyr harp ") the first draft of the famous "Ballad of Agincourt," which he afterwards revised and greatly improved; and here first appeared the stirring ode "To the Virginian Voyage," "The Ode to the New Yeare," and other fine lyrics. "The Legend of Great Cromwell" was published in 1607 (and was included in "A Mirror for Magistrates," 1610).

The 1608 edition of his poems was dedicated to Sir Walter Aston in a sonnet, affectionate and complimentary.

"The triumphs of the Church, the Heavenly Harmonie of Spiritual songs and holy hymns," which appeared in 1610, was in reality his suppressed first book but little changed.

His liberal patron was giving his poet leisure for his greatest work, "Poly-Olbion." Drayton, who had been working at it for years (indeed, Meres mentions it in 1598), must have found the scheme laborious, and he certainly found the publication difficult. The first eighteen books appeared in 1612, dedicated to Henry Prince of Wales, with notes by Selden. In the preface he assures his readers, " My poem is genuine, and first of its kind." This learned and voluminous work, though rising occasionally to the high level of poetry, never really touched the heart of his contemporaries, and has not even yet received its due recognition. He owed much, especially in the early books, to Camden's "Britannia," not duly acknowledged, and he did not travel sufficiently to make his descriptive passages always represent pictures that he had actually seen. His thirteenth song is on Warwickshire, which, containing much personal experience, must remain the most interesting. He speaks lovingly, however, of Tixhall, "which oft the muse had found her safe and sweet retreat," an echo of his acknowledgment in thepreface : "Whatever herein tastes of a free spirit 1 thankfully confess to proceed from the continual bounty of my truly noble friend, Sir Walter Aston."

Prince Henry granted him a pension of ten pounds, recorded in the State Papers, a grant which was continued by Prince Charles, to whom in 1622 he dedicated the remaining twelve books (making in all thirty) of his gigantic undertaking.

He brought out a definitive edition of his poems (apart from "Poly-Olbion ") in folio, further revised and corrected, in 1619, dedicated to Sir Walter Aston, who had been made baronet in 1611. " These my few poems, the work of that Mayden reigne, in the spring of our acquaintance, as it pleased you then to patronize, as I singly set them forth: so now, collected into this small volume, I make the best present that my poor abilitie is able to tender you . . . they were the fruit of that muse-nursing season, before this frosty Boreas (I mean the world's coldnesse) had nipt our flowery Tempe . . . before Hell had sent up her black Furies that in every corner breathe their Venome in the face of cleere Poesie." He added to his "Idea" the fine sonnet, " Since there's no help, come let us kiss and part." He gives an analysis of the "Barons' Wars," and treats of its measure, based on that of " our first late great reformer, Master Spenser." Introductory verses by Thomas Greene, John Beaumont, E. Heyward, John Selden, and terminal verses by Thomas Hassall, Sir William Alexander, and Sir Edmund Scory, praise the author. On the reverse of the title-page is a portrait of the author, in a dress like that shown in Dugdale's rendering of Shakespeare's monument. In this engraving Drayton presents a more attractive appearance than in his portraits at Dulwich and in the National Portrait Gallery. The expression is strong and manly, belying his own description of his "swartand melancholy face" in the legend of Robert of Normandy. The head is crowned with laurel, with flying ribbons. The engraving is surrounded with the legend, "Effigies Michaelis Drayton Armigeri, Poetae Clariss. Etat suae L. A. Chr. C13.D.C.XI1I." In 1622 "Poet Laureate" was affixed to his name, after a copy of commendatory verses to Abraham Holland's " Naumachia."

In 1627 appeared a second volume of his poems, in folio, among which he introduced "The Miseries of Queen Margaret," "On my Lady's not coming to town," the fairy poem " Nymphidia," very popular at the time, "The Shepherd's Sirena," "The Bataille of Agin- court" (a different poem from "The Ballad of Agin- court"), "The Moon-Calf" (asatire), and "Elegies," among which is that on his friend, Sir Henry Rainsford of Clifford Chambers. Of great interest is the "Epistle to Henry Reynolds," in which Drayton passes in review the English poets from Chaucer onwards.

His last work was "The Muses' Elizium, lately discovered by a new way over Parnassus," 1630, a set of ten Nymphals or pastoral Dialogues, dedicated to Edward, Earl of Dorset, to which were appended "Noah's Flood," and other "Divine poems" dedicated to his religious Countess, Mary Clifford.

While so much of the story of Drayton's outer life may he gleaned from his dedications, it is in his poetry that we read the secret of his heart. He was not so fortunate in his love as his master Spenser; he did not wed his fair "Idea," but rather, as Sir Fulke Greville did, he lived single for her sake.

Many writers have taken it for granted that Drayton's "Idea" was but a poetic fiction ; others have thought that, though representing a real woman, her name could not be found. It must have been a very open secret to Drayton's contemporaries.

He had been received young into the family of Sir Henry Goodere, to whose father, Francis, Henry VIII. had granted the site of the ruined convent of Poles- worth. Dugdale says that Henry Goodere was "much accomplished and of eminent note in this country," and adds that he had suffered imprisonment on behalf of Mary Queen of Scots. Both. John Somerville and Francis Throckmorton knew him, and visited him in his home at Coventry. The State Papers concerning the conspiracy of the latter, 1584, refer to Henry Goodere's imprisonment, and his pride in the gold buttons given him by the captive Queen, in remembrance or it. Drayton would be in Polesworth at the time of the trial, and doubtless proved a stay and comfort to the family in his patron's absence. Sir Henry had no son, and only two daughters, Frances and Anne. Both seem to have been born after Drayton's reception, as he speaks of having watched the elder from her cradle. The younger could not, then, have been born before. 1574 or 1575, and probably was born later. The boy would watch the baby as she grew into childhood and girlhood, and become intimately associated with her early development. Probably he assisted in her education. He apparently had not realised before they were separated by his going to London that his affection had become the passion of love. In his sonnet to "Lunacie," 1602, he says that it was "nine years now since first I lost my wits."

In the Fifth Eclogue of " Idea," 1594, he describes his lady sometimes in extravagant terms, as inl

" Read in her eyes a Romant of Delights,
Read in her words the proverbs of the wise,
Read in her life the holy vestall rites
Which love and Virtue sweetly moralise,
And she, the Academ of Virtue's exercise."

The frank, unconscious affection of the girl seems tohave been checked by Michael's fervour, and she was forced to avoid him.

"I follow her that ever flies from me,
Oh love, oh hope, quite turned into despair."

He solaced himself by his art somewhat, however, and exclaimed:

"Now will I make a mirror of my dolors."

This he proceeded to do in "Idea's Mirror," in which he poured forth more consistent, yet not less fervent, adoration, and recorded " Idea's " charms, her coyness, her coldness, her scorn. His love idealized all her surroundings. He takes care to indicate the locality in which she lived. In Sonnet Thirty-two, "To the River Anker":

" Arden's sweet Anker, let thy glory be,
That fair 'Idea' only lives by thee."

Again, in Sonnet Fifty-three :

"Cleere Anker, by whose silver sanded shore,
My soule-shrined saint, my fair 'Idea' lies."

Polesworth, her father's property, was by the Anker. It is true that in his later sonnet, "A hymne to his Lady's Birthplace," he speaks of

"Coventry, that dost adorn
The Country wherein I was born,"

as being specially honoured by the birth of his lady on some 4th of August, at Mich Park. This reference threw some students off the scent, but, as I have shewn, Sir Henry Goodere had a town house in Coventry, and there, Drayton tells us, his daughter Anne was born. That this Anne was the lady of his love, he makes clear in his larger work.

In the Thirteenth Song of his " Poly-Olbion,"Part I. (1612), Drayton describes Warwickshire, and thereleads us back, in italics, to the ever-recurrent "Idea," his Lady:

"The first part of whose name Godiva doth foreread
TV fir it syllable of hers, and Goodere half doth sound,
For. by agreeing words great matters have been found,
But further than this place the mystery extends"

In describing the Warwickshire rivers, he again praises Anker:

"For as the first did tell
Her Sirname, so again doth Anker lively spell
Her christened title Anne."

Nothing could have been plainer in those days of word involvements than that Drayton was possessed by a faithful though hopeless love for Anne Goodere, younger daughter of Sir Henry, of "Polesworth highly graced." Frances, the elder, married her cousin, Henry Goodere the younger, and remained at Polesworth ; Anne married Henry Rainsford, of Clifford Chambers, near Stratford-upon-Avon, at some date not definitely fixed, which can be approximately estimated as in 1595. Michael Drayton was the chief witness to Sir Henry Goodere's will (January, 1595), by which he left fifteen hundred pounds to his younger daughter Anne, "for her better advancement in marriage." Anne Goodere, as one of the executors, proved that will on the 6th of May, 1595; therefore, she was still unmarried. But she must have married very shortly afterwards. On her husband's tomb it is stated that he died in 1622, and had been married to his wife, Anne Goodere, for twenty-seven years.

The period of Drayton's "Lunacie," therefore, we may estimate at four years, from 1591 to 1595. The absorbing passion awakened in him allowed wild hopes of some possible "advancement" in state or fortunethat might have made it reasonable for him, the penniless page, as poet, to aspire to the hand of his patron's daughter. She seems to have been really friendly, though practical enough to show him the utter impossibility of her ever being anything more to him than she was. He was not altogether unhappy, for she remained his friend, and her husband became, to his wife's poetic admirer, even more affectionate than she could afford to be.

P.C.C, Somerset Home, " 30 Scott."

In his "Poly-Olbion," Drayton says that Cliffordl

" Hath been many a time the Muse's quiet port."

Later, indeed, it became his holiday home, and we may safely picture him pacing the streets of Stratford by Anne's side, or dropping into New Place to have a chat with Shakespeare.

When he republished his "Eclogues" in 1606, he adds in the Eighth a suggestive allusion:

"As those two sisters, most discreetly wise,
That Virtue's hests religiously obey,
Whose praise my skill is wanting to comprize,
The eld'st of whom is that good Panape
In shady Arden her deare flocke that keeps
Where mournful Anker for her sickness weeps."

He goes on to say that the younger sister," Idea," had gone to live in Gloucestershire by Meon Hill.

The Gentleman's Magazine, 1825, vol. ii., 136, and Hunter's MS. " Chorus Vatum," vol. iii., give notices of "Goodere and Rainsford."

There is an account of the Rainsfords of Clifford Chambers by Sir John Maclean in *The Transactions of the Bristol and Gloucester Archaeological Society,* vol. xiv., pt. i., p. 50. The dates are confusing, and can only be checked by reference to authorities not quoted. Various grants and regrants had been made from thetime of the Abbot of St. Peter's in 1526, all set aside by the grant in 1562, for the sum of twelve hundred and sixty pounds, of the lordship and manor of Clifford Chambers to Charles, son of William Rains- ford. Charles had three sons, Thomas, Hercules, and Morgan; the second of whom succeeded him in Clifford Chambers and died intestate in 1583, aged thirty- nine. (His father's second wife survived him, and may have been the "Lady Rainsford, aged 62," whom Dr. John Hall attended.) Administration was granted Elizabeth, the wife of Hercules, for his son and heir, Henry, was only aged eight. His widow married within six months William Barnes of Taulton, county Worcester, who seems to have been a good stepfather to Henry and his sister, Elizabeth. Sir John Maclean does not know the date of Henry's marriage, but notes that he was knighted in 1603, and was authorised to impark his free warren in Clifford Chambers and in Alveston, Warwickshire, on the 5th of December, 1616. He died on the 2yth of January, 1621-2, at forty-six years of age. He had three sonslWilliam, who died young; Henry, born 1599, who succeeded him, and married (1619) Eleanora, daughter of Robert Boswell of Eastwick, and was knighted at Tutbury on the I yth August, 1624; Francis, who went to London, lived in St. Martin's-in-the-Fields, married Mary, daughter of Henry Ewer, Esq., and was knighted at Theobalds in 1633. Sir John Maclean states that Sir Henry had lived with his wife twenty-seven years, and gives the flattering epitaph on the tomb, set up by his wife's cousin and brother-in-law, Sir Henry Goodere.

Among Dr. John Hall's tantalizing accounts of his cures we find that his Case lxxxiv. was that of " Squire Rainsford, aged 35, of a Malignant Fever." If we may reckon from his age as eight at his father's Inquisition Post-mortem in 1583, the date of his illness should be1610. But at that date he should have been styled "Sir Henry." Probably Hall used the title he had been accustomed to use in the past. Other Rainsfords, however, appear in Stratford-upon-Avon Registers. Hall's Case xlvii. was that of " My Lady Rainsford, aged 27, beautiful, and of a gallant structure of body." She had lately had a child, and was suffering from indigestion, which Dr. Hall cured. Unfortunately this is not dated. But Hall would not be likely to have called his patient "My Lady" before her husband's knighthood. If it were, then, in the very year of 1603, it would give the date of her birth as 1576, and suggest that she was married at nineteen. If her illness occurred later, she must have been younger; if earlier, Hall must have practised in Stratford earlier than is known.

Her extreme youth, in relation to himself, accounts for much of Drayton's early familiarity and late awakening, and gives new meaning to his Sonnet xliv.:

"While thus my pen strives to eternize thee,
Age rules my lines with wrinkles in my face":

lines that bear resemblance to passages in Shakespeare's Sonnets. It was doubtless when Drayton went to visit the Rainsfords at Clifford that we find him also amongst Dr. Hall's patients. "Mr. Drayton, an excellent poet, labouring of a tertian." He was cured then by the poetic treatment of "Syrup of Violets." Unfortunately the case was not dated. Possibly it was at that time in the spring of 1616, at which gossipy Ward says, "Shakespeare, Drayton and Jonson had a merry meeting, at which, it seems, he drank too hard, for he shortly after died." It is much more probable that at the unhealthy spring-time of the year, after the early floods, Shakespeare also had a tertian ague or influenza, from which his son-in-law could not deliver him, even with " syrup of violets."

It is almost certain that Shakespeare would be an honoured guest at Clifford Chambers, where literary tastes and kindly feelings reigned. In his elegy, Drayton gratefully acknowledged that Sir Henry Rainsford had been a devoted friend:

" He would have sworn that to no other end
He had been born, but only for my friend."

After her husband's death, we hear nothing definite of Anne. Drayton wrote "Of my Lady not coming to town" in 1627.

Probably she came up occasionally to visit her son Francis in St. Martin's-in-the-Fields, and would then see her devoted "Esquire." We know that Drayton still went to see her and her son Henry in Clifford. His last letter to Drummond of Hawthornden was dated 14th of July, 1631, at Clifford, "at a Knight's house in Gloucestershire, to which place I yearly use to come in the summertime to recreate myself, and to- spend two or three months in the country." He returned to town that summer from his last visit, to "sit in the bay window next the east end of St. Dunstan's Church," where Aubrey says he lived. There he shortly afterwards died, and "exchanged his laurel for a crown of glory, 1631." We do not know the date of Anne's death; her place of burial has not yet been found, but 1 think it should be sought in London. Drayton was buried in Westminster Abbey, but there is some doubt as to the exact place. Heylin, in the "Appeal of injured innocence," says, he was "bid to the funeral under the north wall, but the monument was set up in another place." Mary Clifford, Countess of Dorset, employed Marshall to set up a monument to him. Dugdale preserves the verses which are supposed by some to have been written by Ben Jonson. If his, they are no high specimen of his art.

In spite of his good friends and his good work, Drayton seems always to have lived in comparative poverty. It was said by H. Peacham, "Truth of our times," he had but five pounds lying by him at his death, and when his brother had administration the inheritance was only reckoned at twenty-five pounds.

Drayton was much appreciated by his contemporaries. Mr. Fleay and Mr. Elton believe that Spenser refers to him under the name of "jEtion" in "Colin Clout's come home again," 1595, but it is probable (I think) that "JEtion " is Shakespeare. Thomas Greene refers to his "Idea," in his "Poet's Vision and Prince's Glory." Tofte said he "not unworthily beareth the name of the chiefest Archangel, singing after his soul-ravishing manner." Winstanley said," He had drunk as deep a draught at Helicon as any in his time; for fame and renown in poetry he is not much inferior, if not equal, to Spenser." Meres in 1598, we saw, mentioned him several times. "He is held of vertuous disposition, honest conversation, and well-governed language." "We may truly term Michael Drayton Tragoediographicus for his passionate penning the downfals of valiant Robert of Normandy, Chaste Matilda, and Great Gaveston." He is referred to in "The Return from Parnassus," 1602. Fitzgeofirey's "Drake" calls him "golden-mouthed musical Drayton, for the purity and preciousness of his phrase." He was quoted nearly two hundred times in "England's Parnassus," 1600.

Among friends to whom Drayton did not dedicate we may include Lodge, mentioned under the anagram of Golde or Goldey; Francis Beaumont, who died in 1616; Sir John Beaumont, who died in 1627; and William Browne, author of "Britannia's Pastorals." He praises Nashe and Marlowe, as well as Spenser; and though he was evidently friendly with Shakespeare, he does not seem to have duly appreciated him, if wemay judge from his allusion in the epistle to Henry Reynolds, 1627, when, as one Warwickshire man writing of another, he said:

" Shakespeare, thou hadst as smooth a comicke vaine
Fitting the sock, and in thy natural braine
As strong conception, and as clear a rage
As any one that trafficked with the stage."

Insufficient as this may seem as the estimate of a capable and generous contemporary, it may be coupled with other possible allusions that we are not now able to follow. I like to believe that Shakespeare stood out clear in his mind's eye in the last line of the following passage of the Thirteenth Song of "Poly-Olbion," 1612 :

"Brave Warwick, that abroad so long advanct the Beare
By her illustrious Earles renowned everywhere
Above her neighbouring Shires which always bore her head

My native Country then, which so brave spirits hast bred,-
If there be Vertue yet remaining in thy Earth
Or any good of thine, thou breathest in my birth.
Accept it as thine owne, whilst now I sing of thee,
Of all thy later Brood th' unworthiest though I be."

A chorus of praise broke out after Drayton's death. Fuller says " He was a pious poet, his conscience having always the command of his fancy, very temperate in his life, slow of speech, and inoffensive in company." Sir Aston Cokaine's poems, 1658, contain:

"A Funeral elegy on my very good friend Mr. Michael Drayton.

"You Swans of Avon, change your fates and all
Sing and then die at Drayton's funeral;
Sure shortly there will not a drop be seen
And the smooth pebled bottom be turned green
When the nymphs (that inhabit in it) have
(As they did Shakespeare) wept thee to thy grave."

This address to the Swans of Avon is curious, and suggests that Drayton dwelt a good deal by its banks, seeing he was not born there. The Anker runs into the Tame and not into the Avon.

CHAPTER XIV

The Trussells Of Billesley.

In the settlement of the property at Snitterfield, purchased from the Mayowes in 1501 by Thomas Arden of Wilmcote, the second of the Trustees was Thomas Trussell of Billesley. Such an association implied either relationship in blood, connection by marriage, or special friendship. It naturally suggests that Robert Arden's unknown first wife was a Trussell, probably a Joan. The degree of intimacy thus implied, and the close neighbourhood of Billesley both to Wilmcote and Stratford, make the family interesting to us.

The Trussells did not come originally from Northampton as the Dictionary of National Biography says. There were Trussells of Billesley from the time of Henry I.,f when they held a Knight's Fee of the Earl of Warwick. Osbert Trussell held Billesley in the reign of Henry II.

In the reign of Henry III. Richard Trussell was slain at Evesham, but his brother and heir, William, became of great account in the shire. He married Roesia, daughter and heir of William Pantulf of Cubblesdon in Staffordshire, from which marriage the family branched out, making many great matches. Sir William fought at Poictiers, John and William at Agincourt. The willof Sir William Trussell of Cubblesdon, 1379, mentions a bequest to his cousin, Sir Thomas d'Ardene, of the Park Hall family. Alured Trussell, of Billesley, married Catherine, daughter of Sir William Trussell, of Nottingham. William, his heir, sheriff of the county, 16 Edward IV., lived at Billesley. He was made brother of the Guild of Knowle, 1469, and in 1504 Masses were said for his soul. His son was John, whose son was Thomas, sheriff of the county. Thomas married Joane, daughter and heir of William Walton, and died on the 1gth of February, 8 Henry VIII. (1517). This was the trustee for the purchase made by Robert Arden of Wilmcote. His death partly fixes the period at which Leland must have been in the county, for in his "Itinerary," he says, "Mr. Trussell, an ancient gentleman, dwelleth at Billesley, three miles from Stratford." As his son William, who had married Cecilia Curzon of Kettlestone, died before his father, this could not refer to him, nor to his son, Alured or Avery, who was four years old when he succeeded his grandfather in 1517. Alured married Margaret, daughter of Robert Fulwood of Tamworth, co. Warwick, and had a large familylJohn, his heir; Edward, who went to London and became a clothworker; Thomas, Robert, and Henry. There were also five daughterslDorothy, who married Adam Palmer, Robert Arden's friend and trustee; Mary, who married John Gelsthorp; Sisseley, Ursula, and Margaret.

' See my "Shakespeare's Family," page 26, &c. f Dugdale's "Warwickshire," II, 714-718.

Thomas Trussell presented to the church of Billesley in 1498, Alured in 1539, and John in 1574.

John married Mary Grimston, and had three sonsl Thomas, Henry, and George. (John, the son of Henry, went to Winchester, became the Bishop's Steward there, and wrote several historical works.) Thomas, called in the "Visitation " " the Souldier," who married Margaret, daughter of Edward Boughton of Causton, was for atime in the army. He was the author of a little book, which he dedicated to the Earl of Salisbury, requesting his acceptance of the small trifle to suggest means of supplying the King's State. "The Souldier, pleading his own cause . . . with an epitome of the qualities required in the officers of a private company." A second edition came out in 1619.

Thomas, the Soldier, possibly remained a Catholic, and does not seem to have been financially fortunate, as he sold Billesley, the ancient home of his fathers, to Sir Robert Lee, who rebuilt much of the ancient manor house, in which was found a priest's secret chamber with an underground passage for escape.

The name of Thomas often appears in the Stratford Records, where he is described as a gentleman or as an attorney. He brought a case to the Court of Records in 1591. He was the attorney for Nicholas Lane in his suit against Henry Shakespeare, 1587, and in 1592 he drew up the inventory of the goods of Henry Shaw and of Henry Field, in conjunction with John Shakespeare. Among the baptisms at Stratford-upon-Avon are: Rose, daughter to Mr. Thomas Trussell; John, 31st March, 1579 ; Thomas, 13th October, 1580; Elizabeth, 2nd September, 1582 ; Avery, 15th November, 1583; Richard, 19th November, 1585; Thomas, 13th December, 1586; George, 24th August, 1589; John, 27th October, 1591. Among the burials are: John, 8th April, 1579; Rose, 26th August, 1582; Thomas, 26th November, 1587; George, 6th February, 1592; "Johannes filius Thomas Trussell, generosus, 16th June, 1593"; and "Thomas Trussell, generosus, 20th September, 1593." There are later allusions to his son Thomas.

Dugdale says, "How it comes to pass I know not, but the Trussells of Billesley have been reputed lords of the manor of Moreton Bagot for a long time, andhad also an interest in the advowson of the church, as by some records and other authorities appeareth."

Among those who present to the church are "Will. Trussell de Cublesdon, Miles, 1361; Aluredus Trussell, Miles, 1413; William Trussel,Ar., Dominusde Morton Bagot, 1427 ; Humfr., co. Staff. Ratione Minoris setat. Joh. fil. et haer. Will. Trussell, ar., 14330. Trussell, ar., Dominus de Moreton, 1480; Thomas Trussell, Dominus de Moreton, 1485 ; Aluredus Trussell, ar., de Billesley, 1541." Others follow.

Shakespeare introduces the name as "Tressel and Berkley" in *Richard III*r., Act 1, sc. 2.

It may be remembered that Shakespeare's granddaughter, Elizabeth Hall, was married to her second husband, Mr. John Barnard of Abington, at Billesley. Some writers have suggested that it was because she was a Catholic, and connected with the Trussells. But it may clearly be seen that the Trussells had left Billesley long before. Any personal association, therefore, would have been between Sir Robert Lee and Mr. John Barnard (afterwards made a knight). Both were aldermen of London. The registers of Billesley are lost, and it may therefore be entered as one of the possible places in which Shakespeare was married.

11

SECTION 11

CHAPTER XV

The Cloptons.

The Cloptons had been owners of Clopton Hall from the time of Henry III. Their names are recorded among the Guild brethren : John Clopton was Master of the Guild of Holy Trinity, 13 Edward IV.; Thomas Clopton, Master of the Guild of the Holy Cross, 21 Edward IV.; William Clopton granted land to the Brethren and Sistren of the Guild, 9 Henry VIII. The above-mentioned John de Clopton had a license to build an oratory in his manor house for the private exercise of divine service. His elder son was Thomas; his second son, Hugh, went to London, became a wealthy mercer there, was Mayor in 7 Henry VII., was knighted, and by some means acquired possession of the family property. Sir Hugh Clopton was a great benefactor to Stratford, where he built the famous stone bridge of fourteen arches to replace the old timber bridge, said to have been erected by Queen Matilda because she had got wet in attempting to cross the ford. It had become perilous to use. When Leland visited the place, he wrote: "The Bridge ther, of late time, was very s1mile and ille, and at high waters, very hard to passe by. Whereupon in tyme of minde one Clopton, a great rich marchant and Mayor of London, as I remember born about Stratford, having never wife nor children, converted a great peace of his substance in good workesin Stratford, first making a sumptuous new Bridge and large, of stone, where in the middle be a VI great arches for the main streame of Avon, and at eche ende certen smaul arches to here the Causey, and to pass commo- diously at such times as the river riseth" (Leland's " Collectanea," ed. Hearne, vol. iv., part i., p. 16). In another place he says it "was but a poor bridge of Timber, and no causeway to come to it, whereby many poor folks refused to come to Stratford when the river was up, or coming thither stood in jeopardy of their life." Sir Hugh Clopton's liberality and thorough work became a national benefaction. One can well imagine the impetus it would give to the trade of Stratford to have this great bridge built over its river, to make it the main thoroughfare of the county.

Sir Hugh instituted Exhibitions for poor scholars at Oxford and Cambridge, a grant which no doubt helped the success of Stratford School. He also restored the Guild Chapel, and built just opposite to it, for his own use, "the praty house of Brick and Timber" mentioned by Leland, which was to be bought and dwelt in by Shakespeare a hundred years after its founder's death.

Sir Hugh hoped to have been buried at Stratford- upon-Avon, but as he died in St. Margaret's parish, Lothbury, London, he was buried there, 12 Henry VII. He never married, and his property passed to his elder brother Thomas, who was one of the proxies of John Mayowe to deliver seisin of the land at Snitterfield to the Ardens, 1501-2.

His will was proved in October, 1496. One item was: " To William Clopton I bequeath my grete house in Stratford-on-Avon, and all my other lands and tenements being in Wilmcote, in the Brigge Towne and Stratford, with reversion and services and dueties thereunto belonging; remayne to my cousin, WilliamClopton, and for lak of issue of him to remayne to the right heires of the Lordship of Clopton for ever."

This William was son of John and grandson of Thomas, brother of Sir Hugh. A life interest had been granted in the great house to one Roger Paget, on whose death, July, 1504, it was delivered to William Clopton, who left it to his wife, Rose, for life.

On her death in 1525 it fell to her son, William, but in 1543 he let New Place to Dr. Thomas Bentley on lease for a term of years, afterwards altered into a life tenure for himself and his wife. Bentley died in 1549, leaving New Place uin great ruyne and decaye." His widow, by marrying Robert Charnock, forfeited the lease, and William Clopton entered into possession. In the Inquisition taken at his death in 1560 it is designated as his "freehold estate then in tenure of William Bott." He had apparently burdened his property with too heavy legacies, and his son and heir, William, went abroad, evidently intending to retrench, with unfortu-. nate results. In some mysterious way the house became the property of the William Bott mentioned above, a man who seems to have been of an objectionable character. John Harper, of Henley-in-Arden, brought a suit against him in 1564; and William Clopton, being called as a witness for Harper, said that Bott, acting as his agent while he was in Italy, had received his rents, withheld the money, and forged a deed relating to the Clopton property. Very probably he referred to New Place, because in 1567 Bott sold that house to the Underhills.

Another property remained to the Cloptons. Dugdale says that the village of Bridgeton, Stratford-upon-Avon, contained a hermitage, endowed for the repair of the

Bridge, which belonged to the Powers until Christopher Power passed it to William Clopton in 5 Henry VIII., since which time it has been called a manor.

The legendary but unprovable story of Charlotte Clopton, who had been buried too hastily at the plague time in 1564, had regained consciousness, and had been found standing dead by the gate of the tomb, having striven to free herself, may have suggested "Juliet's" terrors.

The William who was twenty-two at his father's death in 1560, married Anna, the daughter of Sir George Griffith. They had two sonslLudovick and William, who died without issue; and three daughters. There is a legend that his daughter Margaret (born 30th September, 1563), through disappointed love, drowned herself in a well at the back of Clopton House, and some have imagined that her fate suggested that of Ophelia.

His other two daughters were Joyce, who married Sir George Carew, created Baron Carew of Clopton and Earl of Totness ; and Anna, who married her kinsman, William Clopton of Sledwick, co. Durham. William Clopton died in 1592, and his wife, Anne, in 1596. Joyce inherited Clopton, and repaired and beautif1ed the handsome tombstone to the memory of her parents, which still remains in the North Aisle of Stratford Church. The registers note the baptism of Ludovicus, son of William, 8th June, 1561; Guiza, daughter, 1yth September, 1562; Margaret, j0th September, 1563; William, son to William Clopton, 3rd July, 1571 ; and of Anne, 9th January, 1576. A William, son to William Clopton, gen., 12th August, 1593, would seem to be the son of the cousin, and an Anne, 12th January, 1596, his daughter. Among the marriages are George "Caroo and Mrs. Jeys Clopton, 3 1st May, 1578 ";" Mr. William Clopton and Mrs. Anne Clopton, 3rd August, 1589"; "Johannes Combes, gen., et Rosa Clopton, 18th September, 1561."

A case of William Clopton's appears in the Court ofRecord, 1591. One incident would give to Clopton House an unenviable notoriety during the poet's time. Robert Wilson held it under a lease from Sir George Carew (afterwards Earl of Totness) and sub-let it in September, 1605, to Ambrose Rookwood, of Coldham Hall, Stanningfield, Suffolk.

It was in Clopton House that Rookwood entertained his fellow-conspirators in the Gunpowder Plot, Wright, Winter, Keyes, Robert Catesby, John Grant of North- brook, and his two brothers (who had been suspected in the treason of Somerville as before related). When the plot was discovered the Bailiff of Stratford went in person to search the house, and in the priest's chamber was found a cloak-bag " full of copes, vestments, crosses, chalices, and other massing reliques," a full inventory of which has been preserved in the Library at the Birthplace. There had not been such a keen hunt for "superstitious relics " since the days of Elizabeth. They now really signified a political conspiracy run to- earth here.

After the death of the Earl of Totness without heirs in 1629, the Countess left Clopton by will to Thomas, the third son of her sister Anna. Thomas entered into his inheritance on the death of his aunt Joyce in 1636. He married Eglantyne, one of the daughters of John Keyte, Esq., of Ebrington, and their son John married Barbara, daughter and heir of Sir Edward Walker. This gentleman in 1675 bought New Place from the executors of Shakespeare's grand-daughter, Lady Barnard, and left it by will back to the Cloptons, through his daughter Barbara in 1677. His will gives some interesting details concerning the transfer of the property formerly owned by Shakespeare.f

In a Recusant Roll of 16 Car. I. Thomas Clopton, of Old Stratford, is mentioned.

t In J. C. M. Bellcw's "Shakespeare's Home at New Place," 1863, elaborate pedigrees of the Cloptons and the Combes are given.

CHAPTER XVI

The Combes.

The Combes were not such old residents in the neighbourhood as were these others. But they were of as old a family. Away south in the parish of Swanscombe, Kent, there was an ancient manor called Alkerdene, or The Combe, so named from the old word "Combe," a hollow in a hill. There, according to Hasted, the historian of Kent, dwelt in old time a family that had taken the place-name. The head of this family, John Combe, or A-Combe, for no recorded reason, left Kent early in the reign of Edward IV., settled in Warwickshire, and is believed to have been the founder of the Stratford family that Shakespeare knew.

The Warwickshire Visitation gives the pedigree of the Combes of Ashley, co. Warwick, and the descent of John Combe of Old Stratford.

The earliest local incident recorded of the family was recorded by Mr. Mark Bullen and published in the *Atheneum.* It is a petition "To the Right Reverend father in God, Steven, Bishop of Winchester, Lord Chancellor of England, 1553-1555.

"The Complaint of Adryan Quynye of Stretford- upon-Haven, Mercer.lThe complainant is seized in fee of one tenement called Barlands House, with one garden, one orchard and one barn in Stretford. Diversevidences and writings relating to this estate have come into the hands of one John Combes (sometimes written John O'Combe) of Stratford, gentleman, who, by means thereof, doth make and convey sundry estates, secretly of the premises, to the disheryson of your said orator." He prays relief in the usual form. (Early Chancery Proceedings, Bundle 1373, Record Office.)

John A-Combe is mentioned as one of those holding a reversionary interest in Clifford Chambers, before the final purchase by the Rainsfords in 1562.

On the 1 fth September, 1563, a case was tried in the Court of Record, Stratford-upon-Avon, John Combes *versus* Humphrey Underhill. He had another suit in 1569.

Other cases in the Court of Record were brought by Thomas Combe, gent., 28 Eliz. (1586); George Combes, gent., 29 Eliz.; Edward Combe, gent., 31 Eliz.; Thomas Combes, gent., 32 Eliz.; George Combe, gent., 36 Eliz. Edward lived at Wasperton, and married Anna, daughter of Stephen Hales of Newland, brother of Bartholomew Hales of Snitterfield.

The Combes' coat of arms, granted in 1584, bore- ermine, three lions passant. John Combe married first, Joyce, daughter of Sir Edward Blount, and second, Rosa, daughter of William Clopton.

The old college of Stratford, which was seized at the Dissolution, passed through many hands before it was bought in 1596 by John Combe, who made it his principal residence. Besides children born elsewherel Edward, Thomas and Georgelthe Registers record the baptism of Elizabeth his daughter, on the 26th of May, 1566; Francis his son, on the 8th of April, 1575; and John his son, on the 2gth of January, 1577.

William, son to Mr. Thomas Combes, was baptized on the 8th of December, 1586; Thomas on the gth of February, 1588; Maria on the 16th of May, 1591; and Jodoca or Joyce on the 10th of May, 1593.

It is probable that this Thomas, who married Maria Savage, and became heir to his brother, was a man ofsome literary taste and a translator, for in the Stationers' Registers it is recorded that on the gth of May, 1593, there was allowed to Richard Field "The Theatre of fine Devices conteyning an Hundred Morall Emblemes translated out of French by Thomas Combe, authorized under the hand of Master Michael Murgatrode, *vid."* If it were his, it is interesting to think that Richard Field was publishing two books for two fellow-townsmen in the spring of the same year.

In May, 1602, Shakespeare purchased for three hundred and twenty pounds from John and William Combe, one hundred and seven acres of land near Stratford-upon-Avon, of which, as he was not in town, seisin was delivered to his brother Gilbert, and in 1610 he bought twenty acres more, the whole being reckoned four and a half yard lands.

John Combe reared a grand tomb for himself, and it has been reported that he asked Shakespeare for a suitable epitaph, who is said to have replied impromptu:

"Ten in a hundred lies here engraved ;
'Tis a hundred to ten his soul is not saved.
If any man ask who lies in this tomb,
Oh Ho quoth the Devil, 'tis my John a-Combe."

It is very improbable that Shakespeare composed these doggerel verses. A suggestion of the epitaph occurs in "The more the merrier. Threescore and odd headless Epigrams by H. P. Gent, 1608." In Camden's "Remains," 1614, are preserved similar lines:

"Here lies ten in the hundred
In the ground fast rammed;
It's a hundred to ten
But his soul is damned."

And Richard Braithwaite, "Remains," 1618, has also a variant of the epitaph.

If, however, Shakespeare did vary the idea to fit thename, it must only have been given as a merry jest, and taken in good humour. It neither hit John Combe too deeply, nor rankled in his mind, because by his will dated the 28th of January, 1612-13, he left the poet five pounds. He also bequeathed twenty shillings for two sermons to be preached in Stratford Church; *61.* 35. *tfd.* to buy ten gowns for ten poor people of Stratford; twenty pounds to the poor; and one hundred pounds to be lent to fifteen poor tradesmen from three years to three years, at fifty shillings per annum, which interest was to be given to the relief of alms. To Francis Collins, sen., he bequeathed ten pounds.

John Combe died at the very time the great fire of Stratford was raging. He was buried on the 10th of July, 1614, in Trinity Church at the upper end of the choir; over him is a handsome monument with his statue in alabaster, and an epitaph recording his bequests.

His legacy to Shakespeare remained uncancelled, but it is possible that the poet never received it, as John- Combe's will was not proved till the 10th of November, 1616.

John's heir William at once took to enclosing at Welcombe; and stirred public feeling to fever heat during the autumn of 1614. On the 12th of November, 1614, at the Common Council it was agreed that "all lawfull meanes shalbe used to prevent the enclosing that is pretended of part of the old town field." On the 5th of December the Council resolved "that six of the company should go with their love to Mr. William Combe at his return home and ask him to forbear." One of the six was Richard Hathaway. A week later they reported that Mr. Combe said "he was to have some profytt by the enclosure, but it was not to be to his own use, that it was to be enclosed by Mr. Mannerynge when the frost passed." A deputation was to be sent to Mr. Mannering, "and I the sayd Thomas Green,the Steward and Councillor for the Borough to assist them against the enclosure."

Shakespeare's attitude towards this has been by some supposed to be favourable, so that he himself were secured from damage. The scheme might materially affect him through the lease of the tithes. Much discussion has arisen over the true meaning of the entries in the note-book of his cousin, Thomas Green, the Town Clerk of Stratford-upon-Avon. Unfortunately these are badly written, and the composition is dubious, but to my mind whether it was "I" or "he," the meaning remains the same that Shakespeare "could not bear the enclosing of Welcombe." This is one of the few colloquial phrases of the poet which have come down to us. (See Dr. Ingleby's " Shakespeare and the Welcombe Enclosures.")

But there is no doubt as to the opinion of the Town Council. In the Records there are several orders made opposing the action of Mr. William Combe of the College. The intended enclosure seems to have been "the north part of the fields of Old Stratford, Welcombe and Bishopton towards Warwick, leading from a certain gate called Clopton Gate, to a certain bush within the fields of Welcombe called Beggar's Bush, *alias* Bragg's, along by a piece of land of Sir Francis Smyth's, knight, in the occupation of Edward Hunt, directly to the upper end of a furlong of tillage ground, lying under Rowley, and so long by the overend of a quickset hedge there lying between Trinity Peece and King's Furlongs, and so from thence to a gate called the Slynge, and also two earable lands now lying in Ford Greene between the land of our Sovereign Lord the King on the west side, and the land in the occupation of Anthony Nash on the east side." Finding their orders neglected the Town Council went in person to resist the enclosures, but William Combe "overthrewthe aldermen who came peaceably to hinder his digging, whereof great tumult arose."

On the 2 5th of January, 1615, Mr. Daniel Baker and Mr. Chandler were sent to London to take advice of counsel against enclosing, and on the 24th of February it was resolved that a case be made out against the riots and misdemeanours, and an appeal to the Lord Chief Justice of England at Warwick. Further appeals secured a reply from Sir Edward Coke that the enclosure was against the law of the realm. Another petition was sent up to the Lord Chief Justice on the 2yth of March, 1616, describing

Mr. Combe as "of so unbridled a disposition" that he continued his enclosures in spite of orders to the contrary.

In the midst of this local storm the poet died. He left nothing to William, but he remembered his brother in his will, February, 1616. "To Mr. Thomas Combe, my sword." (This Thomas died at Stratford in July, 1657, aged 68.)

The disputes about the enclosures continued. On the 14th of February, 1618, an inhibition arrived, signed "Francis Verulam, Pembroke, Naunton, Fulke Greville." (See the Wheler Collection.)

It is strange that in spite of this, William Combe should have been made Sheriff of the County not only in 1608, but in 1616.

On the 1yth of March, 1619, William Combe was requested to view the decays in the parish church, and in 1622 it was agreed that "all the trees of the churchyard should be cut down and sold to repay the cost of repairing" (See the Chamberlain's Accounts). So that we may not even have a fancy that ariy of the trees that waved round the church in Shakespeare's time remain.

Among the recusants 16 Charles I., are entered "William and Thomas Combe of Old Stratford."William Combe lost his wife Katharine on the 21st of June, 1662, at 51 years of age, and he himself died at Stratford on the 30th of January, 1666-7, ag6 80, leaving one son and nine daughters.

Several names of the family occur among Dr. Hall's cases, for instance:|"Part ii., Case xxxiv., Mrs. Combs, aged thirty-six." "Case xliv., Mrs. Mary Comb of Stratford, aged thirteen. Feb. 15th, 1631."

The Register records the baptism of Constance on the 4th October, 1632; Grace on the 20th of April, 1634; Elizabeth on the 20th of March, 1635-36.

CHAPTER XVII

The Underbills.

John Underhill of Wolverhampton had acquired the property of Nether Eatington in Warwickshire in the year of the accession of Henry VIII. (1509) and had died shortly afterwards, leaving two sons, Edward, his heir, and Thomas.

The second son married Anne, daughter of Robert Winter, of Hudington, Worcestershire, and settled at Honingham. He was a petty captain of a hundred men sent by the City of London to the French wars in 1543, but only becomes interesting because of his son Edward, "the Hot Gospeller," who was made a gentleman- pensioner in 1539. In July, 1553, Edward published a ballad attacking the Lady Mary. He was warmly attached to Lady Jane Grey, who, during her short reign, stood godmother to one of his daughters. Her representative on returning from the christening saw all the insignia of state taken down from the royal residence in the Tower. The impulsive poet was arrested in his own house on the 4th of August and sent to the Tower. But, through the influence of his kinsman John Throck- morton on the naturally clement heart of Mary, and the good offices of the Earl of Bedford, whose eldest son, Lord Russell, he had saved from drowning in the Thames, an order for his pardon was granted, on account of his illness, on the 21 st of August. He was not reallyliberated, however (through the suspicions of Mary's councillors), until the 5th of September. Then he took the oath of allegiance to Mary, and helped to defend her loyally at the time of Wyat's rising.

His interesting "Diary" gives a full account of those troublesome times. Much of it has been printed in Strype, and in the "Chronicle of Queen Jane and Queen Mary" (Camden Society). When he inherited Honingham at his father's death he was forced to sell it, as his pension was not sufficient for his expenses at Court.

Edward, the elder son of John, remained in Warwickshire, succeeding on his father's death to Nether Eatington and the Manor of Herberbury. He also became proprietor of certain lands at Stratford-upon- Avon. His elder son was Thomas, a staunch Protestant, favourably mentioned by Fuller in his "Worthies or England." He is perhaps better remembered by the poetical epitaph on his son Anthony, who died on the 16th of July, 1587. There were four stanzas about a vision and death, and the fifth stanza runs thus:

"As dreams doe slide, as bubbles rise and fall;
As flowers doe fade and flourish in an houer;
As smoke doth rise, and vapours vanish all

Beyond the witt or reach of human power;
As somer's heat doth parch the withered grasse,
Such is our stay, soe lyfe of man doth passe."

This epitaph, which formerly hung on the north wall of the north aisle of the church at Nether Eatington, has been traditionally ascribed to Shakespeare.

William Underhill, the son of Edward, brother to Thomas, and uncle of Anthony, seems to have been born about 1523. He studied law, became a member of the Inner Temple, London, and married Ursula, one of the daughters of John Congreve of Stretton, co. Stafford. In 1551, Barton-on-the-Heath (the BurtonHeath of the Induction of *The Taming of the Shrew)* was transferred to him by his brother-in-law, Edmund Bury. Some property in Staffordshire was afterwards left him by his uncle, William Underhill of Shustoke, and he acquired land at Wednesfield near Wolverhampton. After the death of his wife Ursula in 1561, he married the widow of John Newport of Hunningham, and only sister of Sir Christopher Hatton, afterwards Lord Chancellor. When Ferdinand Poulton, the eminent jurist, married Anne, daughter of Thomas Underhill of Eatington, he settled the manor of Bour- ton, Bucks., on Mr. William Underhill and others, in trust for his wife Anne.

It is evident that this William Underhill lived near Stratford-upon-Avon. In an interesting Star Chamber case, 1564, instituted (see p. 216) by John Harper of Henley-in-Arden *contra* William Bott, of New Place, Stratford-upon-Avon, it was testified by William Clop- ton, Esq., that the said Bott, acting as his agent while he was in Italy, had received his rents, withheld the money, and forged a deed concerning his lands. On the same occasion John Walsingham of Exhall, gent., gave evidence that Bott "oppressed divers poor men and took away their cattle, whereupon they went to one Mr. Underhill, a man of law, a very good man dwelling near by, and did desire help for God's sake, as they were utterly undone . . . who did take the matter in hand,

and had it in law a great while, and cost much money. No poor man might dwell by Bott if Mr. Underhill did not assist him."

The house (really belonging to Mr. Clopton, but dwelt in and taken possession of by his agent, the oppressing and dishonest Bott) was New Place, which was sold by Bott to William Underhill in 1567. It was described as " one messuage, and one garden," though sold to Shakespeare thirty years afterwards as " onemessuage, two barns, and two gardens," for sixty pounds.

In that same year Mr. Underhill had acquired more property. The manor of Idlicote had been granted to Ludovic Greville, and his servant, Francis Gyll, who at once assigned his share to his master. (The tragedy that followed is explained in the notice of the Grevilles.) Ludovic Greville sold Idlicote, and also the manor of Loxley, to Mr. Underhill, who at the same time obtained from Mr. Thomas Throckmorton a lease of Newbold Revel for the term of twenty-one years.

In the Chamberlain's Accounts of Stratford-upon- Avon for 1569, there is : " *Item,* paid for a dyner for Mr. Underell at the Swan, 175. *d.*"; a compliment made him probably after some legal help to the Corporation.

His second wife died in the same year. Her will transferred to him the property she held in her own right, in consideration of the advances he had made for the payment of her debts.

He did not long survive his "loving wife Newport," dying on the 31st of March, 1570, and was buried at Nether Eatington, where a marble monument was set up in the church, with the arms of Underhill impaling Congreve, and the following inscription: "Here lyeth William Underhill of the Inner Temple of London, gentleman, of Edward Underhill Esquier, second sonne, and Ursula his dearly beloved wife, youngest daughter of John Congreve of Stretton, in co. Stafford, Esquier, whose life was a spectacle unto all honest virtuous and obedient wives, and she died the 13 daye of May An. Dom. 1561. Upon whose souls Christ have Mercy, Amen."

It is noticeable that this memorial closes with a prayer for the dead, not usual during Elizabeth's reign; and that there is not the slightest allusion to his second wife, who was of higher rank than himself.

Notwithstanding this slight on his family, Sir Christopher Hatton, as a kinsman, in 1571 obtained the wardship of William (the only son of William) who was sixteen years of age when his father died, and consequently the son of the first wife.

The prosperous lawyer died possessed of the manors of Idlicote, Loxley and Barton-on-the-Heath, together with New Place and other houses and lands in Stratford, Hollington, Hardwick, Meriden, Haselor, Dray- ton and Easinghall. He gave stringent commands in his will that there was to be no alienation of his estates except in case of pressing need. He left to each of his daughters five hundred pounds and one silver spoon ; to his second daughter her stepmother's wedding-ring; and to his youngest daughter "a little chaine of gold and one of my first wife's rings."

In spite of the rigid terms of his father's will, shortly after attaining his majority, William Underhill procured a license to alienate the manor of Loxley to his cousin-, Thomas Underhill, of Goldicote and Lincoln's Inn, probably for the "pressing need" of paying his sisters' portions. Not long afterwards he married Mary Underhill, of Nether Eatington, his cousin both by the father's and the mother's side.

He was imprisoned, as a suspected person, on a charge of recusancy in 1579, but being able to give an explanation to Burghley, was soon released. In 1581 "great extremity having happened to the said William Underhill," special permission was granted him to dispose of lands in Hollington and Meriden.

In 1584 Stephen Burman of Shottery, one of the supervisors of Richard Hathaway's will, instituted proceedings against him in relation to a farm at Little Wilnecote, and described Underhill as "a subtle, covetous and crafty man." There was also a long litigation between Underhill and the Stratford authorities, who had granted him a lease of the tithes of Little Wilnecote, the rent of which he refused to pay.

He was nevertheless appointed escheator for the counties of Warwick and Leicester in 1587, an office which must have given him considerable influence.

His wife and cousin Mary died and was buried at Idlicote in 1590.

He settled this property after the death of his wife on his eldest son Fulke, in trust, after his own death.

A curious case was brought against him in the Court of Chancery by Thomas Throckmorton of Coughton, in 1592, praying relief in respect of a bond for 300/., to be paid in three annual sums of 100/. at the manor house of William Underhill at Stratford-upon-Avon, *i.e.*. New Place. Underhill in his reply said that the money was not duly tendered at the proper time, and much inconvenience and loss had arisen to him in consequence.

He and his son Fulke were joined as defendants in a suit brought against them by Thomas Huntbach for not completing the sale of a farm and lands at Shustoke. They pled that the delay was entirely the plaintifFs own fault.

In Easter Term, 1597, Underhill sold his manor- house called New Place to William Shakespeare, the property consisting of one messuage, two barns, and two gardens with their appurtenances.

In July of that same year he was poisoned at Fillong- ley, made his will on the 6th, died the following day, and was buried on the 13th at Idlicote beside his wife Mary.

He bequeathed all his lands to his eldest son Fulke ; to each of his other sons, 200/.; to his daughters Dorothy and Valentine, 500/. each. The executors were George and Thomas Shirley.

Fulke had been baptized at Idlicote on the 28th ofJanuary, 1578, and was therefore still a minor. He died at Warwick in 1598. From Mr. Savage's "Churchwardens' Accounts of St. Nicholas, Warwick," we f1nd that sixpence was received "for tolling the great bell for Vouckas Underhill, May, 1598." He was, however, buried at Idlicote.

It does not seem that, at the time, Fulke was suspected of having poisoned his father, but, either through his own confession or the evidence of others, his guilt afterwards became known. In 1602 a commission was appointed by the Court of Exchequer, "to obtain an account of the possessions of Fulke Underhill of Fil- longley, co. Warwick, felon, who had taken the life of his father William Underhill, by poison."

Fulke had no children, and his brother Hercules, born in 1581, succeeded to the Idlicote estate, and when he came of age in 1602, he completed the transfer of the title-deeds of New Place to Shakespeare, the peculiar circumstances of the case causing some doubt of the validity of the original purchase.

Hercules married Bridget, a sister of Dudley Carle- ton, Viscount Dorchester, and was knighted in 1617, at Compton Winyates. He became High Sheriff of Warwickshire in 1625, and a few years later bought an estate at Halford. He held with the Royalist party in the Civil War, and was forced to compound for his estates by a fine of 1,177*l*. as a Popish recusant. He died in 1657, leaving no children, having appointed as his heir his nephew, William Underhill, afterwards knighted, who married Alice, daughter of the third Sir Thomas Lucy.

The Stratford-upon-Avon Registers give among the baptisms, "Dorothy daughter to Mr. William Underhill, 18th March, 1579; Elizabeth, 10th November, 1585; Valentine, 1yth September, 1586; William, 6th March, 1587-8.

For the facts not mentioned in Dugdale I am indebted to the article on "The Underhills of New Place," by Mr. William Underhill, of Hove.

The Records of Stratford mention cases by Richard Underhill, Clericus, 33 Eliz., and John Underhill, gent., 39 Eliz.

Dr. Hall mentions, Case Ixx., Mr. Simon Underhill, aged forty.

Case Ixxxi., the heir of Mr. Thomas Underhill, of Loxley, aged twelve.

Case xix., the Lady Underhill, aged fifty-three.

Case xx., Squire Underhill, aged fifty.

Case xxxvi., Mr. Thomas Underhill, of Lamcot, aged thirty-nine.

Case xii., part ii., Mr. George Underhill, aged about sixty-four.

12

SECTION 12

CHAPTER XVIII
The Clergy Of Stratford

Dugdale gives a list of the Vicars of Stratford, but it does not seem to be complete, and he does not mention the curates at all. But many interesting references to them appear in the Stratford Records, especially in relation to their having been schoolmasters or ushers, a fact which bears on the social and intellectual status of the schoolmasters of Shakespeare's town and times.

Mr. Roger Dyos, about whom we know little, was appointed Vicar in 1553 by Queen Mary.

The name is uncommon, and it is possible that the following entries in the Chamberlain's Accounts refer to him : " 1575-6. Paid to Sir Roger Dyos for redeeming his portion, 11/.; Paid to Mr. Stuard his charges to London and for counsell to defend Sir Roger Dyos process, 305.; Paid for charges when Mr. Sadler, Mr. Stuard, and Anthony Tanner went to Sir Roger Dyos, their first journey 235. *nd.,* Paid for their charges thither the second journey 235. *1d.* Paid the Sheriff's fees and a copy of the Queen's process brought against the Bailiff and Burgesses by Sir Roger Dyos, *is. 8d.*;

Paid for wax to sele Sir Roger Dyos acquittance and a box to bear the same, 4.; Paid to John Linakers under- sheriffe for the det of Sir Roger Dyos, *1$l. 1js.* 6d."

Mr. John Bretchg1rdle was appointed by Elizabeth on the 2 yth of February, 1560. He was vicar whenShakespeare was christened, and probably performed the ceremony. Among the burials appear: "June 21, 1565, Johannes Bretchgirdle, Vicarius." Among the entries of 1565 are : "Paid to the precher, 205.; To the same precher, *los."* "Dec., 1566. Paid to the Vicar in the absence of assistant, *6s. %d."*

Dugdale dates the appointment of Henry Heicraft, Vicar, as the 1st of January, 1569-70. But there was a "license to preach granted Henry Heicraft, Vicar, on the 8th of January, 1571." In that year the "Vicar's wages" are entered as twenty pounds, and the "assis- tence wages" as ten pounds. There seems to have been a temporary help in that yearl" For 5 weeks to Sir Gabrell for his wages, 205.; to Sir Gabrell for 5 weeks, 385. *6d."* Then comes the introduction of one long known to Stratford, first as schoolmaster-usher, then as curate: "To William Higges for service three weeks, *los. 6d"* "To William Gilbard, alias Higges, Id.j." Thereafter, under various names and titles (Sir Higges, Sir William, Sir William Gilbard, alias Higgs), he received his ten pounds a year sometimes quarterly, sometimes in association with the one pound allowed him for minding the clocks of the town, oiling, winding, and setting them. I have not been able to discover the cause of his signing the cumbrous alias. He was a most industrious curate, always at his post in time of trouble. He was in the habit of saving the charges of a notary to his friends by writing their wills. Among others he drew up those of John Tonge, 22nd March, 1587; Robert Harvey, 10th July, 1584;Thomas Ballamy, 30th October, 1596 ; Joyce Hobday, widow, 28th March, 1602 ; Catherine Welch, widow, 21st January, 1605; Arthur Ainge, shoemaker, 15th March, 1605-6; Richard Balis, fuller, 1605.

Elizabeth, daughter of Mr. Henry Heicraft, Vicar, was baptised on the 8th of October, 1580 ; on the *lyA* November, 1575, Samuel, son to Mr. Henry Heicraft, Vicar.

On the 23rd of October, 1566, he had one daughter, Johanna, baptized; on the 26th of February, 1567-8, another of the same name. On the I3th February, 1593, he buried his wife, Elizabeth, and he was himself buried on the 2nd February, 1611-12.

Richard Barton was appointed on the ryth February, 1584, by the Earl of Warwick. On the gth October, 1586, Richard, son to Mr. Richard Barton, Vicar, was baptised.

John Bramhall was appointed on the 20th November, 1589. The Chamberlain's Accounts note: "Paid Mr. Bramhall, for a sermon, 35. 4." " For his wages, 20/." "To Mr. Jeffreys, 5/." This gentleman was either an assistant or temporary help.

Richard Byfield on the 23rd January, 1596, was appointed by Mr. Edward Greville on the decease of Bramhall. He had a son, Robert, buried on the 28th April, 1600. He transcribed the earlier pages of the Register, and signed the pages down to 1602, when- they were signed by William Gilbard alias Higges, minister, till 1610. In 1598 we find: "Paid to Mr. Byfield for a remembrance sermon, 35. 4., for a sermon on election day, 35. *d"* "For a quart of sack sent Mr. Cooper, a preacher, *1s."* "For a quart of sack sent Mr. Byfield, *1s."* "1605: Paid to a Scotsman for a sermon, 35. 4." The wife of Mr. Byfield, Vicar, was buried on the 23rd September, 1597, and curiously enough he married again on the 30th November, 1597, Margaret Coats, and had a son, Richard, who was baptized on the 24th September, 1598.

Mr. John Rogers is not mentioned by Dugdale, but it is clear from the Chamberlain's books that he had been inducted some time before 1608, for in that year was "paid to Mr. Rogers for the sermon of remembrance for Mr. Perrot, 35. 4." Mr. Venues was paid that year for serving of the cure eight weeks. (Therewere four Oxford men of the name of suitable age.) Mary, daughter to Mr. John Rogers, Vicar, was baptized on the 10th May, 1610.

In 1611 was "paid to Walford that he gave to a precher, *los."* Mr. Edward Brooke, alias Willimore, was appointed assistant minister on the 2gth of April, 1612 ; and Mr. Watts, who had been schoolmaster, in 1614. In that year is recorded the gift so ignorantly commented on by the Baconians, "For one quart of sack, and one quart of clarett wine geven to a precher at Newe Place, *iod."* It only points to the liberality of the owner of the largest house in the town, and the popularity of the preacher there entertained.

On Friday in Easter Week of that year there had been " paid to Mr. Rodgers for a sermon of remembrance for Hamlet Smith, 3.5. 4." A curious entry appears on the 30th January, 1614-15: "Agreed, to have a fit gown of good broadcloth made to Mr. John Rodgers our Vicar, in hope that he will deserve the same hereafter, and amend his faults and failings." One cannot but wonder, if among these "faults and failings" was an uncanonical enjoyment of his great parishioner's plays. The Town Council had made their views clear as to "the inconvenience of plays" on 1yth December, 1602, then on the yth of February, 1611-12, they raised the fine as not sufficiently deterrent from ten shillings to ten pounds, against any bailifflicensing the performance of plays in the Guildhall. The Chamberlain "paid a precher at Mr. Rogers request and per the Company's appointment, Iq5." in 1614. Apparently the new coat did not mend the Vicar, because the burgesses decided on the 4th of December, 1615, that "Mr. Rogers is not to have any more benefit from the burials." The pages of the register bear his signature in 1610; then the Churchwardens had signed till the coming of " Mr. Richard Watts, minister," who signed from 1614 tillDecember, 1616. In 1616 was "paid for a quart of sack, and a quart of clarett wyne bestowed on Mr. Harris for his sermon made here, *l0s."*

On the 5th of May, 1617, the Council petitioned the Lord Chancellor to confirm the presentation by the King of Mr. Thomas Wilson, preacher, of Evesham, to the Vicarage of Stratford-upon-Avon. Mr. Wilson is almost sure to have officiated at the funeral of Mrs. Anne Shakespeare. He had a son, Edmund, baptized in the Parish Church on the 28th of January, 1623-24. (Three of the name had studied in Oxford.)

The Stratfordians were to have even less peace with Mr. Wilson than they had had with Mr. Rogers. On the 6th of June, 1619, he read the articles for avoiding diversity of opinion in the Parish Church ; witnesses, Alexander Aspinall, Richard Hathway, Thomas Green, &c. He was much vexed by citations from the Bishop's Court at Worcester, and the Company appealed to the Earl of Middlesex to try to help them in the matter, both on the 8th of March, 1624, and the 14th of October, 1625. His pay was stopped because of the trouble and loss he caused them, but it was restored when he got Mr. Harris to lecture for them. They agreed that if Mr. Harris of Hanwell gave a weekly lecture in the High Church or Chapel, he should receive five pounds a year. Mr. Wilson was in constant trouble with his parishioners. As, however, the worthy Dr. John Hall supported him, when he took the burgesses to Chancery on the 26th of May, 1634, we may imagine that the right was not altogether on their side. The papers concerning the suit of the Rev. Mr. Wilson, Vicar, against the Corporation, 1635, are among Stratford Miscellaneous Documents, xxxv. Mr. Wilson was suspended for a time on the charge of forswearing against town witnesses, but was soon restored. When he was aged forty, Wilson was treated by Dr. Hall for a rheum in his eyes. Among the medicaments usedwas Sarcecol. "This is remarkable, that a while after it was used on his eyes, he found the taste of the Sarcecol on his palate."

During the troublous times of Mr. Wilson, Mr. Owen was elected to be resident, and serve no other cure, 13th October, 1617; and on the 24th of March, 1619, "Mr. Owen and Mr. Veners stand for election; Mr. Veners chosen."

George Quiney, the youngest brother of the Thomas Quiney who married Judith Shakespeare, was both schoolmaster and assistant for a time. He was baptized on the gth of April, 1600. Matriculating from Baliol, he became B.A. on 11 th May, 1620. He was undoubtedly industrious, learned, ambitious and locally powerful. Therefore, on the 20th of September, 1620, "At this Hall Mr. George Quiney is chosen assistant minister upon probacion of good liking hereafter in his doing of service to the place." And he became entitled to ten pounds salary and one pound for the clocks. In the Wheler Collection, Stratford MS., 112, is a note on " Royalties in Stratford belonging to the Lord Treasurer, and by him challenged," referred to under "Schoolmasters" in relation to Quiney.

In the troubles about the election of an usher, the Company decided on the 1 1th of September, 1622, "to allow Mr. Quiney *1$l.* yearely during the time he continues Reading Minister, if the Company think fit to continue the same. Allso at this Halle it is agreed that at no time hereafter the office of Reading Minister and Usher Schoolmaster shall be supplied by one person." Quiney signed the Registers from the 24th of March, 1621-22, till the 30th March, 1623, and on the nth of April, 1624, he was buried, and his successor, Simon Trappe, signed the pages of the Register thereafter. Quiney was probably of a delicate constitution originally, and overwork of brain and voice, coupled with neglect of his bodily comforts andnecessities, caused him to fall into the care of Dr. John Hall for a "grievous cough," hoarseness, dyspepsia and weakness, at some period undated, which must have been 1623. The treatment ameliorated his condition, but the Doctor adds, "Being not wholy freed from it, he fell into it again the next year; all remedies proving successlesse, he dyed. He was of a good wit, expert in tongues, and very learned."

Mr. Simon Trappe, B.A. in 1623, M.A. in 1626, Oxford, was appointed assistant in his place on the 28th of June, 1624, and signed the Registers until the 26th of March, 1641. He witnessed Dr. Hall's nuncupative will, and was himself buried on the 25th of January, 1641-42. The burgesses had a conference with him about remaining on the 14th of December, 1639.

Henry Twitchet, A.M., 1640, was appointed Vicar by Charles I.; Alexander Beane, 1648, by Cromwell; John Ward, A.M., 1662, by King Charles II.

The Rev. John Ward's " Diary " is the source of some information and more gossip concerning the poet. Coming into the town forty-six years after the poet's death, he knew enough to know that he ought to read the plays, but he did not know how many Shake- speares there were to be confused with our William on the lips of uncertain gossips.

In relation to the Clergy we may mention Dr. Thorn- berry or Thornborough (see p. 40), Bishop of Worcester, who was aged eighty-six, when on the 1 st of February, 1633, Dr. Hall was called in to attend him for scorbutic wandering gout and sleepless terrors. He was treated with good nourishment, and antiscorbutic beer.

The books owned by Stratford Church in Ward's time were the great Church Bible, Dr. Jewell's works, "Paraphrases of Erasmus," Common Prayer Books, Book of Homilies and Canon Book.

The Church House was sold in 1636 for forty pounds.

Among the Clergy also might be included the curates of the various subordinate villages, several of whom are mentioned in Dr. Hall's "Notes of Cases," as for instance, "A child of Mr. Walker of Ilmington, minister, 16 months, afflicted with falling sickness."

But by far the most interesting in one aspect is the Rev. John Marshall, curate of Bishopton. He was reckoned among the students of St. Alban's Hall in 1572, became B.A. 1575, and M.A. 1577. He seems to have been a popular and a learned man. Anne, the daughter of Mr. John Marshall, curate, was buried on the 12th July, 1598 ; and on 2nd February, 1606-7, "John Marshall, Minister of Bisshopton."

He made an interesting will, still preserved in Strat- ford-upon-Avon ; and in view of the announcements made by Mr. Halliwell-Phillipps and others that Stratford was a "bookless neighbourhood," I note that he had at least one hundred and eighty-four books, not a bad library for the time, and these were intelligently priced by Abraham Sturley, Ralf Lord, Francis Ainge, and Thomas Cale.

Of course the majority of these were school books and books of Divinity in English, Latin, Greek, and some Hebrew. But among others there were "The Apologie of Thomas More," "Palengenius Englished," "The Voyage of the Wandering Knight," H. Holland's "Aphorisms," Roger Ascham's "Schoolmaster," G. Gifford on "Witches," Northbrook's "Poore Man's Garden," "The Colloquies of Erasmus," " Morall Philosophy in English," "jEsop's Fables," "The Enemy of Security," "Castell of Health," "A Booke on Fishing, Carving, and Sewing," with the chief classic writers.

See my article, "Stratford's Bookless Neighbourhood," *I1bmrum,* 2jrd February, 1907.

13

SECTION 13

CHAPTER XIX

The Schoolmasters.

The Rev. T. Medwin, in his " History of the Grammar School," refers to the ledger of the Guild of the Holy Cross, which shows that as early as 1424 there was a schoolmaster whose name was John Harris employed by the Guild. In 1477 " Richard Fox, Grammar School master, and Bachelor of Arts, now of Stratford, made brother of the Guild," is the first graduate in Arts mentioned. But this high standard seems to have been ' kept up throughout Jolyffe's endowments and in the re-established school under Edward VI. The charter settled that the school "should be maintained as in past time, and the Schoolmaster have perpetual succession, and be capable to receive and purchase to himself and his successors, a certain yearly rent, pension, or annuity of 20*l*." It was also arranged that he should be allowed to receive another twenty pounds if he could get it. Now, as the ordinary headmasters of the time, such as the Master of Eton, had only ten pounds a year, we may assume Stratford was regarded by "clerks" as a prize, and that it could always command the best men. This must not be forgotten in the estimation of the possibilities of Shakespeare's education, usually so scornfully made light or by his traducers. His father, unfortunately, would suffer in his youth from the evil effects of Henry VIII.'s suppression in the interregnum of the school, but the poet enjoyed its opportunities at its renewed prime.

The masters of the restored School were :l

William Smart, 1554.lOn the 8th of February, 1560-1, was baptised "Gulielmus filius Gulielmi Smart ludimagistri."

William Allen, 1563.lThe accounts of John Taylor and John Shakespeare, 1564-5, record " paid the Schoolmaster, 10/.; paid to Allen for techyng the children, 3/. Paid to the Schoolmaster, 15/. Paid to Allen, 3/."

John Brownsworde, 1564.lThe agreement made with him 1st April, 1565, to serve two years at 20/. a year salary is preserved. John Taylor and John Shakespeare, chamberlains. They have been at the charges of placing him, his wife and his goods. In 1566 there were repairs to the schoolmaster's house : " Paid to Mr. Brownsword, *is"* "TotheScholemaster, 10/." In 1568 the Chamberlain's Accounts refer to "rent for a tenement some time employed as a schole house and for repairs to the old schole. Paid to Mr. Henry Higfer and Brownsword, 40/."

John Acton, 1568.l"Paid to Mr. Acton the schoolmaster, 20/." *"Item.* Paid to Henry Mussel for going with the schoolmaster to Kyllyngworthe, 25." (Chamberlain's Accounts, 2yth January, 1570). "Paid to Mr. Acton the Schoolmaster for his wages, 20/."

Walter Roche, Bachelor of Arts, 1569-70.! "Paid Mr. Roche the Schoolmaster his wages, 20/." (Chamberlain's Accounts, 1571.) "Paid Walter Roche for a tenement, rent by year, 135. 4." (Chamberlain's Accounts, 1574.) He was appointed by the Queen to the rectory of Clifford Chambers on the 4th of November, 1574, which he resigned on the 20th of January,1577-8. But he continued to live in Stratford, where "Mary daughter to Mr. Walter Roche minister was baptised nth of September, 1575." In 1582 the chamberlains refer to "a tenement in the tenure of Mr. Walter Roche."

One of that name is called " Seneschal of the Borough." f "Walter Roche, Mat. Corpus, 16th February, 1554-5 ; Lane. Fellow, 1558; B.A., 1559." Sec Boase, "Graduates of Oxford."

Hunt, Bachelor of Arts, 2gth of October,

1571.l1 purposely leave out the Christian name at present. All writers on the subject call him "Thomas," for which there surely must have been some reason. And Mr. Halliwell-Phillipps, in describing his career, notes that "Thomas Hunt, who had been one of the masters of the Stratford Grammar School during the poet's boyhood, is noted as having been the curate of Luddington in 1584, in which year he was suspended for open contumacy" ("Outlines," 11., 364, note 299). In the Register, Thomas Hunt, curate of Luddington, died on the yth of April, 1612.

On the other hand, I find that Simon Hunt went in for the degree of Bachelor of Arts at Oxford," 30th of March, 1568, and passed in 1569, whereas Thomas Hunt only "matriculated in 1575, aged 18, plebs. Oxon.," and the dates forbid the supposition that he could be the Stratford schoolmaster. Further, I have seen the appointment in the Bishops' Registry at Worcester, and have a facsimile of it, made by Mr. J. W. Gray, who published it in his "Shakespeare's Marriage" as "Simon." That runs: "xxixdieejusdem mensis, &c., anno predicto emanavit licencia Simoni Hunt in artibus bacch. docendi literas instruendi pueros in Schola grammaticali in villa de Stratford-super- Avon." If everything else had not supported the claim of " Simon," we might have supposed it possible the registrar had made an error in the Christian name.

Mr. Gray again finds that a Simon Hunt died about

One of this name was made Bachelor of Arts, Oxford, 1566; Master of Arts, 1569-70.

1598, and administration of his estate was granted on the 3rd of May of that year to Thomas Harward of Hewell in Tardebigg, gentleman. He had two sums of 20/. in the hands ofHenry Morgan and 60/. in the hands of William Harwood. (Probate Registry, Worcester.)

Thomas Jenkins became master about 1577, and repairs of the schoolhouse were made for his convenience. In 1578 there is an entry by the Chamberlains, "Paid to Sir Higges Schoolmaster, 10/.; *Item,* to Mr. Jenkins Schoolmaster his half year's wages, 10/.," and on the 16th of January following he has the other 10/.

This man does not seem to have been popular; so his tenure of office was not long. It has occurred to me as possible that he had a strong Welsh accent which the burgesses did not like, and which may have struck one of his pupils so powerfully, that he reproduced it in "Sir Hugh Evans."

A curious note by Mr. Jenkins is preserved in the Wheler Collection, to the effect that, "Whereas John Colby (Cotton) late of London, did covenant and agree to give unto me, Thomas Jenkins, in consideration of my departure from the School, the some of 6/." He signs a receipt for this on the gth of July, 1579, and the Chamberlain records amongst his expenses, I 1th July, 1579: " Paid to Mr. Jenkins for Mr. Cotton, *61."* In the same year we find, "Paid to Mr. Jenkins for implements and carriage, 105." "Paid Mr. Jenkins the Schoolmaster for his wages, *io/."* So he had two years' " wages " *plus* the *61.* from Cotton, and apparently engaged to stay for two sessions. He was a married man, for the Register states," Thomas, son to Mr. Thomas Jenkins was baptized 1gth of January, 1577."

Mr. Cotton was his assistant before he became hissuccessor, and doubtless offered this *61.* as compensation for leaving the place free.

He i called "John Cotton, 1!.A., 8th of Msy, 1568," in the Oxford Register.

John Cotton, 1579-80.|"To Mr. Cotton Schoolmaster for three-quarters of his wages, 15/." In 1582 an entry runs: "To Mr. Cotton and Mr. Aspinall schoolmasters, 20/.," and Mr. Aspinall was to get the schoolmaster's chamber, as if he were assistant.

Alexander Aspinall, 1583, had matriculated in Brazen Nose College, Oxford, in 1573, aged 20, from Lancaster, Bachelor of Arts, on the 2 5th of February, 1574-75; Master of Arts on the I2th of June, 1578. This master became more identified with the School and the town than any other. Though his relation to Shakespeare could not have been magisterial, he was probably a friend, certainly an acquaintance, and might very well have helped the poet's later culture.

The Chamberlain in 1584 gave "for Mr. Aspinall's Chamber which he now dwelleth in, 1cw.," as apparently the schoolmaster's house was undergoing repairs/ During his tenure of office the Company decided that "School was not to be kept in the Chapel" (14th of February, 1595-6). It is clear that the Chapel was not regularly used as a Schoolroom, but only on rare occasions (when the schoolhouse was under repair).

Mr. Aspinall is mentioned as having been of the Town Council. In 1604-5 ne and James Elletes were Chamberlains of the borough, as well as during the following year. This explains the entry, "For Mr. Aspinall's Charges to London and the hire of his horse, 235. 5/."

Either because of his other duties, or because the school had increased, more attention was paid during his time to assistant masters. Mr. Henry Sturley was appointed "associate to assist Mr. Aspinall, I3th of April, 1603." In December, 1611, the Company resolved to try and get Mr. John Price, of Harvington,to be under-schoolmaster; if not, " Mr. Aspinall to get a sufficient scholar from Oxford." "An under-school- master to be procured, 6th of December, 1612." Aspinall secured Mr. Watts, who afterwards became assistant minister in 1614. " Mr. Harrys allowed to take pains in the schole, as Mr. Hunt and others have done, 2nd of April, 1620." The latter is probably, writes Mr. J. W. Gray, the gentleman referred to below, "One Richard Hunt was cited to appear before the Consistory Court at Worcester on the 14th of June, 1616, for teaching without license at Stratford" (Visitation Book). George Quiney, Judith Shakespeare's brother-in-law, who had doubtless been a favourite pupil of Aspinall, was selected by his old master for his next assistant. Concerning him arose some trouble, probably through his also being appointed assistant minister. Among the "Royalties in Stratford, belonging to the Lord Treasurer and by him challenged," is the following : "The nomination of the Schoolmaster always belonged to the Earl of Warwick and till this very term the schoolmaster continued by the allowance of Sir Edward Greville. His name is Aspinall. Nowe they seeke to put in a newe of themselves, and to displace one Quiney who was formerly under Aspinall, which Quiney is now a suitor to the Lord Treasurer for his helpe by his next right therein." Concerning this dispute the Chamberlain records, "At this Court and Hall it is agreed that whereas Mr. Aspinall hath election of an Usher out of his own means, for that some opposition hath been about the same place between Mr. Queeney, now supplying the place till Michaelmas next, and then Mr. Trap to enter, and the Chamber and Company are agreed to allow Mr. Queeney, *1$l.* yearely during the time he continues Reading Minister, if the Company think fit to continue the same. Allso at this Hall it is agreed that at no time hereafter theoffice of Reading Minister and Usher Schoolmaster shall be supplied by one person, nth September, 1622."

Poor young Quiney evidently had had visions of being headmaster some day, but the next year he fell ill and the following year he died, as is recorded in the chapter on the clergy. His old. master had preceded him by two months.

Mr. Aspinall had married Anne Shaw, probably sister of Julius Shaw (one of the witnesses of Shake- peare's will) on the 28th of October, 1594.

Besides discharging his burgess's duties Mr. Aspinall served as deputy town clerk in 1613-14, and would thus become associated with Shakespeare's cousin, Thomas Green.

On the 30th of November, 1623, was buried "Anna uxor Mri. Alexandri Aspinall." In two months and a week her husband followed her, and was buried on the 4th of February, 1623-24.

The name is uncommon, and I consider it probable that he was related to another of the same profession in the county from which he came. Among the list of recusants in Salford jail on the 22nd of January, 1584, occurs the name of Richard Aspinall, and in the list of convictions he also appears. " Calendar of such persons indicted, arraigned, judged and condemned at Manchester for disobedience to her Majesty, as well recusants as others according to the Statute xx. Common persons ... Richard Aspinall Scholemaster, 240/." The fine is heavy; he would doubtless remain in jail. (State Papers, Dom. Ser. Eliz., clxvii., 47.)

John Trapp, 1624.lHe matriculated on the I5th of October, 1619, as from Worcester, pleb. f., 18; Bachelor of Arts on the 28th February, 1621-22.

She is generally said to be daughter. But Julius Shaw was born in September, 1571 ; married Anne Boys on the 5th of May, 1594 ;was Chamberlain of Stratford 1610; died 1629.

Mr. Trapp succeeded both George Quiney and his master. He was a very capable man. The usual salary was paid him yearly, and " Mr. Trapp is to have Mr. Aspinall's house and his chamber, 2nd April, 1629." The Company made an arrangement with him to increase his free pupils. "At this Hall yt is ordered that Mr. Trap shall have as a newe yeares gift the some of five pounds for this year, provided that he shall full freely teach all such children as are kept within this Borough by any grandfather or grandmother, though the saide children were born without the Burrough ; alsoe he shall teach such children, whose parents are come out of the country to live within the town, 10th January, 1633." Besides the usual salary and expenses duly recorded, the Town Council on the 1gth June, 1637, "ordered that Mr. Baker treasurer, should pay Mr. John Trap, Schoolmaster, 5/. as a free gift in curtesye from the Company for his diligence in teaching school for this year." He was also made Vicar of Weston, and was celebrated as one of the most laborious divines of the age.

Dr. Hall's Case Ixxxii. records the case of "Mr. John Trap, minister, for his piety and learning second to none, about 33 years, of a melancholy temper, by much study, hypochondriac, melancholy and spleen, and saved from the very jaws of death."

This illness must have been before he received the above reward, as Dr. John Hall died in 1635. Dr. Hall had also attended Lydia Trapp, the daughter of Mr. Trapp, aged two, for fever (Case xviii.).

Perhaps among the schoolmasters may be classed Mr. Holyoake. Dr. Hall's Case Ixiv. is "The only son of Mr. Holyoake, which framed the Dictionary." He at least counts as an assistant to teachers and to culture.

14

SECTION 14

CONCLUSION

I Might well allude to many other interesting Warwickshire men of the time, and might have said much more of some that I have but barely mentioned, but space forbids. High over all sat Ambrose Earl of Warwick and Robert Earl of Leicester, whose lives are part of the history of the country. I have worked out the story of the Kenilworth Festivities, which seem to have affected young Shakespeare powerfully, in my "Hunnis and the Revels of the Chapel Royal." Something might have been said of Leicester's brilliant and unfortunate son, Sir Robert Dudley, born 1574, and knighted by the Earl of Essex in his Cadiz Expedition. Leicester disowned his marriage to his mother, Lady Douglas Sheffield, in order to marry the Countess of Essex, widow of the Earl of Essex, who had died, it was believed, by poison from his hands in 1576. Either the workings of conscience or pride in his son made Leicester try to restore his inheritance of Kenilworth and other possessions just before he died in 1588. Sir Robert vainly endeavoured to establish his legitimacy after his father's death, and lived abroad in great honour and distinction, having been made the Duke of Dudley at Leghorn. His second wife was granted the title in England 20 Charles I.

There might have been more said of Warwickshire poets. One at least was doubly connected with Shakespeare, Bartholomew Griffin, who was buried on the15th December, 1602, in the Church of the Holy Trinity at Coventry. His will was proved on the 13th May, 1603, by his widow, Catherine, for his son, Rice (Som. House, 37 Bolein). He, too, joined the sixteenth century school of sonnetteers, and in 1596 brought out a series of sixty-two beautiful Sonnets called " Fidessa, more Chaste than Kind," dedicated to William Essex of Lambourne, Berkshire. He also added an epistle to the gentlemen of the Inns of Court, but details of his life have not been found. His third Sonnet, " Venus with young Adonis sitting by her," was reproduced, with alteration, by Jaggard in "The Passionate Pilgrim," 1599, as Shakespeare's. Mr. Yeatman thinks that he was a cousin or at least a relative of the poet. He might have been one of the Griffins of Dingley, or the son of Mr. Ralph Griffin, the preacher of Warwick, who went out with the Town Council to meet the Queen in her progress thither in 1571, preached a sermon on "Christian Warfare," and gave her some Latin verses. The Queen "caused her coach to be opened every part and side that they might see her." The people let off fireworks in their rejoicing, which burned four houses to the ground and caused great consternation. After great sport at Kenilworth, she went by Charlecote to the Lord Compton's on her return, an occasion in which Stratford would doubtless pour forth to meet her. The " Book of Thomas Fisher " and the "Black Book of Warwick" give much interesting information concerning the customs and manners of the county town.

It might have been interesting to tell more of Thomas Oken, the prosperous mercer of Warwick, interested in good roads, popular education, church music, and protection against fire, who left money to be lent to young tradesmen of respectable character in Warwick, Stratford-upon-Avon, and Banbury; andappointed a feast-day on which a learned man should make a sermon for *6s. 8d.* and the Bailiff and Company should have dinner in memory of him, and a similar feast in Stratford-upon-Avon. Oken died on the 30th of July, 1573, and we often read about the loans from Oken's Fund, and the Stratford officials who managed them. The pleasantest thing I have read about the Earl of Leicester is his conference with Mr. John Fisher, Town Clerk of Warwick, about the affairs of the Borough. He asked what trade there was in the town. Fisher said there was not much ; most of the men had some husbandry, the chief maintenance of their poor households; there were others that "lived uprightly, such as be called Mercers and Drapers, which were the two most profitable trades. And others made corn into malt." "Yea," said the Earl, " I think in making of malt much gain may be raised. I know a town in Essex wherein are four or five worth a thousand or two thousand apiece that have' no trade but malting. But," saith he, " I marvaile you do not devise someways amongst you to have some speciall trade to keep your poor on work, as such as Sheldon of Beolye devised, which methinketh should be not only very profitable, but also a meanes to keep your poor from idleness, or the making of cloth, or capping, or some such like. But I do grieve that every man is only careful for himself. And I think you be most of you graziers and given as in most places men are to easye trades of life, providing for themselves, not having consideration to their posteritye, which should not so be."

Thomas Fisher also describes some of the trials in Warwick, the classes of crimes, charges, defence, and punishments, which let us realise the rough and ready justice of the times that Shakespeare knew.

I might have given a series of contemporary Shake-

speares, even bearing the same Christian name, significant enough when one remembers all the contradictory and sometimes impossible charges brought against the poet. But these I have dealt with in my " Shakespeare's Family," and in various articles in the *Atheneumy* particularly that on "Other William Shakespeares" *(Atheneum,* August, 1906), in which I collect about a score, one born in 1564. There is also much to be collected, and somewhat to be added to the knowledge of all the poet's aunts, uncles, and cousins; but much of that I have already dealt with elsewhere.

Many interesting details are given by Halliwell- Phillipps of the Quineys, the Saddlers, the Nashes, the Wheelers, the Whateleys ; and much more may yet be gleaned from the records of the time. But there must come a period to all work, and I trust that mine has helped beginners to realise the sort of people amongst whom Shakespeare-began his life, and ended it.

INDEX

INDEX.

Printed at

The Shakesfeare Head Tre1t, StratforJ-m-tAvon.

r - . *1*

Lightning Source UK Ltd.
Milton Keynes UK
18 June 2010

155796UK00001B/355/P

9 780217 990738